JUN 1993

The Second Year of Life

The Early Childhood Development Center's <u>Parenting Series</u>

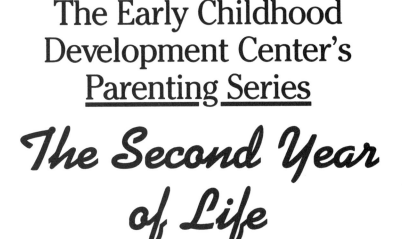

The Second Year of Life

Nina R. Lief, M.D.,
with Mary Ellen Fahs

Walker and Company ☀ *New York*

649.122
LIE

This edition published in the United States of America in 1991
by Walker Publishing Company, Inc.

Published simultaneously in Canada by Thomas Allen & Son
Canada, Limited, Markham, Ontario

Library of Congress Cataloging-in-Publication Data
Lief, Nina R.
The Second year of life / Nina R. Lief, with Mary Ellen Fahs.
262   p.   cm. —(The Early Childhood Development Center's parenting
series)
Previously published by Dodd, Mead & Co. in 1984.
Includes bibliographical references and index.
ISBN 0-8027-1154-5. —ISBN 0-8027-7350-8
1. Parenting—United States.   2. Child development—United States.
I. Fahs, Mary Ellen.   II. Title.   III. Series.
HQ755.8.L532   1990
649'.122—dc20   91-2852
CIP

Photograph credits: introduction, Jim Beecher; text, Marguerite Johnson and Jim
Beecher.

Text design by Georg Brewer

Printed in the United States of America

2   4   6   8   10   9   7   5   3   1

For Amanda Lief Schuster
and Thomas Reade Fahs

Contents

③ Age Eighteen to Twenty-one Months *119*

④ Age Twenty-one to Twenty-four Months *175*

■   ■

Introduction

Much research has been done on the crucial importance of a child's earliest years, but little of the knowledge and understanding derived from this research reaches the parents, who have primary responsibility for the child's care and development. To provide parents with this information as well as with support and encouragement in their roles as parents, New York Medical College and the New York Junior League established the Early Childhood Development Center in 1974.

At the Center, small groups of parents (usually from eight to ten adults) and their children meet with a trained group leader in weekly discussion sessions. The curriculum for the discussions is based on the best current information regarding a child's emotional, social, and cognitive development, as well as on the real-life concerns of parents, as expressed in their questions. The links between appropriate child-rearing methods and developmental theory are continually demonstrated, thereby enabling parents to see how child-rearing techniques directly influence the child's cognitive, social, and emotional development.

The major aims of the Center's program are to assist parents in guiding their children toward healthy personality development and to help mothers and fathers derive enjoyment and satisfaction from their roles as parents. While other programs have emphasized the physical and cognitive aspects of a child's development, the Center is more concerned with helping the parent understand the emotional and social side of that development and the importance of parent-child interaction in this process. The Center recognizes the uniqueness of each child and each family's situation. It adheres to the belief that the most effective child rearing results from the parents' understanding of their own child's needs, temperament, and level of development as well as knowledge of appropriate child-rearing options. Parents come to understand and follow the child-rearing practices appropriate for their own child through the discussions at the parenting sessions rather than from specific directions, as no one method suits all children.

The curriculum used at the Early Childhood Development Center has been published in three paperback volumes: *The First Year of Life; The Second Year of Life;* and *The Third Year of Life.*

This book is divided into four chapters covering the second year of life in three-month intervals. Each of the chapters focuses on developmental highlights followed by discussions as they took place with parents at the Early Childhood Development Center, of a series of topics relating to child development and child-rearing issues, as well as parents' feelings.

Every effort has been made to avoid sexist use of pronouns in referring to the gender of the children who form the subject of this book. This explains why the pronoun referring to the child is sometimes masculine and sometimes feminine, and why the gender of the pronoun appears to change arbitrarily from section to section.

Similarly, throughout the text the parent is more often referred to as the mother, rather than the father. This is not due to any sexist orientation but simply to the fact that the great majority of the parents who provide the major amount of care during the child's earliest years are the mothers. It is our belief that parenting is a shared male-female responsibility, and the word *father* may be substituted for the word *mother* in most cases.

Further, a growing number of mothers of children under three years of age are working outside the home. Because the child's needs regarding nutrition, attention, and discipline are similar whether his or her parents work, topics throughout the book discuss the variety of ways that parents in differing circumstances may meet their children's needs. This is important and possible, whether parents work outside the home or not. The purpose of this book is to foster the healthiest possible growth and development of the child and to make parenting less stressful and more enjoyable.

The Second Year of Life

Highlights of Development—One Year

The child's first birthday has special significance for most parents. Development is still quite varied, however, among children at this age. Some children may be able to take a halting step or two alone, but most still need to hold on to a parent's hand for support. A few are walking alone quite well.

If the parent makes a tower of two blocks, the child will try to build such a structure but often will not succeed. Even the attempt shows an advance. Practice helps the child become more skillful at placing blocks on top of each other, and such play is a good game for parent and child. In a month or so, most children will be able to grasp two blocks in one hand and, therefore, will be able to hold three blocks. These achievements in small motor skills are often overshadowed by the gross motor developments of standing and walking.

The children may be able to put a block into a cup after this activity has been shown to them; soon, they will do it without demonstration. Parents can turn this new skill into the game of putting small objects into larger containers.

When a simple puzzle (of circles, squares, and triangles) is presented to the child without the pieces in place and the round piece is handed to the child, she will look selectively at the round hole, sometimes poking her finger into it. Most children do not put the piece in the correct place unless they have had some practice with the puzzle; they are able, however,

to lift the piece out of the puzzle. In a month or so, most will begin placing the piece into the puzzle. This, too, is a good learning activity for parents to engage in with the child.

When given a crayon, children begin to imitate a scribble; some do it tentatively, and others more vigorously. Parents are often worried about allowing drawing because they are concerned that the child will scribble on everything; but this activity is an important part of a child's development and should be encouraged with supervision.

At one year, most children have a vocabulary of two to four words, perhaps "Bye" and "Hi" or "Ba" (for bottle), in addition to "Mama" and "Dada." They are also beginning to carry on their own conversations using unintelligible words with the intonations of language. Children of this age comprehend considerably more language than they are given credit for or can express; they demonstrate this by pointing to and looking for things on parental request. A good game is "Find the ball" or "Get the doll," which encourages the child's language development and gives the parent a chance to show approval of the child's accomplishments.

The child also likes to gaze at himself in a mirror. If given a ball, he will place the ball against the mirror and look at it as well. In the coming weeks, the child will learn to release a ball toward the parent's open hands. As the child is encouraged to do this, another way of playing by rolling or throwing the ball to each other has begun. This game gives both parents and the child satisfaction and enjoyment.

While being dressed, the children are now beginning to cooperate by holding up their arms to be put through sleeves or holding up their feet for socks or shoes.

Parents' Expectations of This Age Level

The children have made enormous progress in the last year, from complete helplessness and immobility to walking. They are taking on their own unique personalities, yet they are still very young and immature. We have noticed that parents' expectations of their children are often beyond the child's level of development. Are there some achievements you were expecting by now that haven't occurred? Are you surprised at things the baby doesn't do yet?

Weaning

"Yes, I was always under the impression that a baby would be fully weaned from a bottle by one year. My baby is so attached and dependent on his bottle that I don't think I can switch him to a cup for a long time."

Weaning children by one year used to be the practice. We are now aware of the emotional significance of the bottle to the baby. It represents a time of closeness to mother. A baby cannot give up that closeness at a specific time determined by someone else. He should be allowed to give up the bottle gradually as he matures and can take more of his milk successfully from a cup. It must be done on the same maturational timetable as all the rest of his development.

■   ■

"But my mother says she broke me and all of her children at one year. She just threw the bottles out and that was that. She thinks I should do the same. She said we cried for several days, maybe a week, and didn't eat; but she stuck it out and feels very proud of herself for it."

At that time, it was the accepted procedure. Now that we think we understand a child's emotional needs better, we feel that this is not the best way to wean. We feel that weaning from breast or bottle to cup should be gradual and not traumatic. In our view, such abrupt weaning may set up the foundation of depression, interfere with basic trust, and give the child a sense of loss and separation too early for him to be able to cope with it. Because he is still essentially nonverbal at one year, the child really does not understand your expectations and cannot explain his feelings and needs.

"I have been breast feeding my baby and I've been gradually introducing the cup. He takes it well when I hold him in my lap. I give him his milk from the cup twice a day. Is it possible to just wean him to cup feeding without going to the bottle stage and weaning him from that?"

Since you have nursed him as long as this, it is perfectly possible to do it that way. As a breast-fed baby, he has probably had sufficient sucking. When one weans from the breast at an earlier age, before a baby has satisfied the sucking need and before he can take a sufficient amount from a cup, it's advisable to bottle-feed first and introduce the cup later.

"When you say gradually, how gradually do you mean? My idea is to eliminate one bottle a day. Would that be too fast?"

For some babies perhaps not; but in general at least a week should elapse before substituting the cup for another bottle feeding. The parent is the best judge of the interval, because she can tell how well the baby is adapting to the cup feeding. For some children, an even longer interval may be advisable.

Ability to Separate; Parents' Time for Themselves

"What bothers me is that my baby always wants to be near me. He can't seem to play alone. I can't get anything done around the house. I felt that I should be able to put him down for a while or be able to go on and do things in the house that I have to do."

By this age, you expected the baby to entertain himself so that you would have a little more freedom. Then you would come back to him when *you* were ready?

"Yes, and feel that he was all right; but I found out that it is not working at all."

It is not working because at this age babies are not ready to play alone for a long enough time for mother to get the housework or cooking done.

There are reasons for it. One is that they still do not feel secure when they can't see you; another one is that they can't concentrate on any form of play for long enough on their own. They also cannot initiate activities without some help from the parent.

"How long can they play on their own with something like a Busy Box?"

Fifteen to twenty minutes is a very long time for them at this age. Then they have to be presented with something different. Some can be interested in a box with many little boxes, keys, small dolls, or blocks, which they can put in and take out. Others just like to roam about the room you are in and explore objects in it. Some can occupy themselves by turning the pages of a book.

"I'm having the same problem. Even when my baby is in her room, she'll stay for about five minutes and then she comes to look for me. When she finds me, she takes me by the hand and leads me back to her room to play with her."

That behavior is very typical for this age. There are ways, however, to do other things. If you have to be in the kitchen or the living room, you can take the same toy she has pulled you to play with and bring it back to the kitchen. Children need to keep in contact with you all the time. You would like some separation—time to do what you want to do. That's what every mother and father would like. You may be able to do this for a while with three-year-olds. At this age, children are still at the stage of beginning to separate from you.

It is important for working mothers to realize that their children will be acting the same way toward their housekeepers and baby-sitters. It is a good idea to talk with your caretakers and ask them how they feel about the baby's demands for closeness. Let them know that giving the baby appropriate attention is more important than doing all the housework. This is true for parents as well as other caretakers.

"My baby is very demanding of my time on weekends; he won't let me out of his sight. I thought it was because I'd been gone all week. Do you mean he acts like that with his nurse? No wonder the house looks so messy sometimes!"

A neat house and clean laundry are very visible things that housekeepers can show you at the end of the day. That you have kept the baby happy and interested and responded appropriately to his needs are not so easy to demonstrate. It is important to let your caretakers know where your priorities are and to help them to understand your baby's needs as you understand them.

"I sometimes feel that I expect too much when I want my baby to under-stand what I am saying—especially if I take him somewhere and he is a bit frightened. I want him to understand that we are going back home soon,

that everything is all right, that I'm not going to leave him. Or if I am going to leave him, that I'm coming back soon."

At this age, they are hardly able to be in a different room in your *own* house without seeing you. The *concept* of going to a new place and coming home soon is beyond the child's ability to understand. Each child will gain this understanding at a different time, depending on his or her temperament and level of maturation and experience.

"Now that I have stopped working, what I am finding is that when she goes for her nap she will nap for a much longer time, knowing that I'm in the house. She'll also go into another room to play and come back to make sure that I'm still sitting there; and as long as I'm sitting there she'll play for a really long time."

Her separation anxiety is diminishing because you're there.

"Yes, and it's really noticeable in the way she plays with other people now. If I am there, she plays differently than when I am not. My husband says that he is amazed at the difference in the way she's trying to talk and to do things because I am there with her."

She isn't so torn by that anxiety of separation that we talk about and that parents find so hard to accept. It is not that the children are not well cared for or happy while you are away. It is just that their primary attachments are to you and they cling to you. It is still a good sign, for it shows how strong their attachments are. It will probably be a while before they understand and feel secure that you will return when you leave.

What you all seem to be saying is that you were expecting the children to give you a little more time to yourselves. A lot of you are saying that you don't get a lot of free time because the babies want you by their side all the time. But they do have naptime. How do you use that time? Do you use it for reading or rest, or do you use that time for housework? When do you get any rest?

"At night mostly. I go to bed at nine. I'm dead tired and can't get anything done the next day if I don't go to bed early."

"I work while she is napping rather than rest when she does."

"I feel I should get a break then, too, when she is napping."

Mothers should take a break. Anyone working at any other job gets a ten- or fifteen-minute break for coffee. You will find that you are much more patient and enjoy your child more if you take a little time for yourself. The last thing you should forgo is that little bit of rest and relaxation.

"I find that I rest a lot when she plays alone. She does that more now."

"I don't need the rest so much, but I can't even talk to my friends on the phone to relax. She always wants me with her just then."

■   ■

Yes, the telephone is a problem. Most children resent very much when you talk on the phone, because you are physically present but your attention is elsewhere. One of the best solutions is to take the child on your lap and include her in your conversations or give her something to play with on your lap so she doesn't feel left out.

Are there other areas in which you feel your expectations have not been fulfilled?

Communication

"Yes, I always thought that a one-year-old baby communicated more. What I really mean is that sometimes I talk to her and she seems to understand me and sometimes she just doesn't seem to know what I am talking about, even if I've said it before."

Babies need to hear the same word or phrase repeated slowly and rhythmically many times in order to associate it with a specific item or situation. For example, if we say "Bye-bye" to children and wave but do not leave, we don't convey the meaning of leaving to them. We communicate to them by our expression and gesture and by repeating the words. They "catch on" when we have done it in the same way sufficiently often. The baby's readiness for language varies with each baby. Sometimes babies are in a more receptive state and seem to catch on better. The next time you say the same thing, the baby may be working on motor activity and may not respond as well to speech.

At this age, if they say about three or four words besides "Dada" and "Mama" and seem to understand a few others, that is all that is expected. Some children may take longer than others.

Has anyone else been feeling that the children should be further along in speech?

"In our family we speak two languages. We speak Spanish among ourselves at home, but outside the home we speak mostly English. Does that confuse the baby?"

It may. There are some babies who can grasp two languages at once, but most children do better if they learn one language at a time. This is especially true of those who have a slower maturation rate for language. There are some who are just not talkers and do better at other activities like walking or putting things together, such as puzzles.

"I guess I never expected much of my baby. I thought babies didn't begin to talk or understand until they were three or more. So to me, it is a great surprise each time he seems to catch on to a new word. Maybe I'm not stimulating him enough. Do you think I ought to talk to him more?"

It is important for parents to talk to their babies. At this stage, they may not grasp a long, unmodulated sentence all in a single tone, as adults talk to each other. They can understand when you hand them a bottle and say,

"Bo-ttle," or "Here is your do-llie" when you give them a doll. They are at the stage of learning names, identifying objects. They are not yet ready for sentences.

"Would you consider it a word if a baby says 'Bo' for boat and 'Ca' for car?"

This is the beginning. They may not be able to pronounce the whole word. It is important for you to recognize the sound as the word and show recognition and approval by saying enthusiastically, "Yes, boat (or car)." In this way the baby hears the complete word and knows that he has communicated with you and feels pleased about it. Perhaps there are many times that babies do this and parents do not listen closely enough to what the baby is really saying. The baby is looking for recognition and reinforcement. If you don't notice, he may try less. Babies need encouragement and recognition. This recognition adds to the baby's sense of achievement. We will talk more about this on many levels.

Toys—Sharing and Possessiveness

Now that the children are more active, they are playing more with other children. At first, they just play alongside the other child. If the other child is playing with an attractive toy, there is often a tendency to take it. This can prove to be quite a problem. Has this been happening? How do you handle it?

"I'm always having that experience, and I don't know quite what to do. If the other child doesn't protest, then I let my child have it. If there's a protest, then I give it back and give mine something else. He usually still wants the other child's toy."

That is a difficult and important issue. The child who doesn't protest may be getting the message that his things are always going to be taken away from him. He may move away from other children in order to protect his property. We have all seen children who clutch their possessions and isolate themselves from other children. Or the child may feel he has no right to his toys and he becomes submissive and gives everything up. Neither response is healthy.

A good practice is to return the toy to the first child. Then give the other one who took it a substitute, telling him he can have the toy later. At first, there will be a great protest; but if you are consistent and allow the child to play with the toy later, the child gradually learns to wait and trust.

"Shouldn't children be taught to share their toys? Last week, my son was playing at a friend's house. Every toy he picked up, the child would come over and take it, saying 'Mine.' Wasn't that child selfish?"

"Selfish" is a label we apply too easily to young children. A child of that age is establishing his autonomy and identity. He is beginning to know "I," "my," and "mine." The mother could have said, "Yes, it is yours. He is not taking it away. You can let him have a turn playing with it while you play with your other red car."

Another way of negotiating this toy problem when visiting is to bring one or two of your child's toys, so that if the problem comes up, you can give your child his toy and say, "This is yours; that is his." Later, they will each pick up the other's toy and play for a while without difficulty. However, all play at this time has to be monitored by the adults present.

"When I do this, my friends say I'm bringing up a selfish child. I have to teach him to share."

Certainly you will teach sharing, but when he can understand it. Most parents try to teach sharing much too early, before a child has really gotten his sense of self. Acquiring a sense of self is important now. Sharing comes later. You have to supervise; there is no such thing as visiting with children under three and expecting that they are going to be able to manage the business of sharing. If they do, it's really quite remarkable; but you can't expect it.

General Physical Care

Need for Medical Attention—The Ideal Doctor

We know that in the baby's first year, you were all having regular contact with your family doctor or pediatrician or clinic. We feel that continued medical care is very important to your child's healthy development. How often are you visiting your doctors?

"Well, I do take the baby if he is sick. Otherwise I don't, because there is always such a long wait. Even when we have an appointment weeks in advance, we have to wait forty-five minutes or more. It is very hard with an active baby—bad enough when he is well and, of course, more agonizing when he is sick. But my doctor is good, and I trust him. I know he will pay a lot of attention if there is something seriously wrong."

Our reason for talking about medical services is to help you use your doctor's expertise to the best advantage. Your doctor should continue to monitor physical development and give appropriate inoculations and advice about diet, visual and auditory development, neuromuscular development, allergies, injuries, and hosts of other things. A good doctor who knows your family and your child detects such problems in physical examinations because he knows what familial diseases and characteristics to look for.

"I can't afford to go to a private doctor. I have to go to the clinic. Each time I go, I see a different doctor. I know that they try to read my baby's history, but I keep wondering how much they know about her after a brief glance."

■   ■

It is much harder to feel you are getting good medical care when you see different doctors each time. Some clinics have a team approach in which you and your family always see someone from the same team of doctors and nurse practitioners.

"You said babies should be having regular contact with the doctor. What does that mean? How many times a year?"

Every three months in the second year, in order to be sure developmental defects undetected in the first year, such as cardiac murmurs and difficulties with hearing or visual development, will be picked up. Also, during the second year appetites are often poor; nutrition and total growth need to be evaluated.

Poor Appetites During the Second Year

The babies have all grown a great deal in the past year. Their growth rate and weight gain in the second year, while marked, are not as rapid proportionately as in the first year. With the change to table food and a normal decrease in appetite, they may not seem to be eating as much. Have any of you been noticing this in your babies?

"This is a problem I have been having a long time. It didn't just begin this year. My baby has always been a very poor eater. She takes her milk, but only enough solids for a bird. This is one of the things I want to talk over with my pediatrician. I wonder if there is something I can do or should do to stimulate her appetite."

If your doctor were worried about her, he would probably have suggested something himself. If it worries you, however, you should talk it over with him. In general, a child's progress is not measured by weight alone. It's not like putting weight on a turkey to get a good price for the holidays! Although most parents do have the feeling that weight is an important indicator of good development, it is only a small part of the picture. The baby's general health is revealed in her social and emotional responses, her activity level and motor development, her speech—spoken and understood. All these are very important characteristics of development. These are more important than weight and size unless there is something extremely abnormal.

"My baby doesn't seem to care much for the food I give him; but when he sees us sit down to eat, he almost jumps out of his high chair to get it. So I give him some of what we are having: pot roast or chicken or chops, rice, such things. Is that all right?"

There is no reason why your baby has to eat "baby food" if he likes to eat your food. It should not be too highly salted and seasoned and shouldn't contain preservatives that are inappropriate for babies. The only other concern is that you give him small pieces so that there will be no danger of choking.

The important thing is not to make feeding time a battle. Sometimes babies eat much better in the company of their parents when they see adults eating. Often you can interest a baby in new foods this way. If she reaches for some of your food, you may give her very tiny pieces, one at a time. As she finishes each bit, without any eagerness or urging just acknowledge it with, "Umm, so good." In that way, a baby may consume a considerable amount happily, without a fuss being made.

Changing Nap Patterns

At the same time as babies seem to be developing poor eating patterns, their sleeping patterns may be changing as well. Gradually during the first year, your babies have been sleeping less and less but generally for a longer stretch at night. Most of the babies during the past months have been taking a morning and an afternoon nap. Are they still doing this?

"It's funny you should bring this up now. For the last three days my baby has refused to sleep in the morning, so we've gone outside earlier. By the time we get home, he is tired and falls asleep over his lunch. His schedule is all off."

In that case it may be better to come back earlier so he can eat his lunch and then nap.

"My baby is doing the opposite. She still naps in the morning but won't sleep in the afternoon. By the time my husband gets home, we've played all our games twice and we are both 'basket cases.' I don't know what to do with her."

Your babies have given up one nap, but they seem to get tired without it. This is a developmental change that the children are unaccustomed to— and so are you. When they begin to nap less, it is important to see whether the one remaining nap can be lengthened. If not, then it is often necessary to try to do something quiet with the baby at the time of the former nap: listening to a soothing record or looking at picture books. Sometimes the babies will fall asleep in their carriages or strollers if you take them out at the former naptime. Usually, after a week or so, both you and the baby will settle into a new routine that has only one nap but less strain than at first. In general, the babies seem to need less sleep now. You may also find that, as they walk more and get more exercise, they sleep better at night.

"I look forward to that! Now that the baby walks around he gets into everything. When we're outside, he's constantly on the go. He comes in tired, but I'm exhausted. Yesterday, we both slept for two hours!"

Sometimes when the children first give up the second nap, they may still miss it. They are not quite ready to be active that much more of the day. Sometimes parents plan too many activities with the new time and overtire the children, who become irritable and need a quiet time. Each of you will have to experiment a little as you rearrange routines to accommodate this new development. It is also a good idea for those of you who are not home with your children all the time to discuss these changes in napping and eating patterns with your caretakers.

Attachment and Separation: The Child's Needs

How Attachment Develops

The babies are now at the beginning of their second year. Let us review for a moment how their attachments have developed. Gradually, as they are cared for by mother, father, or other caretakers, they become familiar with these persons. This familiarity establishes the baby's sense of security and attachment. Generally, one person takes primary care of the child and the child becomes attached to that person.

Many of you decided that you wanted to be the one to provide the primary caretaking and that you enjoyed child rearing. You have decided to stay home with your children and provide the quality of care that is very hard to replicate: the full-time care of the mother. The babies have become primarily attached to you, but they have also formed attachments to the father and other relatives as well. This was a good decision for you and your children, and this job you have undertaken should not be considered "nonwork" or any less professional than a paid job outside the home.

Others of you felt the need (for economic or professional reasons) to continue working outside the home. We advised you that it was best to return to work before the baby had formed such a strong attachment to you that leaving him or her would create great separation anxiety. We advised that you go back to work when your child was three or four months old, so that he or she could form a strong attachment to the substitute caretaker as well as to you and the father. Some of you have done this. You have found that the baby was able to become attached to each adult in a special way because of the particular routines that each has with the baby. Your babies have come to depend on you because of this special relationship, and yet they feel secure when you leave. In this way, they have not had to experience the trauma of premature separation. The baby has learned which adult fills which part of the daily caretaking and feels secure.

"You know, I do think it has worked. I was afraid my baby would be attached to the sitter and not to me. I know now that she is attached to all of us."

She *should* be attached to the caretaker. It is important for her to form an attachment to the person who gives her consistent care. Most children will form a different and very special attachment to their parents if they give the child regular and consistent care in their own special ways and times.

■   ■

By now, whether the parents are both working outside the home full time or not, one would hope that the babies have established feelings of attachment to both parents and caretakers. Those of you who have been home all the time may be thinking that this is about the right time to go back to work or get out of the house more with your husband and friends. You are feeling ready to separate yourself from your children, and you are thinking the children should be ready as well. In fact, many of the children have recently learned to walk and seem only too eager to toddle away from you. Often their exhilaration in being able to move away confirms your feelings that they are ready to be away from you. Actually, the children are not as independent as they seem; they move away from you, but they prefer that you be stationary—a secure "home base." If it can be arranged, part-time work would probably be better.

"I am not thinking of going back to work. Eventually I may feel that way. What is the ideal time to consider going back to work?"

Ideal Time for Separation

When you ask about the *ideal* time, we think that *from the child's point of view* the child should be about three years old. Children need a consistent mothering person around them until they are about three, the age at which most are able to function independently. By that time, they are able to talk and communicate their needs and to feed themselves. Most are also toilet trained and able to spend time playing alone or with friends. They are ready at that age to start nursery school or a day-care program and are able to separate more easily from the parents.

We are talking now about the ideal situations from the child's point of view. There are two of them: either to have a nearly full-time parent for about three years (we say "nearly" because everyone needs time off, and it is good for the child to get used to other caretakers for short periods of time) or to have the consistent care of another relative or baby-sitter or housekeeper who shares the caring role with the working parent(s) during the first three years. We recognize that it is often very difficult to achieve these ideals. The most important thing to remember is that children will experience feelings of separation anxiety and abandonment if the parent or other caretaker leaves them too abruptly before they have become accustomed to the new caretaking situation.

"My husband is not working. Very soon I may have to go back to work. Is there something special in the baby's behavior that I should be prepared for?"

You have all noticed that often, when a mother leaves her child, the child clings to her on her return and needs undivided attention. A baby who has become accustomed to his mother's care will protest at her leaving. After being without her all day, no matter how good the substitute care, this child will at first cling to her. She needs to expect this and plan to spend time with him.

Helping Child Adjust to Substitute Care

"Is there some way to ease the baby's anxiety and make it easier for him?"

The best way is for the change of caretaker to be gradual. Sometimes the mother can find work and the father cannot; so he can care for the baby. In our experience, fathers are very good caretakers. Sometimes, when both parents work, their schedules can be arranged so that one of them can care for the child while the other is out—at least, most of the time. Grandmothers, sisters, and other relatives make good caretakers because they have a sense of affection and responsibility toward the child.

If no member of the family is available, then you have to hire a caretaker either to come into your home or to care for the child in her own home. It is best if she can be at home with you for a few days, watching your way of caring for your baby and gradually taking over some of your functions. In this way, the baby gets to know her and becomes accustomed to her way of doing things with him. During this time, you can go out for short periods, so the baby begins to learn that you will return.

Many parents may not be able to find an appropriate person to come to their homes to care for their children. Another solution for children of this age is called family day care. This means care given by a qualified person in her own home. Regulations vary in different states, but generally, licensed family day care strictly limits the number of children who may be cared for by one person and assures a certain level of competence. Care in a day-care center is also a possibility, but we feel it is a less desirable alternative *for children of this age* (actually, center care is rarely an alternative, since few centers take children under two years of age).

Whether you leave your children with another mother, in family day care, or in a day-care center, the process of separation should be gradual. The child then becomes familiar with the new caregiver, the new routines, and the new environment while the parent is still available for support. To make the transition, it is necessary to bring a few of the child's own toys from home, especially a special one such as his blanket or other favorite object. In the long run, extra time spent at the beginning of different care is time well spent in maintaining a child's sense of security and well-being.

Child's Reactions to Parents' Absence

"But what if you have to make a change in a hurry? You have no choice."

We know that happens sometimes. You must then be prepared for the baby to cling to you, cry a good deal, and not let you out of sight when you come home. You just recognize that this is his way of saying, "I missed you; I was afraid you would never come back," and give the child your undivided attention for a while when you come home. Don't feel that the child is too demanding and being naughty and nagging just to upset you. If you react that way, the child will pick up your negative feelings and his anxiety will increase.

"What about the mother who comes home after a hard day's work? Isn't she entitled to some peace and quiet?"

You mean that after working she feels entitled to some relaxation; she feels the baby should realize how hard she has worked and that she is working for him? The child simply cannot understand that concept. All he or she understands is "Mommy has been away and I want her back."

"Usually I work part-time; but yesterday I worked all day and I came home exhausted. I did play with him, but I had the feeling that he was angry at me, and that made me angry."

That is another way children show how much they have missed you—by being angry. That is because they are not yet verbal and cannot say, "I missed you; I'm glad you are home; please play with me." Parents should be prepared for this kind of response and not get so upset by it. If the parent can understand the child's needs, he or she can deal with them upon arriving home. The child needs special attention and time after a day's separation from the mother (and father).

"What if I have to do the cooking, or the laundry, or some marketing when I get home?"

You can do all those things *after* you have given the baby some undivided attention *first.* Have a snack together or play for a while. Then involve the child in whatever you have to do so that he or she does not again have the feeling of being left out. It is also important to realize that you don't have to be a "superwoman." Perhaps the marketing and laundry should wait until the weekend; or the baby's father can help. You know we believe that parenting is a shared enterprise. Planning your time so that you get some relaxation is important. Sitting down and looking at a book with the baby may be a good change of pace for you. The baby will be so pleased with your attention that she may be willing to play with some toys near you. You will be surprised at how cooperative the baby can be if she feels close to you.

"You were saying that until they are two and a half or three most children are not ready to separate from the parents once they are attached. That seems like a long time. I'd like to be doing something else part-time earlier. Parenting sounds like a job I am going to have forever!"

Yes, that's right. Once a parent, always a parent! But getting your child off to a good start in the early years should make the job easier later on. You see, the generation gap can start here if early separations upset the child's development of basic trust and self-confidence. You need to understand that your going away upsets him. You will then expect clinging and you won't think he is naughty and react with anger, thereby adding negative feelings to his feelings of distress at your absence.

"It sounds like parenting should be a twenty-four-hour job. Can't the mother and father have some time off?"

No mother and father—no matter what the age of the child—can be with the child all the time. Most fathers and many mothers work outside the home. Parents also need time to pursue activities that they've always liked to do as adults. No one can do the same job well twenty-four hours a day, seven days a week. No profession requires that. No lawyer, businessman, nurse, mechanic, or doctor keeps those hours. Each needs relief and change; this enhances one's ability to do the job well. It is so with parents, too. Each family has to work this out in a way that suits its needs best. That is not the issue here. What we are trying to emphasize is the way the baby may respond to separation and how best to deal with his attachment and separation in order to cause the least difficulty and the most positive personality development. We want our children to be self-reliant, self-confident, trusting, and compassionate individuals. The foundations for these character traits begin in the early years.

Parents' Feelings About Parenting Roles; Mothering as a Profession

"No-win" Situation for Mothers

Some of you have decided to take off from your jobs to be full-time mothers; others have made the decision to continue in your professions. As you know, we hope to help all of you to raise your children with the minimum of stress and the maximum of pleasure, no matter what your decision about your jobs. We wish to be supportive of all of you. We do find it startling that the women who work outside the homes are labeled "working mothers," while those who stay home and care for their children, husband, and home are considered nonworking! We believe that full-time mothering requires as much, if not more, stamina, ingenuity, knowledge, understanding, diplomacy, and common sense as other professional positions. We stress the importance we place on full-time mothering because the value of mothers and homemaking is often downgraded. At the same time, society in general has made mothers who work outside the home feel guilty. It's kind of a "no-win" situation for young mothers right now.

"I enjoy this age more, but it is much harder in some ways. What annoys me is that people at a party ask me what I do. When I say I take care of my child, they look at me and say, 'And what else?' That gets to me."

■   ■

That is something to overcome. This is an area in which we have to enlighten society: that being a mother is just as important a profession as any other. As we have said before, and we will have to repeat often, mothering (parenting) is the most important profession because it is the profession on which the success or failure of our society depends. This recognition of the value of parenting has to be fought for.

"I've noticed that when a woman goes to register to vote, if she says she is a teacher, doctor, etc., that is well regarded. If the woman has no paying job, then housewife *is entered in the book with a little disdain."*

Motherhood Requires Versatility and Skill

It is not recognized in our complex society that being a wife and a mother requires a great deal of versatility and skill. When you are in the kitchen preparing dinner, you also have to have your mind on whether the child is safe. Or maybe you have your mind on whether what you are doing is a way to teach your child a new experience. You also have to think of things to do to divert the child if he is getting in your way. This really takes a lot of ingenuity, much more than you have to use in the average paying job. Mothering is a far more responsible and demanding job than is generally recognized.

"When it's put that way, it raises my self-esteem no end. It's such an important job; what if we make mistakes?"

Everyone makes mistakes in all areas of life; that is how we learn. Recognizing the importance of your role should make you want to know how to do it better. For instance, if you were a pianist, it wouldn't scare you because you couldn't play a sonata the first time you tried it. It's the same with mothering (parenting). It's not fatal if you make a mistake once or twice; the danger comes when we keep repeating the same mistake.

"I agree that being a parent is a complex job. I was a schoolteacher and I prided myself on my ability to understand preschoolers and conduct a class with pleasure and satisfaction. But let me tell you that nothing requires as much patience, understanding, and savvy as bringing up your own child. This sounds 'corny' to my friends who are still at work and have no children. I understand them, because that's the way I used to feel."

"I never wanted to be a mother, and I frankly don't think I'm a model one. I don't enjoy it all that much, but I could never let anyone else take care of my child. No one would do it the way I would like it done. Besides, I've had a career in advertising. I was succesful, but I would not go back to it. When my son is older, perhaps I'll find another career. At the moment, my child is my job. Certainly, I like my time off a couple of afternoons a week. I shop or visit with friends, but my son is so glad to see me when I get home that I know my being there makes a difference to him."

That is an important discovery. Many more mothers need to be able to understand that so they will take pride in their efforts and feel worthwhile.

■   ■

We believe women should be able to choose how to lead their lives. That includes seeing motherhood as an occupation of value.

"There is another aspect that I'd like to emphasize because I am a 'working mother.' When you are single and you work, there is only one job to do. When you marry and work, there are two jobs: keeping house and working. But when you have a child, too, then it's quadrupled because you have just as much work at home—a husband rarely pitches in sufficiently. Even if he doesn't mind a little housework, there is the job, the child, and the responsibility of getting across to your caretaker what you want done for your child."

"I think too much is expected of women without at the same time giving them the credit they deserve for raising a family. In the law office where I worked, women were often passed over in promotions because they were not considered as continuously employed if they took maternity leaves. So, I just left. When I go back to work, I'll begin with another firm."

"It's quite unfair. Women are passed over for promotion in industry for the same reason. No provisions are made for a 'buddy' system, so that two people can do the same job. The excuse is that the fringe benefits would be too expensive."

We are living in a period when more and more women, including an increasing number with children under six years of age, are entering the work force. Insufficient provisions are made by society for the care of these children. They may be given the least effective care at the time when intelligent care is most important. The first three years are considered by most experts the most crucial; that is why we concentrate on that period. The extended family with a grandparent or aunt available to take the mother's place when she goes to work is a rarity. In many cases, the grandmother is working, too! In some areas, one can find a good day-care center small enough and intimate enough to give children of this age adequate individual attention and appropriate physical surroundings and equipment—at a fee that parents can afford. But that is quite rare, especially for children under three.

"Well, I have decided not to work, even though we could use the money. My husband has had to take two jobs; but he is willing to do it, and I am willing to spend a lot of evenings alone because of it. We think it is worthwhile because we have been observing the children of our neighbors who work and leave their children in day-care centers or in a relative's house. They don't speak as well as our son; they don't socialize well; they cry a lot. They just don't seem to be happy. Those who do seem to be doing well relate to their caretakers as though they were the parents. I wouldn't want my child to do that; I want to have his affection for me, not for the caretaker."

"Suppose a mother does have to work for whatever reason. Does she necessarily lose her child's affection? Isn't she still the mother?"

She is still the mother; but if she is away most of the time and the baby's needs are met by another caretaker, that person may become the "psychological" parent. It is important, however, that the child establish an affectionate relationship with the caregiver. The relationship indicates that he is well cared for and that he feels secure and is developing basic trust. That does not mean that the biological mother has lost her role or the child's love. She may fill her role in another way when she returns from work. She has to establish her own way of spending quality time with her child. As we have discussed before, the mother should, upon first returning, spend time with the child, playing with him, talking to him, having a snack with him and later involving him in any household chores. She can also spend time bathing and putting him to bed, either by herself or with the father when he returns. Parents can establish special pleasant play and bedtime routines in the evening. Working parents will then be establishing different roles for themselves with their child, but ones that are *just as important* as the one with the caretaker. Weekends are another period that can be used in expanding one's parenting role with the child.

"But isn't a mother who works all day at some job or profession—no matter how interesting—too tired to be patient and involved with her child? Isn't that asking too much of her?"

It is true that the parent may be tired, but she is tired of doing her outside job. There is plenty of energy left to do a different job at home, especially if one regards it as a pleasure to be with one's child. We all know that after work tired businesspeople have enough energy to go swimming, play tennis or squash, ride bicycles, or jog. The tiredness is from doing the office job. There is plenty of energy left for other activities, and caring for one's child can be one of them.

"It is true that the 'working parent' can establish a good relationship with her child. But doesn't she miss a lot of the firsts: the first step, the first word—all the new things a baby learns? I have had that thrill. I wouldn't have missed it for the world. It only made me sad that my husband wasn't home to share most of these 'firsts,' too."

These are all important considerations. But each family has to make its choices according to its needs and compensate in other ways.

Working Mothers Need Help with Housework

"It seems that mothers have to take the major burden in any case—and if you work you feel guilty."

Our society seems to place the major burden on mothers. Research shows that the increase of women in the work force has not been paralleled by an increase in male participation in housework. But it need not be so. We believe parenting is a shared responsibility. Household chores and baby care are not something that only a woman can and should do. Societal

■   ■

attitudes have to be changed. Fathers are equally capable of caring for children—given the time and the inclination. Fortunately, some fathers are getting more involved with child rearing. If parents understand child development, child care can be an exciting challenge, not a chore.

A rather radical idea, but one that would relieve many of our present tensions, would be to pay mothers to stay home if they wished to take care of their *own* children, while at the same time learning how to do this better. This would be an enormous step forward in our society. It would be more economical than day care for very young children. Courses on child rearing would help as sources of information, as support groups, and as an economical way for early detection of children's difficulties. This approach would begin to educate society to advocate the appropriate care of children in the preschool years and beyond.

At the same time, greatly improved and expanded day-care services should be made available, especially for preschoolers aged three to five. Parenting education classes should also become a part of the day-care system, to help these parents meet their children's needs.

Such a dual system would give all women the *real* choice of remaining at home to rear their own children, especially in the early years, or joining the work force with the feeling that their children are being adequately cared for. In the meantime, it is our concern to look at this dilemma as objectively as possible. Our purpose is to enhance parental understanding of child development so that good parent-child relations can be established. In that way, parenting can become a happier, more satisfying role and the child can be helped to reach his or her maximum potential, whatever the family's particular circumstances.

Discipline: A Teaching Process

Your children are now more mobile and are exploring and trying to manipulate more of the objects in your houses. Many of these objects are dangerous for a child of this age. What do you do about it?

Toddlers Don't Understand Consequences

"We are having quite a time with that. Our baby can feed herself with a spoon. We are proud of that. But she starts walking with the spoon in her mouth and I take it away from her and give her something else. She throws herself on the floor and looks as if she's about to have a tantrum, and she is not satisfied with the substitute. She isn't even certain what it is; but whatever it is, she doesn't want it. She wants what she had before."

Children are very insistent on continuing their activity, and they do protest. That is normal. We want them to understand that walking with a spoon, pencil, or other object can be dangerous if they should fall and jam it into their eyes or throats. We want them to understand this and be

■   ■

reasonable. That would make life easier for us. However, we cannot expect it of children this age. They cannot foresee such consequences, and therefore they do not comprehend our concerns.

One way to make such an incident easier to handle is by offering the child something more attractive to hold: perhaps a small soft toy, ball, or a small jar with a block in it. Then, as the baby reaches for the toy, remove the spoon instead of pulling it away and give the substitute before the baby has begun protesting.

"But that way you are not teaching the child that it is dangerous to walk with spoons and such things."

The children are too young to comprehend this danger, but you may begin trying to get the idea across to them if you don't expect too much. After the spoon has been taken away and when the child is not protesting and can hear you, you may say, "Spoons are for eating. We don't walk with spoons. We walk with dollies or teddies."

Importance of Safety and Exploration

If a parent is consistent and persistent, the child learns in time that some objects are not allowed in certain situations. It takes patience. It is not easy. Once this understanding comes, it is a very important milestone. Homes should be arranged so that you do not have to limit the child all day long. When the children were younger, we talked about the dangers and mess associated with their increasing motor ability. Now the children are even more mobile; most are walking and some are beginning to climb a little. The danger increases for pulling things over and getting into cupboards with medicines or poisonous cleaning materials.

We do have to try to confine the restrictions we place on children's exploration to matters of safety rather than whims of ours to keep our houses neat. Precious objects should be put out of the way for their preservation. If they are too large to be moved, then the baby has to learn to avoid them and be given interesting substitutes to play with. In the kitchen, for example, the stove and certain closets are off limits, but one cupboard can be made safe for exploration with a set of cups, pans, measuring spoons, and jars. Most children are fascinated with these domestic utensils, often preferring them to elaborate toys.

The important thing to remember as children reach this stage is that they need to explore. Their curiosity about the world around them and their understanding of the properties of objects—what makes things work—comes from their manipulation of the objects around them. This understanding and the desire and drive to understand are not enhanced if everything the child tries to do or touch evokes a stern parental "No." The parent can become a real guide during this phase. The child begins to learn what is dangerous and what is safe, what is appropriate and what is not; he learns what his parents approve and what they don't approve.

■   ■

Child's Need for Approval

Parents often emphasize limitations and disapproval with a firm "No" or, in frustration, angry words. Approval is often not overtly expressed to the child.

How do you show approval when your children are doing the right things? Do they get the message that these actions are approved?

"I say, 'Yes, very good, nice!' "

Do you say it dramatically enough so that it is more important than the "No"? That's the key, to make your approval much more important than the "No." When the child is doing something that we like, many of us just smile. The child may not see it and may not get the message. The child must really hear the "That's good," so that she will know that you approve of what she is doing. That approval gives children a sense of self-esteem or well-being about themselves. Not only is this sense of self-esteem important, but parental attention for *approved* behavior is an important pattern of parent-child interaction. If we pay attention only when our children are "naughty," then our attention is counterproductive—and the relationship becomes one of an "angry alliance." If we pay more attention when children behave appropriately, or as we approve of them, then our relationship can be positive. Children look for attention and approval and will work for it. They will try to avoid disapproval; they will see that they don't have to be "naughty" to get attention.

Often you see your child about to touch something, then he looks at you because he wants to know if you are going to say "No" or "Yes." Have you seen this yet?

"I have seen my child do that. But I thought he knew he was not supposed to touch the light cord and that he was just teasing me. So I became angry and slapped him."

It is very common for parents to mistake the child's testing of limitations as teasing. Children need to be shown over and over again what is approved and what is disapproved. Children will work for the approval. The trouble with us is that we're often much more emphatic about the "No"; we sometimes shriek and yell! We feel the child is bad and we give the child the feeling that he is bad.

"Well, isn't the child being bad when he does what he isn't supposed to?"

He is not bad. He is just trying to find out what is right or wrong. We, the adults, are the teachers. We have to repeat the response until the baby learns. Some children learn after twenty times; some may take what seems to the parent like two hundred times! It depends on the child's neurological maturity. At this age he doesn't have control of his impulses. He still needs the parent's *help* in *not* doing what he is beginning to sense is wrong. That is why he looks back at the parent. He is not teasing. He is looking for his parent to help him control his impulses.

"I have tried to be firm, but sometimes I'm gentle and say 'Please.'"

You cannot vacillate; you have to be *very* firm right from the start. It has to be a firm "No" instead of a gentle "Please don't, dear."

"He often cries and cowers away from me. Then I feel guilty and give him a hug. A few minutes later he goes back."

You are giving your child a double message. You are being very stern and scaring him; then you are cuddling him. He feels your ambivalence. So you really haven't accomplished anything. It is important to say a very firm "No." The impulse to do something is there; you have to give another outlet for that impulse and show your approval for the substitute. When you understand that you are teaching your child an important lesson for her future life, then you will realize that you don't need to feel guilty about imposing limits.

Importance of Substitute Activities

"I used to be able to substitute a toy when my baby was doing something wrong or harmful, but now that won't work. He always likes to be in motion since he learned to walk. He used to be able to play with a toy, sometimes for forty-five minutes."

In that case, a motor activity has to be the substitute for him. For example, take him to find something in another area of the room. Your child has achieved a new level of development. He is concentrating on motor activities now, and you must utilize this level to absorb his interest. Parents have to move with the child's level of interest. Different responses are needed at different stages—this is called "cuing in" to your child.

"Are they too young to understand that if they do something bad, they won't get a cookie; and when they are good, they will?"

That is a very difficult way to set limits, even with an older child who is verbal. When a child is removed from some unacceptable activity and is happily engaged in another, a cookie may be offered to reinforce the pleasant atmosphere. Cookies should not, however, be offered as rewards. If this has been the usual procedure, the child may begin to associate approved behavior with oral gratification. This is a habit best not initiated.

"I just think a lot of the time is spent diverting. I find, too, that my son likes to be in the same room with me. If I'm in the bedroom, then he must be there, and I'll give him a brush or some knickknack to play with."

Yes, for effective diversion an adult has to be there in person.

"I like everything to be very neat when I get home from work. I get annoyed at the baby-sitter when the house is a mess. I wonder if that attitude is making her say 'No' too much to my daughter."

■   ■

That is possible. It is very important to try to limit saying "No." We have to accept the fact that a house with a baby cannot be as neat as it was before the baby arrived. But it doesn't last forever. If regarded as part of the child's growing and learning, it may be seen in a better perspective.

"I guess I'd better discuss this whole business with my sitter. I need to be more understanding of her. And we both need to agree on how we discipline my baby."

That is a very good idea. It is very important for everyone involved with the child's care, especially mothers, fathers, and sitters, to be consistent in their teaching of discipline. Inconsistent discipline—like the ambivalent messages we discussed earlier—can be very confusing to a child and will slow down the learning process. Different adults have different personalities and styles; each will interact with the child in his or her own special way. But in some areas like discipline, there should be as consistent a message as possible. Inconsistency in our responses to children is, in our view, what "spoils" them.

Different Cultural and Ethnic Attitudes Toward Child Rearing

Do you find that some of the attitudes we discuss here are quite different from the way your parents and neighbors view child rearing? Is this upsetting to you?

"I find that when I tell people I attend parenting classes with my baby, they say, 'What's wrong with you?' "

"Yes, I get the same thing. 'Why do you have to learn how to be a parent? That just comes naturally.' "

Why Teach Parenting Skills?

Parenting in our complex society does not come as naturally as it does for the lower animals. Parenting has always been taught. From the beginning of time, the care of children and the teaching of the culture and mores of tribes, peoples, and nations have been passed down in families from generation to generation. The phenomenon that has seemed so new in the last decades is the teaching of parenting skills by people *outside* of the family, a trend made necessary by the many changes and far greater mobility of our society.

In the past, when several generations lived in the same house, or at least nearby, there were family members around to help the new parents. Most young mothers had also had experience caring for younger brothers and sisters and cousins. Now families are more scattered. Most of you have had little experience with children until you had your own, and families

are not usually around to help except at the very beginning, and then only
if you are lucky.

Appropriate Attention Is Not "Spoiling"

*"My father-in-law used to tell me that my child was going to be a spoiled
brat if I kept picking him up when he cried. He is a strict, European
disciplinarian. My husband tries to support me, but he wonders sometimes."*

As we have said before, *appropriately* attending to children's needs does
not spoil them. Crying is the infant's only language. He cries for a reason:
because he is hungry or wet or lonely. When the parent or caretaker
satisfies or gratifies this need, a child learns to trust the people around
him or her and gains a sense of confidence and security. She learns how
to "communicate" and interact with the world around her. Actually, the
children who do not get picked up when they cry as infants, and do not
have appropriate attention paid to them, often become the demanding
adults who fume in restaurants and stores if the service is not quick
enough. They are still afraid their needs will not be satisfied.

Your father-in-law's attitude is not too different from the attitude
promoted by American pediatricians some years ago, or that advocated by
behavioral psychologists. They believed that children only cried more if
parents "rewarded" crying by responding. Other psychologists have demonstrated the opposite: that children whose cries are attended to become
more trusting and cry less, and those who are ignored tend to become the
clingers and "cry babies."

Development of Trust and Self-esteem

*"My family also objected when I picked up the baby when he cried. They
said that does not relate to a black child. They said, 'They have to learn to
wait out in the world and you have to let them know it right away.' "*

What they are saying is that the world is much harder for a black child
than it is for a white child and that he's got to learn this early. Unfortunately, they are probably right about the first part. But what will help a
black child—or any child—succeed or overcome difficult situations in life
is a sense of trust in his parents, self-confidence, and self-esteem. A child
who does not develop a sense of attachment and trust because his needs
are not met has a harder time. A child whose parents value him and
respond to his needs learns that he is recognized and develops self-
esteem. This child is willing and able to strive for further achievements
with confidence. If parents do not respond and build trust, the child can
become "turned off" from other people as being of no help or can become
angry and disappointed or unnaturally submissive and ingratiating in order
to get attention and care. We believe that this is what all parents, including
black parents, want to avoid.

■   ■

You have a real job helping your friends and neighbors understand that all children have similar needs, whatever their race or ethnic group. There is no biological difference in infancy other than that ordinarily found among all children, because each child is unique. It may interest black parents that some of the early studies of infant attachment and the infant's need to be picked up by the mother were done in Uganda. These studies were repeated here in the United States and form the basis for what we have been saying about attending to a baby's needs as soon as you can, no matter what his or her color or national origin. There are few differences between one infant's needs and another's. It is *our response* to those needs that can change his or her personality development. We can enhance it or hinder it. It is up to us in our own immediate families and in our religious institutions and in our community organizations to help people understand children's basic needs.

"Well, this helps me. Now I also understand a little better why my child cries when some of my neighbors try to touch him or play with him. Their whole approach is rough and tough; he is afraid of them."

"I have the same problem with my in-laws, who come from Europe."

Many people have the same problems, because the ideas of past generations and different cultures have been that you have to toughen kids to face a tough world. Well, you don't toughen a child at four weeks or at four months or at two years. First, children have to develop a sense of security, a relationship to their families, and a sense of their own worth. If children don't begin to develop these within the first three years, they are beginning with deficits that make it harder, if not impossible, for them to develop to their fullest potential.

"Doesn't this idea of being tough apply more to boys than to girls?"

That is another one of the "sacred cows" that we have to overcome. Many people still believe that boys will be sissies if they are not toughened up early. Actually, boys of this age need the same attention and protection as girls.

"You say boys need the same protection as girls. I would say girls need to be toughened as much as, or more than, boys. It's a man's world; our daughters need to be tough to get ahead."

"I come from a Spanish culture, and there, too, the idea that a boy has to be tough and continue to be so as a man is the accepted attitude."

First, we must consider the child's developmental needs. Response to children must be adapted to their age. At this age, all children need attention and protection, not toughening. Instead of making girls and women fit into the old male stereotype of being "tough," however, perhaps we should be thinking of how we can help boys *and* girls to become competent and self-confident and sensitive to the needs of others—as well as the other qualities we admire in men *and* women.

Spacing of Children

Some of you are beginning to think of having another child. What are your thoughts?

"The only reason I would think of having another child is to give my son company and keep him from being an only child."

You think you are going to provide a playmate for your child. You may find, however, that the children are rivals and are not such good friends after all. The spacing can make a lot of difference. If the first child is too young to share his parent's attention and parents are insensitive to his needs, his initial resentment to the new baby may linger on.

Ideal Spacing: The Child's Viewpoint

"What is the best interval to have between children if you plan to space them for the best interests of the child?"

Each family has its own way and reason for the spacing of their children. However, thinking of what is best for the child, the ideal spacing is about three years. The reason for this is that a baby needs a great deal of attention for the first three years. A child of three usually has developed many competencies. She is verbal and can communicate, saying how she feels and what she wants. By this age most children are independent and can feed and almost dress themselves. They are probably toilet trained and, most of all, can separate from their parents and socialize with their peers. A child is in a better position to cope with and enjoy a new baby when he has a sense of self and is more ready to share his parents with another child.

"Logically and developmentally, I can understand and appreciate what you are saying; but my doctor has warned me that I must have another child right away because of my age—I'm thirty-five."

After thirty-five there is increasing risk of difficulties in pregnancy and fetal abnormality. That is a medical issue for serious consideration. However, we are discussing what is best for the child. One must realize that a child of eighteen months usually does not have the capacity to understand the situation as well as an older child. She will not be able to tell you how she feels or to express her resentment or hostility toward what in her eyes is an "intruder." There will be times when she needs your attention, but the new baby's needs will have to come first. It is more difficult for the mother to take care of an infant and a toddler who is not yet ready to separate.

■   ■

With appropriate expectations of each child's needs, you will have a much better chance of coping.

"I am interested in what you say because my husband and I want to have all our children close together so that I can go back to work before my training is useless. It sounds like it will be harder—but possible."

It is possible, but harder, as you say. You may need more help from your husband and other members of your family. It may even be necessary to employ help in caring for the home and children.

Why Have Another Child?

"This just makes me feel more than ever that I am not sure I want another child. I enjoy our baby, but he takes so much time and effort. Why should I have another child?"

The best reason for having another child is that the parents want to have one. You should not have a child because somebody else thinks you should or because you would like company for the first child. Each child should be wanted for himself. The best reason for having a child is that you love children and look forward to bringing up more than one child—you think you will enjoy the challenge of having two (or more) children, each with a different personality. For those who feel this way, it is exciting.

"I love my son so much. I don't think I could love another. I still feel that I couldn't put the time and energy into another child that I have into him."

This is a very common feeling; one can't imagine loving another child or going through all those sleepless nights again. But remember you are now an experienced parent, and probably the things that you found very hard the first time will not be so hard the second time. You know a good deal of the mechanics now that you didn't know the first time. So you will probably be more relaxed.

"We can't afford another one now, although we would like to have another baby someday. If we do, we will have to move, because there just isn't room in our present apartment—and that will add to the expense, too."

"I really feel now that I would like to get back to school and do the things I couldn't do before. That's my reason for not having another child."

Each family has to make its own decision. Now that our whole society is working toward population stability, there isn't that pressure for everybody to have large families.

Only Children

"Isn't it bad to have an only child? Aren't only children usually spoiled children?"

Only children are not necessarily spoiled children. It depends on what you mean by spoiled. We feel that children are spoiled when their needs are

■   ■

not consistently attended to—sometimes getting attention and sometimes not. This can happen more easily in a family where there are many children close together, with no one getting sufficient or consistent attention.

"I read some research on only children in which they seem to think only children might be better off than other children. Is that true?"

There are reports that indicate that the first child in the family is the better achiever. In effect, he has had the advantage of being the only child until his siblings arrive.

"One of the things you associate with only children is that they always seem to want to be the center of attention. I call that spoiled."

Only children spend a good deal of time with adults. When adults are around they expect to be involved because they are used to being with adults.

"Don't parents of only children have to make more of an effort to see that their children have companions?"

That is, of course, one of the extra responsibilities of having an only child. However, there is no reason why an only child's day should be so different from other children's. Many people have no choice about having another child—or not having one. All of us can learn to adjust. Only children can have happy, cheerful childhoods; sometimes a child with brothers and sisters can be lonely. There is no *one* best number of children. It depends on how parents respond to children's needs and on each family's circumstances.

"Well, I can tell you that I wish I had heard this discussion long ago. This is my second baby, and there are only two years between the two. It is very hard. One year more would have made quite a difference. My reasons were wanting to get back to my profession and have child rearing over faster. I'm learning to manage, but it's hard. I would tell someone else to think it over carefully."

As we have said before, each family must make its own decisions. Some are based on emotions or economics or age factors; some are cultural or religious. Each family, if well informed, can be prepared to cope effectively for the good of the entire family.

Emergency Measures for Accidents: Poisoning, Cuts, Splinters, Head Injuries, Burns, Choking

During the second year, children often have more accidents because of their increased mobility and exploration. Knowing simple first-aid procedures will help you to keep calm and enable you to reassure the children while coping with the emergency.

Poisoning

The best way to deal with accidents is to try to prevent them. All poisonous cleaners, detergents, or paints should be put on high shelves or in cupboards with safety catches or locks (with the keys kept well out of reach). This same precaution should be taken with all medications. As you probably know, even drugs commonly used for children, such as children's aspirin or vitamins, can be toxic if taken in amounts over the normal dose for age and weight. Care should be taken not to leave medications in purses. Children of this age enjoy exploring mother's purse when it is left in an accessible place and sampling its contents. (Lipstick can make a mess, but a parent's medication could be lethal.) These precautions seem self-evident, but too many of these avoidable accidents still occur. Parents may feel that the medicine cabinet is "safe" because the child is not a climber. But there is always a first climb or another new development that enables the child to get into trouble. Therefore, parents must get into the habit of observing these precautions. In this year, the need to watch the children carefully is more demanding on parents because of the children's natural curiosity. We don't want to inhibit this exploratory drive, but at the same time we want to keep the children safe.

"What if the child, no matter how careful you are, does get into a poisonous substance. Then what should you do?"

There are certain precautions you should take to be ready for such an accident. One is to have the number of the Poison Control Center in your area posted near the telephone. If there isn't one, then you should have the number of the nearest hospital emergency room and your doctor's number posted. (It is a good idea to have these numbers in your wallet as well, so they are available when you are out visiting or shopping.) The second precaution is to have on hand syrup of ipecac, a medicine to induce vomiting, in case you are directed to give it by the doctor. It is also useful to keep sufficient cash for taxi fare posted near your phone so that you or the sitter can get to an emergency room or doctor. When the child ingests something that you suspect is poisonous, have the container in hand as you phone so you can read off the ingredients. If Poison Control or the doctor advises giving ipecac, give one tablespoon to a child of one year or over with a glass of water. If no vomiting occurs in twenty minutes, the dose may be repeated *once* only. If there is still no result, then take the child to the nearest emergency room or doctor, taking the container or label with you. Keep the child upright, so that if he or she vomits there will be less chance of choking. *Ipecac should not always be given,* so it is best to consult Poison Control or the doctor first. If the ingested material is caustic, such as lye, for example, ipecac should not be given. Instead

■   ■

you should give milk or water, anything to dilute the poison, and go to the emergency room as soon as possible. You can call your doctor from there.

The same procedure of calling Poison Control or your pediatrician should be followed if the child ingests too many baby aspirins or vitamins or any adult medication.

Cuts and Splinters

"Could you talk about scrapes and cuts? Because that's my son's problem. I know I should wash off a scrape, that soap and water is the best treatment, and if there is dirt in it that I can't get out, to see a doctor. But he raises so much more fuss now than before and kicks and screams. I was wondering if it wouldn't be just as good to simply put some antiseptic on and a Band-Aid and let it go at that."

It is very unpleasant and unnerving when the child puts up a fight against first-aid measures, but the parent still has to do the right thing. The compromise may lead to unnecessary smarting of the wound by an "antiseptic" that may not avoid subsequent infection because of the contamination of the wound by the remaining dirt and germs. Washing the area involved with soap and water is the best procedure. Then the wound should be covered with a light sterile dressing or Band-Aid. If the accident occurred outdoors or in the street and there is soil embedded in the wound, your pediatrician should be consulted to make sure the child's immunization for tetanus is up-to-date. While attending the child, the parent must bear in mind that the child is frightened and needs to be assured that the parent understands and is going to help, not scold.

Another way to ease the situation is to get the child involved in the process. As many of you have probably discovered, the children are entering a period when Band-Aids are a kind of magic "cure-all." There are some kinds that have decorations on them—stripes and stars. After getting the child calmed down, hand her the box of Band-Aids and ask her to pick one. Explain that before the Band-Aid is put on, the cut must be washed. Then you can partly open the Band-Aid and let her get it out. Talk about the colors or stars and then make a little ceremony out of the Band-Aid.

"Now that you mention it, I did see a child in the park with about five Band-Aids on his leg. He kept looking at them and touching them. I think they made him feel more comfortable. I will try that."

"I will, too. But you know it is so hard not to scold the child, especially when she hurts herself doing something that I told her not to do."

That is very understandable. But parents must remember that children of this age, while they may be aware that they are doing something forbidden, still do not have the self-control to resist. So parents must control their first impulse to scold, and comfort the child while they are administering the appropriate help.

■　　　　　　　　　　　　　　　　　　　　　　　　■

"My trouble is when there is a cut and a lot of bleeding. I get excited. My baby fell and hit his mouth, and his teeth cut his lip. I remembered to soothe him but I couldn't remember whether to wash his lip or press on it or what."

Bleeding usually washes away the dirt unless it's a very jagged, dirty cut that needs professional attention. Usually, just applying pressure for a few minutes with a clean cloth or dressing is sufficient to stop the bleeding. Constantly washing the cut after the first cleansing only washes away the clot and the natural clotting substance that stops the bleeding. If the cut is large, open, or continues to ooze or bleed for more than five minutes, it is best to see a doctor, since stitches may be needed. If the blood is not oozing out but spurting out, apply pressure above the bleeding point and go to a doctor or a hospital emergency room at once. An artery may be cut, and this requires immediate medical attention.

"My baby stuck a tack into his finger. There was a hole and it didn't bleed at all. My doctor took that very seriously."

Puncture wounds that don't bleed are often overlooked. They can be the most serious, however, because the puncturing objects may have been carrying infectious germs, pushing them deep into the wound. To avoid infection, the child may even need an antibiotic or a tetanus injection, depending on the last immunization date. A doctor should be consulted to determine the treatment.

"We have a wooden floor on the porch of our house. Sometimes, when our child plays on it, he slips and falls and gets a splinter in his hand or leg. We try to keep him on the rug, but it doesn't always work. We remove the splinter with a tweezer if we can and then wash the area clean. It is a trauma all around, however, because our child cries and screams. Some friends have told me that small slivers work their way out and that I am causing more trauma than necessary. Is that so?"

It is best to remove a splinter. Wash the area first with soap and water, then wash again after the splinter is removed. If the splinter isn't easily removed with tweezers, or leaves a deep hole, consult the doctor.

Head Injuries

"My big worry is that my child will fall or hurt his head seriously because he insists on climbing. I try to keep hold of him when we are in areas where he could fall down stone steps and really hurt himself. But just in case—what about head injuries? If a child bumps his head really hard, should you try to keep him awake or let him fall asleep?"

In case of head injuries, rest is the most important thing. If the fall causes unconsciousness immediately or later, consult the doctor at once. The child should not be shaken to keep him awake because further damage may be done. It is best to keep him quiet and take him at once to the

■   ■

nearest doctor or hospital. If there is vomiting, bleeding from the ear or nose, pallor, or unequal size of the pupils of the eyes, immediate medical attention is necessary. None of the child's symptoms can be assessed well if the parents are too excited themselves. The most important thing in an emergency such as this is to reassure the child that you are there and that you will take care of him. Then assess the situation and get proper help. Keep the child as calm and quiet as possible as you go to the doctor or the emergency room of the nearest hospital.

Nosebleeds

"My little girl fell while we were visiting yesterday and came running to me with her nose bleeding. I don't know how it happened. My friend got very excited, laid her down, and put a cold compress on her nose and one at the back of her neck. But it didn't help much and the baby kept screaming. I tried to soothe her. Then I remembered that it is best for the child to sit up while you squeeze her nose closed."

That is the correct procedure. In case of a nosebleed, the child should sit up while you squeeze the nose closed by pressing the nostrils together, where the soft part meets the bone. This stops the bleeding. It is better for the child not to lie down, because then blood may run into the back of the throat. Most children hate cold compresses on their faces or necks, so their use is often counterproductive for nosebleeds. If nosebleeds are prolonged or frequent, the doctor should be consulted.

Burns

"I was able to keep my baby from going near the stove by saying 'No, hot.' But now he's so active I'm afraid he'll run into me when I am cooking and tip over something hot that I'm lifting before I can warn him away. In fact, he did tip over a cup of hot soup, but only a little splashed on his hand, leaving a small red spot. I just put a cold cloth on it. But if it had been more severe, should I have used butter or some salve? That's what my mother always did."

For just redness, which is a first-degree or superficial burn, use cold water or an ice cube or cold compress until the stinging pain subsides. Then a nonadhesive dressing, such as Saran Wrap, can be put on to protect the area. If blisters form, the burn is more serious. The blisters should not be broken or opened. The child should be taken to the doctor or emergency room. If burns are more extensive or severe, remove the clothing around the burn, apply cold compresses, and get to the hospital as quickly as possible. If the trip is long, give fluids in sips frequently on the way. At no time should butter or oils or powders be applied. Oil applied to the hot flesh will continue the burning action; ice, or even cold water, will stop the actual burning process. In addition, oils complicate the proper cleaning of the area and may serve as a culture medium for the growth of bacteria, thus causing infection. The first impulse may be to put on a salve, but it is better to wait for your doctor's instructions.

One can't reiterate often enough that matches must be kept away from children and that children should never be left at home alone, because they can start fires by playing with matches or tipping over electric lamps and heaters. If you have to leave the house, even for a few minutes while you think the baby is asleep, it is better to wake the child and take him with you. In addition to having an accident, the child could awaken and become frightened at finding himself alone.

Convulsions

"My baby had a cold, sore throat, and very high fever and suddenly he had a convulsion. I took him to the emergency room. They gave him a cool sponge bath and some aspirin and, I think, a sedative. He was better the next day, but it was frightening. Is there any way to be prepared? Does that happen often with small children?"

Some small children do not tolerate high fevers well and have convulsions whenever their fever gets high. Your doctor can best advise you what to do for your child. In general, it is well to give something to control fever, such as Children's Tylenol (whatever your doctor recommends), at the first sign of fever. Be prepared to give cool baths or sponge baths if the fever gets high. Any child who has a convulsion should be seen by a doctor to determine the cause. During a convulsion, parents should keep the child's head inclined and the tongue extended, to avoid choking or aspiration.

Choking

"My child is at the stage of putting everything in his mouth. I'm afraid he'll choke on something or swallow something harmful. What is the best thing to do?"

It's best to keep an eye on him. But even so, we can't always prevent swift action on the part of the child. If the baby actually swallows a small, smooth object, the most important thing to do is keep calm and not frighten the baby. Then, it is a good idea to give her something soft to eat, such as bread or thick cereal, so that the object will be coated. If the object is sharp or jagged and could cause a perforation, you should also give the child something soft to eat and then get in touch with the doctor immediately.

If the child is choking on an object or piece of food, again it is most important to keep calm and not frighten the baby. The first emergency procedure is to quickly inspect the baby's mouth to locate the object. If it can be reached, it should be pulled from the mouth immediately. If it is in the baby's throat, do not try to dislodge it with your fingers, because you may push it farther down and cause more difficulty. The best procedure is to make use of gravity by inverting the baby and slapping his back firmly.

■   ■

A good way to do this is on your lap or along your extended legs. If the object is not dislodged, place the baby facedown along your forearm (or, for a larger child, you may use your knee) so that his abdomen rests against your arm (or knee). Then, quickly and firmly press down three or four times with the heel of your hand between the child's shoulder blades. This usually causes the baby to cough up the object so that you can remove it from his mouth.

If these emergency measures fail, take the baby immediately to the nearest hospital emergency room. Even though an object is obstructing the baby's throat, enough air may be getting through to allow him to breathe. Soothing and calming the baby is important at this point, so that the spasms or crying are not intensified. Crying itself constricts the throat muscles, creating less air space.

We have talked about these emergency procedures to help you feel prepared. It is always important to remember that the child is even more frightened than the parent. Therefore, the first step is to soothe and comfort the child. Then assess the situation as calmly as possible so that you can take the appropriate measures.

Socialization

As the children are getting older, your social life may be increasing and the children will be introduced to new situations. At this age, the children can begin to enlarge their social horizons. They need to emerge from the confines of the immediate family into the world of friends and neighbors. Have you been venturing into new situations with them? How is it going?

"We've been trying to get out on weekends with the baby. Sometimes we just go for a ride in the car, and he likes that. It gives us a change of scene, and we can show him things. It works all right."

"We've had some trouble visiting friends. Whenever we go to a different place, a place the baby has not been before, he stiffens up, cries, and seems frightened. We've almost decided not to go out at all with him. What should we do? We want to get out, but we can't have baby-sitters all the time."

Children's Responses to New Situations

Many babies don't feel secure in new surroundings. This is normal because the new or unknown is strange and can be frightening. Your baby responds vigorously to change; other children become very quiet and clinging. Some babies are wary of strangers and strange places because they have been frightened by well-meaning but overenthusiastic friends or relatives who rush up without giving the baby time to get used to them. Even some babies who have not had that experience are very cautious of strangers;

some sense that the parent may allow the stranger to pick them up and hold them.

If your baby responds fearfully to new places and people, you can help him feel more secure by holding him close to you. Instead of not taking him out and increasing his isolation, you need to help him learn about new situations. Talk to him. Show him interesting things about the new place. If the baby doesn't relax, then stay a short time and repeat the visit another time.

"I think our problem is just the opposite. We took our baby to visit friends. She made herself right at home. She was into everything. The house was so 'unbaby-proofed' that when we weren't holding her she had to be in a playpen, which she hates. So either she was in the playpen or we were following her like policemen. We had no time with our friends."

When babies of this age (twelve to fifteen months) are taken to visit friends, the parents must not expect the same kind of relaxed visit, with uninterrupted adult conversation, that was possible before the baby was born. It is inappropriate to expect the baby to be quiet and not explore interesting new surroundings. Actually, this exploratory behavior indicates healthy curiosity and appropriate cognitive development. Visits at this age have to be more baby-centered than adult-centered.

"I think we could manage visiting when we have the baby if my husband and I could take turns watching and playing with him; but it doesn't work that way. Before I know it, my husband is deep in a political or business conversation, and he just doesn't seem to know the baby is there. I get so angry. I've just given up, and don't think it's worth the trouble getting all the gear together and then minding the baby just as I do at home all week."

Child rearing is a shared parental activity. Some fathers do need to get more involved. Before going out, it would be a good idea to talk about your expectations. Explain that you would like to participate in the visit, too. One of the ways to encourage the father to be more involved is to indicate how he can show your friends the baby's achievements and the games that he and the baby play together. It also sounds as if you need to get out a little by yourself. Some mothers, without realizing it, actually prevent the fathers from being involved with the baby because she never leaves the two of them alone together. Why don't you try going out for an hour or so on the weekend and let the father take full charge of the baby?

"That's what I've been doing. I go out each Saturday afternoon for a while. Now my husband has a much better appreciation of how tiring the baby can be. But they have also developed some special games on their own. When we go visiting now, my husband really does share."

"We are having trouble with older children. When we go to the park, there is no place just for little children. Sometimes older children of five or six play roughly and knock the little ones over or take their toys. I've made it

■   ■

a practice to sit at the edge of the sandbox. I'm the only mother who does that. I know the others think I am overprotective. Is that overprotective?"

"Overprotective" is a very commonly used expression of disapproval of mothers who are concerned about their children's welfare. There is a great difference between appropriate protection or anticipation of trouble and overprotection. In this case, you know that the sandbox has a mix of children both older and younger. Some older ones, either inadvertently or purposely, are dangerous to children of this age. You can't expect a baby to protect himself from an older child, or even from one of his peers who may poke at him innocently. It is the parent's job to be available to intervene before an unpleasant encounter has occurred.

"My husband says that if I always stand up for our son, he won't learn to stand up for himself and I'll make a 'sissy' of him."

From our experience it seems that quite the contrary is true. If young children are exposed to situations that are frightening and perhaps even dangerous before they are old enough to have developed coping mechanisms, they may always be afraid of situations that involve encounters with others. Such children will hang back and will develop the characteristics that have been labeled "sissy" or "crybaby." Other children may respond by becoming overly aggressive and punching other children without provocation. In this situation, as in so many others, parents must respond appropriately for the child's age. At this age, your children need protection. If you help them now, they will gain the ability and confidence to cope on their own later in life.

Child's Need for Reassurance

Some fathers feel that little boys, particularly, should not be treated in this way. They are more willing to be protective of their daughters. Both boys and girls need protection and help while they learn to socialize. A boy who cringes and cries when threatened by another child should not be considered a sissy any more than a girl would be. Many tend to think it's okay to be protective of little girls and comfort them when they cry; little boys of the same age are often scolded for crying. Parental attention and protection must be age-appropriate and not determined by the sex of the child. At this age, your children need your help as they learn to cope in social situations.

What are some of your experiences? What are your ideas about intervening when children play?

"I guess I expected too much and didn't intervene soon enough, because my child begins to whimper and cling to me as soon as she sees other children approach her. They may not be stopping, just passing by, and she seems to cringe and cling to me. I pick her up and hold her till they pass. How can I help her overcome this?"

■   ■

When a child has had an unhappy experience, one has to be very supportive and stay close to her until she begins to feel secure again. As she has good experiences with other children and matures, she will feel more secure.

"What should we do when our children are playing and start to pull toys away from each other? Some people say to let them settle it themselves so they will learn what to do."

The adults have to intervene. Children of this age cannot settle things themselves. They are not verbal. They do not yet know how to play with other children.

"You know, I think that may explain something that has puzzled me. I do take my child to the park on weekends, and she cries when I take her to the sandbox. Perhaps my sitter did not intervene soon enough."

For those of you who work, it is a good idea to discuss these ideas about beginning socialization with your relatives or sitters. It is important for the child to receive this kind of help and support from caretakers as well as parents.

"My policy has been to ignore it unless the child protests when the toy is taken. You are saying that is not a good idea?"

What you have been practicing is "peace at any price." Actually, you may be giving the nonprotesting child a feeling that his rights are not recognized and are not important to you. He is simply *not* protesting. If this happens too often, the child may become apprehensive at the approach of other children. He may draw back from other children because they have come to mean that he has to give up his toys. The nonassertive child becomes the victim and the assertive one is rewarded. Projecting that to older children, we can see that this is rewarding the "bully." That is not the attitude we want to foster. We have to be sure that the nonprotesting child is protected as well as the one who loudly protests. This is all part of the gradual process of developing social skills, in which the parent or other caretaker plays a very important guiding role.

Outdoor Activities

Now that the children are older, the way they behave outdoors changes, too. Some are very content to be wheeled in their carriages or strollers. Others, now that they can walk, are no longer so willing to sit still— causing parents some concern. How are you managing now when you take the children out?

"I have a great deal of difficulty keeping her sitting down. She wants to stand up in her carriage. I have to keep her harnessed. I'm afraid she'll fall out."

■   ■

"My son doesn't like walking. My husband is always telling me, 'Make him walk, make him walk.' When we're out in the street, he likes to be held. Sometimes he'll get down and walk for a couple of feet. Then he'll lift up his arms, and I usually pick him up. Is that okay?"

Children do like to be picked up and carried. It takes a while before they can do as much walking as we expect. In the house they run around, and you think they'll be able to take a good walk. But when you take them out for a walk in the street, they get tired. They're not ready for much walking in the street yet.

Need for Autonomy and Protection

"I have a different problem. When my child gets out of the stroller, she refuses to hold my hand and starts to run. Fortunately, she's not too fast yet."

Now that the children can walk, they are feeling more independent. Their unwillingness to have their hands held does present concerns about their safety. Parents must be very firm in order to protect the child. Sometimes at this age you can use a special harness that allows the child to walk without having his hand held. In this way, the child feels independent, but you are still able to maintain some control over how far away from you the child can get. Another technique is to hold the child's hand until you are nearly at the playground and then say, "Okay, you may walk by yourself now." You can do the same thing as you are returning to your apartment or home entrance.

Tantrums Caused by Frustration and Fatigue

"My son hates to have me hold his hand. When I insist, he lies down on the sidewalk and has a tantrum. People stop and look at me; it's embarrassing. I don't know what to do."

"My child did the same thing the other day. I got so mad I shouted at him and smacked his bottom. Then he really started to cry."

This is very typical behavior at this age. Children feel more independent and they don't like to be restricted. Or they may have been walking quite a distance and they get tired. Lying down and refusing to get up are common responses. If you are in the middle of the street, you simply have to pick the child up and carry him or her. If you are on the sidewalk, sometimes you can just let the child lie there for a few moments. Then you can say that it's time to ride in the stroller, or time to go for lunch, or time to look in the store window. One must handle these outbursts in the same way that one does a tantrum in any other place. It is also important to try to keep your cool and remember that everyone on the street who is a parent has probably been through a similar episode. It doesn't help to get angry yourself and to shout or hit. Children having tantrums are often

■   ■

frightened by their inability to control themselves; they need your help in regaining control. You will be most effective if you keep yourself under control.

From this age on, it is important to find a good playground where the children can run around safely. A playground should have a fence around it and only one entrance. Then you can watch your child from a distance, giving her the feeling of freedom and independence. At first, the child may wander outside the entrance. This provides another teaching opportunity. You say firmly, "No, we play in here," and lead the child back into the playground. Gradually, children will learn to stay there.

Mobility of Child Demands Vigilance

In the next few months, the children's motor abilities will be improving. At the same time, some will begin to separate more from the parents. These combined developments will mean that the children move farther away from you and that they have the ability to move faster. It is therefore very important to be vigilant in the playground. If they are near the entrance, they can dart out quickly. Or if they are near the slide, they can suddenly be at the top. If one sits down to chat with friends, one must always be watching and ready to dash to protect one's child.

"You are right. My son loves the playground, but I see it as a million hazards. Sometimes I'm sorry that he's become so mobile. It used to be so peaceful to be able to sit on the park bench in the sun and know the baby was safe in the carriage. Those days are gone for good."

Those days are gone for good. Just as one gets used to the child's level of development, she reaches a new level that requires adjustments on the part of the parents. The stage that the children are coming into now is quite trying: they have lots of energy and no idea of the consequences of their actions. Most of the learning at this stage comes from doing and action. Gradually, as the children approach two years of age, more of their learning will come from observation and thinking.

Cuing In to the Child's Needs

Are you finding it difficult to understand your child's new level of development? Are the changes frustrating to you?

Accommodation to Child's Needs

"I think I had the notion before the baby came that I would have the baby fit into our way of life. I learned that it led to an irritating situation between us, and I've gotten used to doing what he needs and not feeling upset."

I think you are right. The baby cannot totally accommodate to the adult world. The adult cues in to what the child can tolerate and needs on the level at which he or she is—that's the whole idea. You know, grown-ups think that they are going to train children to fit into their lives at once; but you can't do that. You have to recognize the various levels of development and adjust your behavior accordingly. This doesn't mean that there will be no adjustments by the baby. Each family has a somewhat different life-style, and by trial and error you are all finding out how much you *have* to adjust and how much the baby *can* adjust. Some of you work part-time or have regular times you go out, so your children have gotten used to being cared for by a grandmother or a baby-sitter. In other families the fathers work late; so you have helped the children to develop a schedule in which they take long afternoon naps and may stay up late to be able to play with Daddy. In some families both parents work outside the home, and a similar schedule is usually worked out: the evening becomes the child's playtime with the parents. These adjustments are made gradually by both parents and child—with the parents taking into consideration the needs of the child for adequate sleep and time with the parents. This kind of scheduling does put an extra burden on parents who have a busy, tiring day. Spending quality time with your child, even when you are tired, is the adjustment you make to the child's needs.

Although you can't train a child to fit completely into the pattern of your life as it was before the child was born, you can, with some adjustments, find a new pattern for your life as a growing family.

Making adjustments for the child's needs does not mean that the child "rules the roost." There are many areas in which you are teaching the child to accommodate to the values of your family in particular and of society in general.

The main thing that children must conform to at this age—and they learn to conform only by consistent training—is that there are certain things they cannot do because they are dangerous to themselves or to others.

Accommodations to New Levels of Development

In all other areas, you should be cuing in to them at their level. You cue in to their level of development regarding what they can eat, how many hours they can sleep, how long they can play with a toy, what toys interest them, and how much they can socialize and separate from you. At the same time, you are also trying to stimulate them to go to the next level of develop-ment. As their central nervous systems mature, they will move to a new level. They need the opportunity to advance step by step at their own rates, not at the rate the parent might find more convenient or pleasurable.

"I have had to say 'No' when something was dangerous, but I felt like a heel. I avoid the negative as much as possible. I guess that makes me pretty inconsistent; but I so want to avoid being like my parents, who were so strict."

■   ■

We are not suggesting that you be strict in the sense that left an unpleasant memory for you, but that you be firm and consistent about a few necessary limitations, such as touching a hot stove or pulling over a large lamp or plant or hitting another child. The important part is to limit and offer a substitute activity appropriate to the child's level.

"But won't the baby be angry with me? I want my baby to love me."

Your child will not be angry with you because you are firm. One can be firm without being harsh, mean, or angry with the baby. Consistent limitations give the child a sense of security as he or she begins to learn what is forbidden and what is allowed. It is the parent's duty to set limits.

"Can the baby understand why you are setting limits? If my baby climbs on the couch and falls off, will she understand the next time I stop her that it is for her safety?"

At this age children do not understand the why, the reason. That understanding comes much later, when they begin to learn the concepts of cause and effect. They are just at the stage when they are beginning to discover that a toy falls down if it is pushed over the side of the high chair.

"Is it wrong, for instance, if while she's playing with something and I can sort of tell that she is about finished, to get her interested in something else before she's fretful?"

To be able to anticipate like that is very good. It is something that parents—and nursery school teachers—learn to do. When parents have difficulty in doing this, the child can become cross and fretful or frustrated. It is very appropriate to change the activity when you see it is reaching an unproductive stage. Often it is possible to show the child a new way to play with a toy. For example, when a child looks as if she is tired of rolling a small ball back and forth, you may pick up a box and let the child drop the ball into the box. A little later, you can show her how to roll the ball toward the box.

Gratifying Needs Is Not Spoiling

"How can you anticipate the baby's every want and need? If I could, wouldn't that spoil her? Does she have to have every need gratified?"

We are not talking about gratifying every wish. That's not possible. If we can anticipate some of them, it makes life run more smoothly for the parent and gives the child a sense that the parent is there to help. It fortifies basic trust. We are talking about children who are nonverbal and can't always express their wishes or needs clearly. It is indeed the parents' job to anticipate as much as they can. If the parents get it right even half the time, that gives the child a feeling of trust and security.

I think you are touching on another aspect of this question when you mention spoiling. Gratifying a child's need is not spoiling. Often, when parents are trying to anticipate or meet their children's needs, they are concerned that other people will think they are spoiling the children—in fact, some people may even tell the parent exactly that.

Very often in crowded places such as shopping centers, buses, or trains, children will be restless. Sometimes they cry and the parents have difficulty discovering what is needed to quiet them. They often want to run around and explore; or they may be frightened by strange places or people. Parents often feel embarrassed and often appear to be placating the other adults rather than satisfying the child's needs. The child is scolded, told to be quiet, sit still, and stop bothering. Does this sound familiar to any of you?

"That has often happened to me. Especially on a bus. My baby will cry and want to get down or tug at the newspaper of the person next to us. I feel embarrassed and try to quiet him down to avoid disturbing others, but he only makes more of a fuss. It's a hassle. It's not every time; some days he is fine."

It's a natural thing for us to say, "Now, sit down and be quiet. There are other people around and you must be quiet," trying to show the other adults you know how to bring up a child. At the same time, you imply that your child is at fault. Your child senses this and protests more vigorously.

"What should one do? What would be the proper procedure, given that situation?"

To respond to each situation, one has to know the child's state. Is she overtired? Is she hungry? Has she been confined for too long? Is she frightened? One must assess the situation. If the child is overtired, she needs soothing—a little patting, soft talk, some rocking. If she is hungry, a snack or a bottle is in order. It is always important to have a few diverting things in one's purse or bag—a toy or book and a snack.

"I have trouble in the supermarket. My baby tries to reach for everything she sees as we pass the shelves. She cries if she wants to touch something and I won't let her. Once, a woman came up to me and said, 'What your baby needs is a good sound smack on the hand.' She made me very angry. But she said it so emphatically, as if she knew so much about raising children, that I began to wonder if she was right and if I am spoiling the baby by not slapping her."

Alternatives to Slapping

Slapping or hitting is never a satisfactory form of teaching. The baby is attracted by all the brightly colored packaged items on the shelves and wants to explore. The trip to the market can be a very important part of the baby's day. As you take down an item and put it into the cart you can name it. Try to give one or two small things to the baby to hold. Talk to the baby and describe what you are going to get next. In this way, the

■   ■

baby becomes involved in what is happening. She absorbs what you are saying, and the entire activity can be productive instead of aggravating.

"When I do that I feel self-conscious. I think people are looking at me as though I were crazy."

You seem to be worrying more about what other adults think than what your baby is learning from this experience. Think, instead, of enhancing your baby's understanding of the world around her and of your increased communication with her. What the other adults think doesn't matter. How your child feels does matter to you.

"I can do that and enjoy it when I have a few things to buy; but I can't do it when I have to do the shopping for the week. It takes too much time, and the baby gets tired or fussy."

That's true. If at all possible, the baby should not be with you for a long shopping trip. If someone can't watch the baby while you shop, it might be better to rearrange your shopping. Do a little each day so that the baby gets used to the routine without getting overtired and irritable.

This is what we were talking about earlier. You can't expect the baby to accommodate completely to your needs. You need to cue in to how much the baby can tolerate. Several shorter shopping trips a week may, in the long run, be better for both you and the baby.

"I guess I fall into the trap of being more tuned in to the adult than my baby when we have company. Somehow, at that time, she seems to want the most attention. I feel that the guest's needs are more important than hers, that the baby should wait."

Waiting is something we learn as we mature. The younger the child, the less she can wait. It is a sign of maturity to be able to wait. Our babies are now at the stage when they can delay gratification of their needs only briefly. It is the adult who should be patient. Parents have to be on the child's side—and not expect more of the child than she can deliver. Children who feel that their parents are on their side—helping them get what they need—develop trust and self-confidence. Children who feel that their parents are always disappointed in them or not satisfied with them take on these feelings about themselves. The way one responds to one's child, therefore, goes beyond the resolution of the immediate situation. It has a lot to do with the development of the child's personality—his feelings about himself and about others.

Dealing with the Child's Fears

New Places and Situations

Are your children beginning to show fear in certain situations?

"Yes, I was going to ask about that. I find now that when we go to a new place my baby shows much more anxiety than he used to. He cries and pulls me away from a house where we have not been before, or where we have not been for a long time."

The important thing is to reassure the child. Pick him up and hold him so he feels secure. Point out things he might be interested in. Tell him you are going to stay a little while and that you will be going home soon. Make your visit very short if he doesn't overcome his anxiety. Try not to give him the feeling that he has done something wrong. This anxiety is age-appropriate behavior. It indicates that the child recognizes the difference in his surroundings and that the "known" is different from the "unknown." It indicates an advance in cognitive development. Some children are more anxious or shy than others in accepting newness. Many parents give children the feeling that they are naughty and that they are displeased with them. If you return to the same place again and the child has not been forced to accept it the first time, it will be easier the second time. As he matures, he will be more ready to explore and socialize. Some children are not yet as ready as some parents would like them to be. We can make them more apprehensive by forcing too much exposure too early. That does not mean we should not try new situations. We should, however, respect the child's apprehension and reassure him.

Loud Noises

"My child is afraid of loud noises. Whenever we are in the street and a car backfires or a loud truck comes along, he starts running to me and cries. So I pick him up till it passes, and then he is all right until the next time. I always say, 'Mama's here; everything is okay. The truck will soon be gone.' As it disappears, I say, 'Bye, truck.' That seems to make him feel better."

Many children are afraid of loud noises. In fact, some people seem to be more sensitive to noise and even as adults will be startled when they hear sudden loud noises. The important thing is to comfort and reassure children that everything is all right. Gradually, they learn that loud noises per se do not hurt them. Again, one must not belittle children for this kind of fear.

Elevators

"My child has fears, too. Especially of the elevator. The door makes a noise as it closes. Right away, the clutching begins."

Elevator phobia is not uncommon in large cities and can start early. Once you know that some elevators bother your child, you must be prepared to distract the child with something interesting to do. One could say, "Let's look for Mommy's keys so that we can open the door" or "Let's look in our bag for your car so that you can play as soon as we get up (or down)" or

"Let's watch the numbers light up." Counting the numbers up and down is a particularly good game when the children are a little older. Another good diversion is to show children how to push the button (in a self-service elevator) and let them do it. Say, "We push the button and the door will close. Here we go up to see Granny." When there is an operator, one can say, "Let's watch the man drive the elevator. First he shuts the door; here we go up, up, up."

Of course, for small children there may be too many strange things at once. They may be afraid of the elevator operator as well as the elevator itself. We are often beset by people who are trying to be kind but sometimes interfere.

"You're right. My daughter was frightened by an elevator man who suddenly poked her in the stomach and gave a big laugh. I guess he was trying to be friendly, but my daughter was terrified."

Some people come upon children too quickly. We need to hold the children and reassure them that we will protect them. What is fun or funny to an adult is not always funny to a child. Children do not understand jokes, or sarcasm for that matter, until they are much older.

Animals

"My little girl just became afraid of dogs. One day when I was taking her home, this very big collie started barking excitedly. She was very frightened of him. Now she is afraid of all dogs."

Fear of all animals—dogs, cats, and horses—is a very frequent fear. One of the most common errors adults make is to try to make the child pet the animal. This often intensifies the fear. The best thing is to hold the child and move away from the animal. Let the child observe from a distance until he is older and has seen you or others pet the animal. It's a good idea to give the child a small toy replica of the animal and show him pictures of the animal. Gradually he may show some desire to get close to the animal and you will allow him to do it. Often, a lifelong fear of animals is started innocently by forcing a child to make contact with them before he is ready.

"I think my child is afraid of dogs because she senses that I am. Is it possible that she knows? I try to hide it."

We know that children are much more sensitive to our moods and feelings than it might appear. Even though you try to hide your fear of dogs, you may be startled or become tense. If you are holding your child, she will literally feel these physical responses on your part. In this case, it is a good idea for both of you to remain at a distance looking at the dog and talking about his actions. Discussing the fear is hard at this age because children do not understand exactly what you are saying and they are not able to express their own feelings, except by crying. By the third or fourth year, you will be able to talk together about the child's feelings—and your own as well.

When one encounters a dog in the park or on the sidewalk, one should not let one's child rush up to it, no matter how small and friendly looking it is. Sometimes the dog's owner will actually say that the dog is frightened of children and may bite. Others will say the dog likes children and encourage you to introduce your child. Again, the most important thing is not to force the child and to let him or her observe from a distance.

Strangers

"My son is frightened of people, strangers who come up and talk to him. They say 'Hello' and he hides behind me. It's embarrassing."

The best thing to do is for you to say "Hello" in a friendly way and move on. Some parents stop and insist that the child reply. These children are really too young for that. When the child is older, having watched you model the greeting procedure sufficiently, he will be able to do it on his own without coaxing. Parental insistence lowers the child's self-esteem and intensifies his reluctance to meet new people because he senses your disapproval of his behavior.

"When my little girl sits on my lap, she is very friendly; but she won't go to anyone. If anyone comes too close, she cries and pulls back."

Adults have to be warned that they must let the child get used to them first, that children need to "size them up" as it were. The child makes the approach to the adult when she is ready and feels comfortable. A little patience on the part of the adult will be well rewarded.

"My child is afraid of her grandfather, who has a muscular condition and walks with a limp. He uses a cane—he is not steady on his legs and he sort of falls into the chair. When he wants to pick her up, she shrieks. I think she senses his weakness."

She notices his disability. The cane and his unsteadiness may scare her; she may sense your concern. This is very hard to explain. Instead, you can explain that children are very often afraid of grown-ups if they are not used to them. Make it general, so Grandfather isn't hurt; but still make it comfortable for the child. After a while, instead of picking the child up, Grandfather should be encouraged to hand her a toy or roll her a ball.

"That reminds me of my childhood. I can still hear my mother say, 'Shame on you; say hello to so-and-so.' I still have a funny feeling when I'm introduced to strangers, but the grown-up part of me goes through the formalities. Are we helping our children to avoid this? Are we sowing the seeds of easy social poise by being supportive of the children at this age?"

Yes, that is exactly it. We are trying to help them deal with their age-appropriate anxiety by recognizing their need for support.

■   ■

"This seems to be an age of lots of fears. When will it end?"

As you reassure the children about one set of fears, they will gradually overcome them. Then suddenly you will discover that there is something new they are afraid of. This is part of growing up and learning about the world.

The Water

For example, you take your child to the beach this year and he loves it, running into the water without fear. Next year, you may take him back to the very same beach. He will be a year older and will be frightened. You just can't understand what it is. This is the year he realizes how large the ocean is and how big the waves are. You have to get him used to the water in gradual stages.

Masks

Halloween masks are something else we might mention at this point. From this age until children are about three or four, they will be very fearful even of other children wearing masks. If children wearing masks come to your door, you should ask them to take off their masks so the baby can see their faces. Even if they see the other child's face, that child is "gone" and the "pussycat" or "witch" is back as soon as the mask is replaced. Even when as familiar a person as daddy puts on a mask or a Santa Claus beard or even sunglasses, he is no longer daddy to a child of this age— even though all the rest of daddy is showing. Daddy should not be hurt. Everyone must realize that this is a phase of development that all children go through.

The Dark

"One fear we haven't mentioned yet is the dark. Our baby screams now if her room is dark."

Yes, and that is a fear that may last several years. Some of you may already have started using dim night-lights. You can get either a small lamp or a little bulb that fits into a plug—the kind that many people keep lit all night in a bathroom or hallway. A little bit of light helps the child to see the familiar objects in the room and feel reassured. Fear of the dark is probably the most common childhood fear of all. As with all other fears, one must reassure the child.

Some children are quite independent and can always do many things on their own and not get into trouble. Others are more sensitive and need more emotional support. Parents have to tune in to each child's needs in these situations. With parental reassurance, fears are gradually overcome.

The Child's Daily Routines and Activities

Now that the children are older, do you find you are able to spend time together in more satisfying ways? Is there any difference from when the children were younger?

■ ■

"There is a world of difference. At first, I was so busy just making sure he ate, slept, was bathed, changed, and kept reasonably entertained. Then when he began to walk, it seemed all I did was run after him to keep him out of trouble. Now he is beginning to talk. There is communication, and I feel I'm spending time with a real person; I am having a great time. This is what I thought having a child would be like. We can do so many things together."

"My son seems to want to be on the go all the time. From the minute he wakes in the morning he is ready to go out in his stroller. Of course, I dress him and give him his breakfast first. That he seems to be able to wait for, but then he wants to go. I feel frustrated because I would like to straighten up the house first and get some cleaning done. That was my old pattern when he was a baby. Now I know that if we go out first, he is happier. I get a little marketing done before the stores are crowded. If it's nice, we go to the park for a while. Then he seems tired and ready to come home for lunch. Then he naps and I do the laundry and some cleaning . . . and then we go out again. By the time his father gets home, we're both pooped! The only good part is that after some quiet play with his daddy, he goes right to sleep."

"I also go to work. My son eats breakfast with his daddy and me. Then we dress him. Both of us get up early so as to avoid too much rush before we leave. Then his sitter comes; her main job is the baby—not the house. She plays indoors with him, if the weather is bad, or goes out to the park. In the afternoons it's a walk outdoors again, or maybe she gets together with another sitter and baby and they play indoors. Then I get home and take over: bathing, supper, and bedtime about nine. Sometimes my husband is home in time to join us. Then it's easier and more fun. I'm trying to take it easy and have more fun; a lot of housework just doesn't get done."

"I used to work full time, too. But it was too much of a hassle for me, so I decided to work part-time, just in the morning. Now I can take my child to the park, or we visit a friend or play games at home. Sometimes we go to the children's room at the library. Now I feel I'm giving my child the stimulation he needs, which I wasn't sure the baby-sitter was doing. The best part is that I have been around to see most of the 'firsts.' We talked before about how a working mother may miss these."

Importance of Play Versus Housework

It seems that those of you who leave your children in the care of others worry that the child may not be getting appropriate stimulation, while the "at-home mother" is there all the time and can make sure. However, some of the mothers who are at home seem to have difficulty tearing themselves away from household chores and seem overburdened. Others seem more willing and able to accommodate to the child's needs and put housework aside. Each one has a choice to make. We believe that the child is more important than the house.

■   ■

"I'm glad to hear you say that the child is more important. It's what I feel, but my husband says his mother always kept a neat, clean house and she had four kids."

We don't know exactly what her circumstances were or what other help she had. Often it is easier for adults to get things done in the house when there are several children in the family who can play with each other. But your child can't be expected to entertain himself for very long. He won't be able to for some time, in fact.

We believe that child care should have priority over housework both for the parents and for caretakers. Most mothers will make that choice— or wear themselves out trying to do both. Housekeepers may get the idea, however, that the house is their priority. After all, it is easy to see when the laundry isn't done or the kitchen floor is not washed. It is not necessarily so easy to show the results of a walk in the park or time spent looking at a book or playing games with a child. To show that the child— and appropriate stimulation of the child—is more important, parents should make a point of asking about the child's day and what activities the caretaker and child have engaged in. It also doesn't hurt if every once in a while you come home when you are not expected, to see what is actually going on. This occasional checking up on the child's daily routines and welfare is also a good idea if the child is left regularly with a neighbor, in family day care, or in a day-care center. Remember, your children are too young to tell you what is actually happening to them.

Children who do not see their parents all day do need time with them in the evening but, after working all day, parents need some time to themselves as well. Though a caretaker may not be as exciting as the parent, she can provide some stimulation and outdoor activities.

"I'm afraid my baby-sitter doesn't have much imagination. I know they go out when the weather is good, but I guess I will have to make some suggestions about games for rainy days."

"Of course, the rainy days or sick days are hard, and the child gets restless and cranky. I have a bag of some new toys he hasn't seen before that I save for those days. I have also put away some old ones. He has a ball trying to play with the discarded ones in a new way. It gives him quite a lift and me a breathing spell."

"A cranky child is no worse than a cranky, demanding boss. Some days at work are just as trying. It seems that every minute of life can't be a thrill, either at home or in the office. You just 'roll with the punches'—it's a challenge."

There is no doubt whether one is an "at-home working mother" or an "outside working mother," it is a challenging job. It takes patience, ingenuity, creativity, and knowledge and understanding of the level of your child's development, his personality, special needs, and how to accommodate the child's and parents' needs. No one ever said it was easy to be a parent, but it can be interesting and fulfilling. No profession—and parenting is an important profession—is without its hard and dull days, its frustrations and annoyances. The difficulties need to be examined thoughtfully so that they can be minimized. Often, that can be profitable.

Daily Routines Should Be Pleasant for Parent and Child

Emphasizing the negative, however, and not focusing on the positive aspects of any job can be destructive. That's why it is important for parents to work out their priorities and establish a consistent framework of daily activities that is pleasant for parent and child. Pleasant daily experiences enhance the relationship between parent and child or housekeeper and child. The child needs the security of familiar activities and the stimulation of new ones. For example, children enjoy becoming more proficient in rolling a ball; at the same time, the game becomes more interesting if they roll the ball into a box, or even try to throw it.

"I just couldn't take the routine at home. I am much better off working all day. When I come home, I am glad to see my son, and he is glad to see me and his father and plays with us. Before bed, we take time to get him simmered down. On the weekend we take turns taking him to the playground. One day each; we can take it. His father is better at it than I am. We both relax when he naps. He seems to be thriving, except that we notice he doesn't talk as much as some other children his age. Can it be his rate of development, or isn't he getting enough speech stimulation?"

Language Stimulation

Some children develop one area more quickly than another. Your child sounds as though all his energy was devoted to motor activity. There probably is no cause for worry. However, one needs to know whether he is getting sufficient speech stimulation so that when he is ready, he will achieve appropriate language development. Some caretakers may not stimulate speech sufficiently. If that is a concern, then the parents can try to make up for it when they are with the child at night and over the weekend.

"I'm afraid we have the same problem. Our housekeeper is Spanish-speaking and she apparently doesn't talk much to our little girl—although she is fine in every other way, gentle and efficient, reliable in everything one would want."

Your housekeeper may feel that you don't want her to speak Spanish to your child. Actually, it may be a good opportunity for your child to learn two languages. Usually children who learn two languages at the same time learn both more slowly, but they can learn both well. The important thing is for your child to be spoken to, to hear language, and begin to say words and communicate. It is much better for her to learn Spanish from your

■   ■

sitter than not to have any verbal communication while you are gone. Reading books that have pictures with names or simple captions underneath may be a good way for your housekeeper to learn some English, too. With encouragement from you—and some help in pronunciation—your housekeeper may find she enjoys this activity.

"I like that idea. I'll try it. Also, I think we need to talk more to our baby ourselves. I did not realize it would make so much difference."

We've been hearing about the many different ways that parents plan for their child's day. Each family has to make the appropriate adjustments to suit the child's and their own needs. Routines will vary, depending on the time parents can spend with their child, their own emotional needs, the child's endowment, and the kind of substitute care that is available. All of this takes a great deal of thought. The important issue to bear in mind is that the child is dependent upon the parent. Each child has his own endowment, but the parent supplies the environment in which the child develops and flourishes. Not every day will be great; but as the children mature and, as some of you have said, "get to be real persons," more days can be happy and productive for both parent and child.

Marital Relations: How to Revive the Romance

How do you feel the care of a child has affected your lives? Has it been what you expected?

"Well, I'll say it's changed our lives enormously in a way we didn't expect. We knew the baby would be an added expense, but we figured that we could manage; and that part is okay. But we didn't figure how much time he would take away from our doing things together, such as going out to dinner, or entertaining, or just talking alone together. The baby himself is a joy, and we are getting to understand his needs better. The older he gets, the better it is getting. But we rarely are alone together—and when we are, we're too exhausted for romance and sex."

"We find this, too. We can't be spontaneous anymore. We have to plan on the baby's needs and then ours. It's a growing experience, I suppose, to look out for another before yourself. Sometimes I wish I could just think about myself."

Certainly, raising a child is very time-consuming and demanding. Many of you are experiencing some satisfaction, even though there are times of frustration. Occasionally, the frustration comes from unrealistic expectations of what child rearing will be like. Other times, frustration comes from unrealistic expectations about what marriage will be like and what each partner can realistically offer the other. Sometimes, a husband may expect his wife to be just like his mother, and the wife's care of the child interferes with the care he desires. The same may be true for a wife.

Much more common, however, are the cases in which parents become fatigued by the many responsibilities of child care, housework, and jobs. "Romantic love" then becomes lost in the other pressures of the marriage. Sometimes, parents don't know what to do about this—or don't recognize the lack for what it is—and develop feelings of anger and frustration toward each other and the baby. Toddlers are very active, and often their sleep is still disturbed by dreams or teething. Parents therefore are often tired and have no energy left for lovemaking, or even for affectionate gestures toward each other. As soon as couples notice such feelings, they should discuss them with each other.

"We had that situation after the baby was born. It took a long time before we were able to talk it out."

Each one has feelings of concern and regret or resentment. If one doesn't discuss one's feelings, it is easy to think that the other doesn't notice or care. Often, it's hard to find the appropriate time for such a discussion because you are so busy getting the child to bed, doing the laundry, and other chores.

Parents Need to Discuss Their Feelings

"We have found we spend most of the time discussing what the children have done or what my day was at the office—and not addressing our feelings. The whole business of being affectionate to each other got lost somewhere. My wife was so busy being cross because I wasn't helping enough; she didn't seem to be making me the center of attention. I thought she ought to, because I'd been imposed upon in the office. I wanted to come home to a haven, and it's not a haven at all—so I was terribly disappointed. I didn't realize that was the trouble until we talked about it."

In all our relationships—whether professional, social, marital, parental—we have to think of the other person's feelings, just as we have to think about how the child is feeling. Each person has to consider how the other one is thinking and feeling about the marriage as well. When the husband comes home and says, "Dinner ready?" and the wife says, "No, it isn't," and he says, "Why not?" then she starts telling him that she hasn't been wasting her time, that she has been busy all day. He can't understand the outburst because he doesn't fully understand what she has been doing and that she feels overworked and unappreciated. At the same time, she may not know what has been happening to him.

"That is exactly the scene in our house. My husband expects dinner to be ready and our son put to bed all between the hours of 7:00 and 7:30. Our baby doesn't finish eating until 6:30. Then I have to bathe him and get him to bed by 7:00 so I can clean up and get dinner ready in thirty minutes. It's a mad rush; so when my husband comes in I'm feeling harassed—and certainly not loving."

Parents Need to Help Each Other

This kind of situation does not need to go on. Parents can try to work out their time schedules and help each other a bit. If it's the mess that bothers the

■   ■

father, it would not be a big deal for him to toss the toys strewn about into the toy box. Sometimes the mother and toddler of this age can do it together as a "cleaning-up time" before bed. Simple dinners can be planned that can be cooked while the mother is tending the baby. It takes a little forethought and planning, but it can be done. Such planning will help to avoid an angry welcome home that is unpleasant for parents and baby alike.

"We overcame that situation by sharing the bedtime routines. I cook while my husband takes over and plays with the baby. Then we put him in his bath together while dinner is cooking. Then one of us reads or sings to him, whichever he seems to want that day. Usually a little holding or quiet play works best; and he is off to sleep. Then we have a quiet dinner alone and talk over the day. Sometimes we make plans for going out and getting a baby-sitter. I think we are really getting to feel good about being parents, and good about being with each other as people and parents. Somehow we expected that from the start, but it took work to make it come out that way."

"My husband and I seem to be on different wavelengths. He was always loving, but in a way that made me feel like a child. Now, as a mother, I feel more grown up and want to be treated that way—not criticized all the time, no matter how tactfully, and I'd like a little praise."

It may be that your husband was brought up in the way that many of us were brought up—if you don't like something, you say so; but if you like it, you make no particular comment. There are many people who will tell you when something is wrong. If it's right, well, that's the way they seem to expect it. If you are really looking for a compliment from that kind of person, then you are doomed to disappointment. It's not that such a person doesn't recognize what you have done and doesn't approve of it; he simply doesn't think to express approval. He may never have had the experience of being overtly approved of in his own bringing up. Therefore, he can't express what he has never experienced.

"I guess that is our situation. I recognize it; so now I will understand better if there is never a compliment. I'll try to consider the lack of criticism as a compliment."

That is a way to deal with the situation. However, it may also help if you express your appreciation for whatever your husband does; it may make it easier for him to respond the same way. All of us like to be recognized and praised a little. If we can do it with our children appropriately, then perhaps we will raise a generation with fewer people who can make only a critical response. In addition, we have to realize that as parents we are growing, too. *We* must be able to recognize when we have done something right ourselves. Then we will not be dependent on others' recognition, although it is always nice to have it. Truly mature individuals recognize their own achievements without being smug.

■   ■

Parents Need Time Off Together

"Isn't it possible that sometimes parents can't get time with each other because of the demands of the household and that they need time away from home?"

That certainly is often true. That is why we have always advocated that parents should spend time alone together regularly one afternoon or evening a week. Occasionally, parents should plan a "mini-vacation," such as a short weekend alone in a hotel in the city or at a resort with friends or relatives in the country. The best way to do it is to have someone the baby likes stay with her in the familiar surroundings of your own house so her routines and sense of security are not disturbed. Then separation will be as painless as possible for the baby.

"What about longer vacations? Would the baby be too upset at this stage?"

It all depends on the individual child and the arrangements the parents can make for baby-sitters. Having the baby at home with a capable baby-sitter whom the child knows well or a family member is best. Leaving the baby with friends or relations whose home he is used to and who knows how to carry out his routines is next best. Sometimes close friends and neighbors carry out these services for each other on an exchange basis. If the child is experiencing separation anxiety in general and is very clinging already, that would not be the best time. If parents have no alternative, then they will have to understand the repercussions of the baby's separation anxiety and deal with them on their return. When the parents understand that often the baby feels abandoned when they leave for an extended period, they can respond patiently and appropriately when they return. They can help the baby deal with the separation by allowing clinging and giving extra attention and reassurance.

It is when we get angry and impatient with the baby for expressing his normal feelings that we get into trouble. A vacation should make a parent feel more relaxed and willing to spend more quality time with the baby. Many parents, in fact, find it nicer to be home with the baby than away from him.

"We went away for a week and left the baby with his regular sitter. When we came home, the baby turned away from us at first. After about twenty minutes, he seemed to recognize us and was all smiles. Didn't he know us?"

My interpretation would be that he was letting you know that he missed you and was possibly a little angry. As he is still not very verbal, he could express himself only in that way.

"Now I understand why our baby is so cross when I first come home after a business trip. It makes me feel better to know that that is his way of expressing that he missed me. I always expect him to get excited and smile; and I'm so disappointed when he doesn't. When my husband is away on a trip, he does the same thing to him."

With children of this age, it is best to take frequent "mini-vacations" rather than an extended vacation. When the child is older, you will be able to be away longer.

■   ■

Even if you are not able to get away, you should make a point of getting out occasionally in the evening. Also, it is important to stop your work while you are home—at least a couple of evenings a week—and talk to each other. Sit down and relax with each other. If, after supper and the baby's bedtime, both parents continue to do work—whether office work or housework—until bedtime, they will be too tired to think about enjoying any intimacy with each other. The decrease in sexual relations between married couples because of other life pressures and fatigue is very common, but it can be overcome with a little effort and mutual consideration. Ultimately, the best thing for the child is to grow up with parents who are happy with each other as well as with him.

Recognition of the Child's Personality as Unique

Now that the children are well into their second year—walking and perhaps saying a few words as well as understanding much more about the world around them, they are beginning to have more distinctive personalities. They are also able to express their likes and dislikes more clearly. Many are already showing early expressions of a desire for autonomy. This is a normal progression in child development that catches many parents by surprise.

Some of you have commented that they are beginning to be "real people." By that you mean that their character traits and personalities are becoming increasingly distinct and individual. Many of you have expressed enjoyment and interest in this development—often when the child begins to express himself or herself in ways that match aspects of your personalities. For example, active, athletic parents enjoy active children; and more verbal parents are especially thrilled when their child begins to say words and communicate. Often, however, children's personalities are quite different from one or both of their parents', and this mismatch can cause difficulties. The active, energetic child can be exceedingly tiring and may appear abnormal to the quiet, reflective parent; similarly, a cautious child can be a total puzzle (and embarrassment) to the active parent.

Have any of you found this to be true in your family? How would you describe the match between yourselves and your children?

"My husband is quiet and likes it that way. I'm more exuberant, and so is our little girl. So I find I have to try to counteract his attempts to keep her quiet; I try to strike a happy medium for her."

"We have just the opposite situation. Our boy is quiet, sensitive, and emotional. I can accept that, but my husband can't understand it. He thinks a boy should be all "go." Gradually, he is becoming reconciled and can see the baby's progress in other than muscular development now that he is beginning to talk. I think he is still disappointed."

Temperamental Differences

It does make it difficult if a parent's temperamental makeup is different from the baby's. It is important to remember that the baby is a unique individual, not a duplicate of the mother or father—or even an equal mixture of both. If one recognizes his uniqueness and respects it as the child's normal endowment, then some thoughtful adaptive arrangements can be made to ease the frustrations that differences can cause. For example, if a very active baby is really troublesome to a quiet mother but enjoyed by the father, the father can assume major responsibility for the outdoor activities that cause the mother anxiety. The mother can concentrate more on the quiet activities such as looking at books and playing games, which are also important to the child's development, while understanding that her son's attention span for such activities will be quite limited.

Mothers and fathers who like quiet may be lucky to have quiet, reflective children. Those households will appear quite subdued to others. Other children may be rather noisy at times. Before they learn to talk, there is a period of screaming. That is the way children express themselves. Also, they simply do not know how to modulate their voices or talk in a whisper. It helps for quiet parents to realize that this behavior is a normal part of development, and not a malicious attempt on the child's part to disturb their peace; and it should be allowed at certain times, such as in the park. Sometimes a child becomes very noisy and disruptive to gain attention; so parents should be sure they give enough attention to the quiet behavior they claim to appreciate, and not use the child's quiet periods as times to ignore him.

"You are right. My daughter is sometimes most exuberant when my husband is reading and paying no attention to her. When he stops his book and reads to her, she quiets right down."

While it is important to recognize and respect the uniqueness of each child's personality, this does not mean that one cannot also encourage a child to develop in areas where natural inclination is not evident. For example, the active child may learn to enjoy quiet activities once in a while. With appropriate encouragement, the quiet, sensitive child can learn to take more interest in more active games. The way to do this is not for the parent to force motor activities on the child and berate him or her for being reticent, but to encourage more activity gradually and gently. Children should be exposed at the appropriate ages to all kinds of activities, such as sports, music, dance, and art. Parents cannot assume that children will have the same interests as they have; but often children develop similar interests if the activities are presented without pressure.

Child's Need for Appreciation as an Individual

"Our son is adopted, so we have no idea about his natural endowment, whether he is artistic, mechanical, musical, or what. He seems to us to be bright, but we really don't know what his potential is. We plan to introduce him to lots of things to see where his talents lie, though I guess we will probably concentrate more on the things we enjoy and understand ourselves. But we love him for himself."

■   ■

That is an attitude that would be healthy for all parents to have regarding their children. A child can have a wonderful personality or talent that, if unappreciated or misunderstood by the parents, can be inhibited or prevented from developing to its fullest potential. There is nothing sadder than to see a perfectly competent child who doesn't "measure up" in his parents' eyes because he can't do what they want him to do.

Growth is a two-way proposition. Children with different character traits and talents cause parents to grow and develop with them. These differences make child rearing a dynamic, interesting interaction between parents and child. Very often parents become interested in new things through their children's interests. If our children were just like us and did just what we always expected, life would be nice and stable and probably a bit dull.

"I'm glad you said that. I was getting the feeling that differences only cause trouble. My husband and I are quite different, and I think our daughter is an unusual combination of two grandparents. It is quite fascinating and fun to watch her develop. We love it."

"You seem to be happy that your child resembles the grandparents. In our case it is just the opposite. I worry that my daughter will be just like my mother-in-law—dictatorial and opinionated! I think I may be mistaking our child's natural development for imitation of her grandmother, and I may be squelching the natural development of her personality."

Often parents may see in their children characteristics of relatives, or even of themselves, that they do not like. It is important to recognize that in most cases these are just associations you have made. They may cause you to relate to your child in such a way that you are always emphasizing the characteristics that you do not like rather than recognizing all the other likable characteristics of your child. In some cases, the very thing you don't like because you associate it with someone you don't like may, with proper guidance, become an asset to the child.

There is much to appreciate about each individual child's personality and achievements. Parental approval stimulates further growth and development in a winning cycle of parent-child interaction. Disapproval and inappropriate parental expectations produce just the opposite: the vicious cycle of the "angry alliance" between parent and child or the child who lacks self-esteem. None of us wants to do that, but sometimes we need help in fully appreciating our children when they are very different from our expectations or from us.

The child whose individual traits and personality delight his or her parents will gain a sense of acceptance and self-worth and self-confidence. Each child develops somewhat differently and needs to be accepted at the level that he or she has achieved. Children thrive when their accomplishments are noted by the parents and when they receive the appropriate mixture of challenge and support.

Age Fifteen to Eighteen Months

Highlights of Development—Fifteen Months

Most children have now advanced from standing and holding on to furniture and taking a few steps to walking alone. Some may have abandoned creeping except for climbing up stairs; most will begin climbing down stairs backward. Greater small motor dexterity is evident in the child's ability to put a marble into a small jar without prior demonstration and to help turn the pages of a book.

When given several small blocks, the child can make a tower of two and can put six blocks in and out of a cup. Putting small objects into larger containers is a favorite activity of this period and is therefore a good game for parents and child.

The child can now grasp a crayon more firmly and may begin to imitate a line as well as a scribble drawn by the parent. She can also place the round piece in the puzzle without demonstration.

The child's vocabulary may have increased to four or five words; some children will have many more words. Most will still be using jargon, unintelligible words with the intonation of speech, much of the time.

While a child's language is related to his or her own maturational timetable, it can also be enhanced by parental stimulation and language modeling. There is still more understanding than production of language. When looking at a book, the child now pats the picture, indicating recognition or interest; parents should name the object to which the child points.

The child may grasp his dish when his food is served and need to be inhibited from spilling it. He may respond with some version of "thank you" occasionally if it has been modeled for him. He now points at things that he wants. He likes to show or offer a toy but then may not actually give it up. He may throw a ball or refuse to throw it. These options are more complicated than parents often realize. Knowing he has the ability gives the child the choice of doing it or not. Learning to throw is very exhilarating; but the child still has no appreciation of what is appropriate—he will need to be intercepted if he decides to throw his dish or food.

Language Development

Language at this age consists mostly of naming objects. A child's vocabulary is normal if he says about five words, including names, at fifteen months. By eighteen months most children have a vocabulary of about ten words. Most parents expect more, and indeed it would make life simpler if children were more verbal earlier. However, although children are not able to say much, they do understand a great deal more than some parents realize.

"I must admit I expected more speech by this time. My son knows 'hi,' 'bye,' 'Daddy,' 'Mommy,' 'car,' 'hot'—and that's about it."

"I am just realizing that my son knows a lot more than I think he does."

Toddlers Understand More Than They Can Express

Children do know a good deal more than they are able to express right now. They take in a good deal more than we recognize. They have a large store of receptive speech and many concepts that they cannot express.

"Yes, I had a good example of that when we were eating out last week. I have never given my daughter a spoon, mostly because I do not have the time. But we were in a restaurant, and she picked up a spoon and put it straight into my mouth."

She really knows what a spoon is for; and if you are eating, then she is going to help you eat. The concepts are getting there. They aren't always as fully developed as we expect them to be; but if the children are given the time and opportunity to experiment, the concepts will come.

"I think I'm doing the same thing with my daughter. I will say to myself, particularly when I'm reading a book, 'She won't know that is an elephant.' So I'll say something simpler. Maybe I'm not really being fair to her."

She may not be able to repeat the word, but you should say "elephant." Finally, one day when you point to an elephant, she will name it—and you will be surprised and pleased.

"My inclination is to say 'No, say cat' if it is a cat, because I feel the child won't learn if she is not corrected."

Correction like that sets a tone of disapproval when what is needed is approval and good speech modeling. You say the correct name when you point out the animal. The child will do the best she can, and one day you

■   ■

will realize that she is saying the word correctly. Then you should recognize her achievement with approval. There should be no attitude of disapproval if the sounds do not seem quite correct to you.

Appropriate Speech Stimulation

"So you are saying that I shouldn't correct her?"

At this stage children need encouragement, not disapproval. Their vocabulary is very limited, and "dog" means all animals. If he says "dog" now for all animals, you don't say "no." Later, they will be able to differentiate.

"What should you say in that case?"

Just say "Um" in a sound of acknowledgment and go on to the next picture. You don't correct him; but the next time, you say, "There is a dog, and there is a cat, and there is an elephant." He looks at the book and may still say, "Bow-wow, bow-wow" or "Doggie." For him, bow-wow represents all animals. Later on, as you point out things, he will learn to say the correct name. In another picture you point out that this is a moon, or this is a star. He may say "moon" for everything. Don't say "no," because that makes him feel that he is doing something wrong. Then the next time you show the picture, you say "moon" and "stars" again. You may have to do that for several months, until one day he is saying "moon" and "stars" for the appropriate items. When he does this, it has really registered and he has been able to put together the physical ability to verbalize the visual image. The brain center has matured, and he has reached the stage of being able both to differentiate and to express it. In the beginning, it is enough if he says "bow-wow" for every animal. It is also enough if he says "dada" for every man.

"I guess we are all too impatient. You keep telling us that each child matures at his or her own rate and we have to allow for it."

That's the message. The difference in rates of development is especially evident in speech. The baby will develop speech as soon as his central nervous system matures sufficiently in that area. His speech will follow the parents' model but will also contain a lot that is original to the child. Children learn to name objects from hearing them named—there is no other way to do it. They learn how to put sentences together from listening to others talking. They also have the innate capacity to put words together in a way that goes beyond imitation and is original, as we will see in their speech toward the end of this second year.

Language Development in a Bilingual Family

"We speak two languages at home, Spanish and English. My husband and I generally speak English to each other, since we were born here and went to school here; but my mother, who speaks only Spanish, came to live with

■   ■

us last year to help with the baby. We noticed that our baby seems to be slower in saying words than some of the babies here. That worries us a little. Do you think that it is because he is confused by two languages?"

Some children in bilingual families do begin to speak later. They understand words in each language, but are slower in expressive speech.

"Is it bad? Should we speak only one language to the baby?"

There are speech specialists who believe that it is best to concentrate on one language at a time. That is especially important if the child is having difficulty with speech. However, there are many children who are able to learn two languages at the same time and can distinguish between them from a very early age.

Parents have to observe their child. If they observe that the child's speech development is quite late, even though they speak slowly and clearly to the child in each language, they may want to consult a speech specialist. In that way, they will be properly advised whether the problem is due to the use of more than one language. If it is, they can then concentrate on speaking only one language to the child.

"My native tongue is Swedish. I always speak to my son in Swedish, and he is learning very well. My husband speaks only English; so our child says words in English, too. I do not see how it can be bad to learn two languages at once—in Europe, it is common to do that."

It is not bad to learn two languages at once. In fact, it is very nice if the child can do that. It is also important for parents to communicate with the child in a language the parents are comfortable with. However, there are some children who cannot do this. For them, it is better to concentrate on one language until they have acquired it and can use that language for communication.

"Which language should the parents choose? I want my child to know French because that is the language we use in our home. But when we go to the park to play, she does not seem to understand the children very well. Will that be a handicap for her?"

At this age, there is not a great deal of verbal communication among children. It is mostly gesture and crying. If you speak your native tongue at home, she will learn that first. As she gets older and associates more with children, especially at nursery school, she will learn English and will achieve a knowledge of two languages. She will have the advantage of the background of your language and culture and will learn ours, too.

"How can you tell if the baby understands what you say? She says so little that it worries me, especially since we speak two languages at home. I am worried that it confuses the baby."

One way to tell is to ask the child to look for something that you mention every day and that you think the child should know. For example, "Where is the shoe?" or "Where is the light?" The child will turn toward that object or walk toward it. Then you know the child understands, even if he cannot repeat the word yet in whichever language is used.

"Well, my child can do that whether I say it in English or Spanish. I guess it will just take time, and I can stop worrying."

That is right. We always have to remember that each child has his or her own maturational timetable. Some children are so endowed that they develop speech later. These very children may be walking early; others may both walk and talk later. Each child is different. So, while we have to bear in mind the effect that being exposed to two languages may have on the child's speech, we must not forget that each child's natural endowment and timetable for development is unique.

However, no matter what the child's endowment, and no matter which language we use, we should talk to our babies. We should name things for them slowly and with a rhythm and intonation that they can pick up and imitate as soon as they are ready.

Organic Causes of Speech Impairment

"Aren't there some physical things that are sometimes the reason why a baby doesn't talk?"

An important function for speech is good hearing. Deafness retards speech development. Normal hearing can be interfered with by ear infections. So ears should be checked during bad colds, and hearing should be checked after each infection. Then, if hearing seems impaired, proper measures can be taken.

"Is there anything else?"

The issue to be most concerned about is understimulation. The child who is not spoken to early or clearly has no speech models and little opportunity to practice language. All children make sounds, but those sounds do not become a specific language unless the child has a speech model. Earlier we spoke about what may be overstimulation, the introduction of two languages; but we must not overlook the fact that some children are not sufficiently stimulated to speak even one language. For each child the parents are the first models and teachers. Stimulating speech does more than teach the child the cognitive skill of language concepts; it also develops the social and emotional skills of communication.

Appropriate Play Activities and Toys

Some parents enjoy playing with their children; others set up the toys and hope the children will play alone so that they might have some time for

■   ■

themselves. Some parents find playing games with children of this age boring and some enjoy it.

How much are you playing with your babies now? What kind of games do you play?"

"I put a bunch of his toys in his playpen or crib and let him do what he wants. Or when he is on the floor, I put them down near him and let him crawl or walk over and get them. But that doesn't keep him quiet very long—he soon tires of the toys. Is there some way of getting him to spend more time playing on his own?"

Very often parents give children too many toys at once. Children often can't deal with that. They don't know what to select and just give up and cry. They need the parents to show them the way to play with one or two things. For example, at this age putting some small blocks or small animals into a box or other container and then taking them out is very entertaining. The child then does it on his own—often many, many times. This is also an instructive activity because it is giving the concept of "in" and "out," especially if the parent participates and verbalizes "in" and "out."

"I just don't seem to know what to do, either. What are some of the other things to play with them now?"

At each age, one has to utilize the level of the child's interest and development. At this age, children also enjoy handing things to you and getting them back. Sometimes they want to give the parent several items and then have them given back. This giving and receiving is the beginning of sharing and getting a sense that giving is not a loss, because the toy will be returned.

Games for Toddlers

"My daughter started that. We do that all the time and I thought it was silly. I couldn't understand why she got such a kick out of it. Now I feel differently about it."

Rolling a ball back and forth serves the same purpose. It is a game that can be shared with the parent and gives pleasure to both parent and child. When the ball rolls out of reach, the child can go after it. If this, as well as catching the ball on the roll, is recognized as an achievement, the child's sense of mastery and the parent's sense of pride in the child's accomplishment are enhanced. In addition, the "rolling ball" game is a precursor of later "catch" games and gives the child experience of what rolls and what does not. This game also leads to the game of hiding and finding things when the ball rolls out of sight. It also helps children to learn the concepts of "in front of," "behind," "on top of," and "under."

The child's limited level of understanding about looking for objects may surprise the parents. At first, parents will see that they need to hide the object while the child can see where it is being hidden, even leaving part of it exposed. Then say, "Let's find it," and the child will excitedly and confidently find it. If you hide the object without the child's knowing about it, the child may have no interest, for the hidden object seems to be "gone." After some experience, the children get to the point where you can hide the object and they can look for it without seeing where you put it. But when you first begin hiding things, you have to let them see where you hide them. Children also need the experience of hiding things from you. At first, they will put the object right in front of you, and you have to pretend that you have looked and found it. This game increases in complexity when you put the object "in front of" or "under" something and say, "The ball is under the cushion. Let's look there." Or, "The ball is in front of the table." This variation helps teach the concepts of different spatial positions.

Even if you play with the children for just a few minutes, you as parents can make their games more stimulating. Then their play becomes interesting to you because you see that they have learned something new. By participating in this way, you make their play more challenging and more interesting for both of you; such play is no longer a boring routine.

It is the same with books. Children love to read the same book and point to that same moon or house over and over again. But they need to find out about other pictures they haven't noticed before. You can point out something new to them each time you look at the book. Then the next time you read the book, the child has something new to name. The child will gradually develop a repertoire of things of special interest, and you will be interested to see if she can find these in the book. Then she will find her favorite items in other books. In this way, children enlarge their experience and vocabularies, making the reading of the same book over and over more interesting to you as well.

Children will still enjoy tactile games such as "This Little Piggy" and "Pat-a-Cake," which they can now do more competently than before.

Songs and Nursery Rhymes

At this age children may also like to listen to nursery tunes, and may even sway to a tune. Some parents have been singing the baby to sleep for some time, so singing may be a more familiar form of play in some families. Some children are now beginning to recognize favorite songs and rhythms and like to sing some of the words and clap hands or dance.

"My baby is learning to do that. If I sing and stop before the end, sometimes he will put in the word. It is such a thrill."

That's very good; that is one of the ways to learn to talk. Sometimes, when they are in the kitchen and they're bothering you, you can starting singing a song and they will become interested in putting in the words you leave out. In this way, you get them occupied and diverted from doing the things that you don't want them to do. Some children are ready to play in this

■   ■

way now; others will do it at a later date. Most also enjoy listening to children's songs on records. They all want to touch the phonograph, but they are not yet ready to handle it safely. The phonograph, therefore, should not be put in a place that is accessible to them.

They are getting to the stage of beginning to play "Ring-Around-a-Rosy—All Fall Down." While they can't say all the words, they may enjoy the movement to the song. Some children can respond to this now; others are not quite ready. Parents should not be disappointed if their child is not ready now; they can try again in a week or two. The change in responsiveness may be quite remarkable, and parents will find that their children are suddenly understanding and remembering much more than they expected.

"I know all these things and I always thought I would be playing a great deal with my baby. But somehow one gets caught up in household chores and neglects to play."

That's a rut one sometimes gets into. That's why we like to remind you that household work can wait. The child's developmental stages will not wait, nor can they be hurried. So parents need to be tuning in to their own child's readiness for play activities, and not letting important learning opportunities pass by.

Toys and Play

Have you noticed that your children seem to be less interested in their old toys and are less easily distracted by them? What are you doing about that?

"I was out shopping to pick up a few things for the baby. There aren't too many things available for this age."

"There are many things that one can make, however."

"Yes, but I just don't have the time."

It's often hard to find time to make toys for your children, but some things that you have around the house make wonderful toys. For instance, your measuring cups, the ones that fit into each other, make interesting things for children's play. At first they will only separate them. Gradually, they will learn to fit them back together.

All kinds of household objects can be used for the "in and out" game described earlier. Spoons, clothespins, little empty boxes, small cookie cutters, and jar covers—as well as small blocks, toy animals, and cars that most children may already have—can be put into (and then taken out of) pots, plastic containers, and jars.

They also like to play with a comb and brush. They try to comb their own hair and that of their dolls. They like to play with toys that simulate the things parents are using.

■   ■

"My baby only wants to use the phone. So we got her a plastic one that is a pretty good imitation and that keeps her busy for a few minutes when I want to use the phone."

That is a good toy. Another one that simulates something of yours is a pocketbook. An old purse with a few keys, a small change purse, a little box that can be opened and shut are all things that one can find in the house. They keep children entertained and stimulate their manual dexterity, parental imitation, and concept formation.

Books

"My baby likes books, but I find it difficult to get the right ones. Most are too complicated for him right now."

Although there are many good books for children, most are too complicated for this age. *(A list of books appropriate for the second year of life can be found on pages 241–43.)* When you or your child notice something in a magazine, such as an apple, a baby, keys, a cup, or a shoe, cut it out and paste it on a piece of cardboard. Shirt cardboards can be saved for this purpose. Sometimes you can make up a story, using these pictures of familiar objects. The stories that children like best are the ones you make up about their own experiences. For example, you say, "This morning *(child's name)* went for a walk with his daddy. They went to the store and they bought an apple." Point to the apple. "Then they went to another store and bought shoes. When they came home, Daddy put a key in the lock, and here is the key they used. They opened the door, and there was Mommy at home waiting for them." Children love this sort of story. At this age, it is best to have a single picture on each page of the book. You turn to that picture as the story is told. Soon, the children will be turning pages, mumbling their own version of the stories, and naming the objects.

Other Toys

"How about blocks? Are they good toys for this age?"

Blocks are always good toys because they help in organizing spatial relations and assist in manual dexterity. Small blocks about one inch square are good for small motor coordination and for putting inside other objects. If the child is at a stage of throwing things, it is a good idea to make blocks by cutting up a sponge. These can be covered with cloth or left as is. Such blocks can be cut into various sizes and shapes and the child will enjoy arranging them in various ways.

Toys that can be pulled are also very good for this age. Some, of course, can be purchased; you will see all kinds of pull toys in the stores. But most children are very happy pulling a shoe box with a string attached. It is very exciting for them to have it filled with small items such as a doll, a small car, or a few small boxes. They like to make stops, taking things out and putting other things in as they move around the house.

■   ■

Other toys that interest children of this age are the large snap-lock or pop-it beads (they will be able to pull them apart but not snap them together); bath toys such as bath boats and fish; and stacking rings (again, don't expect stacking in correct order yet). Some children of this age may also be ready to play with a small doll's house, with a few people to go in it. As they get older, more people and furniture can be added. Some parents may be able to construct this kind of house themselves.

Toys that provide stimulation to the larger motor skills, and ones that parents can begin to introduce with supervision, are small riding toys. Parents should make sure that the child's first riding toys are well balanced. Some are too high and narrow and tip over, causing the child to fall. For maximum safety, the toy should be low and not too narrow. Among the best designs are several types of toy cars, because they are broad and low to the ground—the design of some riding horses is too narrow and unstable. These toys should not have pedals but should be the kind that the child propels by his or her feet on the ground or floor.

We have been talking about a number of new toys that will interest and stimulate your children, but it is important to remember that children like to keep their old toys around as well. Sometimes a parent will throw out some scruffy old toy that the child seems to have discarded, only to find that it is very much desired again. When children seem to be bored with their toys, it is a good idea to remove them. A month or so later, going through such a box of old toys can provide a wonderful rainy-day activity of rediscovering "old friends." As children mature, they often find new ways to play with old toys.

When we speak of toys, we must remember that the greatest "toy" and stimulant for the child is the interaction with another human being, particularly his parents (or their substitute). Playing with parents, and then gradually learning to play with other children, is the most important kind of play. Interesting toys and objects that the child learns to manipulate and understand are valuable for the child's learning experience; but children need the physical and verbal interaction with people in order to develop emotionally, socially, and intellectually.

Independence: Autonomy Versus Limitation

The children are getting more competent now that they are between fifteen and eighteen months old. They are walking quite well on their own and exploring more and more of their surroundings. To some parents this means that the children are "getting into everything," and this is not too welcome a development. Some children insist on feeding themselves and refuse to be fed; others are refusing to get into their strollers and instead want to push them; some want to walk only in a certain area or toward a certain part of the park. They are beginning to show a desire for indepen-

■   ■

dence—for autonomy. This is a normal stage of their development. At times, their wishes are in harmony with the parents', and all is well. However, when the desires and expectations are contrary, there may be a confrontation—with a resulting angry parent and tearful, screaming child. Have you had any incidents like this yet?

"One of the problems I am having with my son is that he wants to climb up every step he sees. When we are going outside, I hold his hand; but in the house he wants to climb upstairs alone. I can't be with him all the time to watch that he doesn't fall. I'm always in a frenzy at home when I can't see him."

That is a problem. The steps are very tempting. However, one cannot expect that an admonition will work when the parent is not present. One has to anticipate that the child will want to climb the steps. To avoid accidents and constant conflict, gates have to be installed at both the bottom and top of the stairs.

"We have gates in our house. But when I go to someone else's house where there is no gate, then what?"

In that case, you have to keep your child close to you and occupied with a toy. If it is possible, close the door to the stair hall or put up some makeshift barrier to the steps, such as a chair on its side.

Saying "No" Too Often

"I think I've reached that stage with my baby, too. I find I'm beginning to say 'No, no' most of the day."

When you are always saying "No, no," the children may begin to think that the parent is a person who always says "No." They may just tune you out. The good relationship that you've had seems to disappear. They need to know that a parent says "No" but she also says "Yes"—that she does recognize the good things. These have to be recognized with a more emphatic voice, with much more enthusiasm than the "no" things. You must also remember that many of the "bad" things are quite interesting to the child, and learning to stop doing them takes time. If you are aware of this, you may have more patience; you will also learn to avoid certain situations that lead to confrontation.

"I'm having a tough time with my son. When he can't have his own way, he gets mad. Sometimes he will grab a glass and try to throw it on the floor!"

In such an instance, the child certainly has to be stopped. You can't let him do that; you have to say "No" firmly and give him something he can do. He will fuss, and he may scream and kick and try to get what he wants. If you get mad at that point and raise your voice, this only intensifies the situation and it becomes a battle between the two of you. The only thing to do at this point is to say "No," and give him something that he can do.

■　　　　　　　　　　　　　　　　　　　　　　　　　　　　　■

Let him cry and fuss; let him bang something safe. This is a stage that children have to go through: learning what they can do and what they can't do. If you continue to be firm about a *few* important issues, the child gradually learns. If, on the other hand, confrontation becomes a pattern between you and the child, the relationship with you is always going to be one of conflict. Conflict will become a part of the child's way of relating; he or she will act in this combative way with friends, with siblings, with teachers. This sets the stage for the development of the angry character structure.

"Is this what happens if the parent always makes too much of a fuss?"

It may, if a parent emphasizes only what is not approved and does not recognize just as emphatically the good things the child does.

"Should you say 'No' just firmly, or loudly?"

It has to be loud enough so that the child can hear it. Very often parents say "No" and smile. That confuses the child. You must say "No" very firmly and look firm. Then offer a substitute, saying, "You can have this (or do this)," and you make "this" very appealing—and smile. Or pick him up and take him into another room where there is a new interest for him, "something special." Change his entire focus. Finding an appealing substitute takes a lot of effort and patience; and no one says it is easy. This is one of the hardest things to do, but it's one of the things that pays off in the long run.

"Suppose you go visiting in someone else's house. They allow the child to take things off the table, and you don't. What do you do then?"

When you are visiting and you see objects that are dangerous for your child to have and that you don't allow to be touched in your house, you have to make the same restrictions. You have to be consistent, even if the host doesn't mind whether the baby does some things he is not allowed to do at home. You explain your standards and see that the baby carries them out in another home. Then you have to help your child in a strange house. The easiest way is to remove the objects that are fragile or dangerous.

"What if a mother and father do not have the same standards? That's what happens in our house."

Need for Consistent "No's"

You can't say "No" and have father saying "Oh, let him do it." Or father saying "No" and mother saying "Oh, he's only little and you're too strict with him." You have to establish uniform standards that you both are going to accept; both father and mother have to establish these together. You may find that one day while father is with the baby and mother is in the kitchen, father says, "No, you can't do that." You can't rush from the

■   ■

kitchen and say, "I always let him do that." You can talk to father afterward; but in front of the child there should not be any kind of disagreement.

If limits are not the same, the child may become manipulative later, playing one against the other. Setting consistent limits is very important for the child's personality development.

"We seem to be able to do that. It seems to me it only takes a word on my husband's part and the baby responds, but I have to scream."

It may be easier for father to be consistent and firm and get a response, because father's manner is often firmer than mother's. However, if mother uses the same tone and is firm and doesn't scream, the child learns she means business, too, and responds just as well. Sometimes, because he sees less of the child and wants to be loved, the father tries to ensure the child's affection by being less firm than mother.

"We are having a different kind of irritating time with our baby. She is just learning to pile up her blocks. She gets up to three, but when she tries the next one they topple over and she gets very upset and screams. I try to soothe her by putting the blocks up again, but she will have none of it."

They are at the stage now when they want to do things by themselves but they are not competent enough. They aren't helpless babies, but at the same time they can't do all the things they want to do on their own. It is a very difficult time for them and for the parents. If a parent knows, for example, that the baby cannot pile more than three blocks, give her that number and let her feel success. Then, in a week or two, give her a fourth. Having had success, she may then be able to handle the frustration of its falling off. With the passage of time and practice, she will reach the point where she can manage four, or will let you show her how to manage. A difficulty at this stage is that children are often not competent enough, but they won't accept help, either. Another situation that arises frequently at this age, and later, is that children are given toys that are too complicated for them to play with. A parent needs to be aware of this and be ready to put away those toys and reintroduce them when the child is ready.

"Does that mean that children should never be given anything that is difficult to do—that they must never be frustrated?"

No, that is not what is being advocated. Children should not be given things that frustrate them beyond their tolerance. Parents have to observe their children, understand their level of frustration tolerance, and help them overcome it by tuning in to the child's level of development. This will vary with each child. Some children can tolerate their blocks falling down and will try over and over again to set them up. Their frustration tolerance level is high; that is their endowment. Other children become upset quickly; their frustration tolerance has to be patiently increased by slowly introducing more difficult tasks. This is what good teaching is all about; and parents are the most important teachers the child will ever have.

■   ■

"Is what we have been talking about the beginning of what some people call the 'terrible twos'? Are we approaching that time?"

It seems that you are. What we are trying to explain is that the twos need not be "terrible." Parents need to understand how to permit and encourage the independence that is necessary for development; they need to find appropriate areas in which the child can express his or her independence and sense of autonomy and achievement. At the same time, they need to set consistent limits when the child's desires can harm him, others, or valuable property. This principle remains the same throughout life, though the items may change with growth. This is a time when the child's desire to do things is not equal to his ability to do them for and by himself. The parents need to understand the child's level of development, his or her level of competence. If they also tune in to or anticipate some of the child's desired activities, parents can tactfully help the child handle the situation—or prevent him from getting into a situation that will be too frustrating or dangerous.

More on Autonomy: Eating and Dressing

One of the areas in which parents can sometimes come into conflict with their children as they assert their growing autonomy is eating. Are any of you beginning to see signs of this?

"I am having that problem, I think, especially when he spills his milk. I leave a cup of milk on his high-chair tray so he can have some whenever he wants it. When my back is turned, he just picks it up and pours it on the floor. Of course, I scream at him, but he does it all the time. He seems to enjoy the battle."

Avoiding Conflicts About Eating

It seems you are setting up a situation for an angry confrontation. For him it is a new experience; it gives him a sense of achievement to pour something. If you want to teach him to drink his milk from a cup, give him a small amount. Sit with him until he finishes it and recognize the achievement by some comment such as "Good, you drank it all up." Give him more if he seems to want it and repeat the recognition when he finishes. Let him learn that milk in a cup is for drinking. Then, when he is in his bath, let him have a few small containers that he can fill with water and pour out. He may pour some on the bathroom floor, but that can be absorbed by the bath mat. In the bathroom you teach him to limit his pouring to the tub. The point is that he needs to be given an appropriate outlet to get a sense of achievement in pouring. He needs to have a chance for exploration, without angry confrontation all the time.

"My problem with independence also concerns the way the baby eats. It drives me wild. She won't let me feed her anymore. Most of the time, if I

make her cereal thick enough, she gets it into her mouth by using the spoon, which is usually upside down! Sometimes cereal drops on her table. Sometimes she mushes it up all over the table; after she has done that, she'll eat it with her hands. Other times, she just loses a lot and won't eat it from the table. Can I just let her go on like that?"

All babies are messy eaters. In most cases, if they are hungry and they like the food offered, they will eat enough. We expect them to like the food warm and eat it neatly from the spoon. But warm food and neatness are not important to them now. It really doesn't matter from a nutritional point of view if they eat with the spoon or with their hands, or if the food is cold or has been smeared over the tabletop first.

"Is there any way to teach them to eat from the spoon?"

The mother can fill the spoon and help the child guide it to her mouth. She should then make some favorable comment such as "Good" when the child is successful. That may reinforce interest in eating with a spoon.

If one is too fussy about neatness, it sometimes diminishes the child's interest in eating. Teaching manners will come later. Now the child needs to develop the skill of eating by herself and to have the satisfaction of that competence.

"But what if she just takes a few mouthfuls and then begins to smear the food over the table and doesn't eat it?"

A parent can usually tell when the child is hungry and interested in food. If she begins to smear it about, just remove it. The less fuss made the better. When she eats, make a favorable comment.

"Shouldn't a child be made to eat his food? It is such a waste to make good food, which is now also expensive, and have him waste it all. My mother says she always made her children eat what was set before them. If they didn't finish it, she just gave them the rest at the next meal. Sometimes I am tempted to do that."

That is not really an appropriate way of handling a poor eater. There are several things to consider. In the first place, one has to remember that at this age, in the second year, appetites usually diminish. A baby who was an avid eater before may become much less interested in eating. That is a natural physiological process that occurs in most children. So, of course, they should not be forced to eat. If they are forced to eat when their appetites are poor, they may become resistant to eating. Then when their appetites normally improve, they will not resume eating as they ordinarily would have if they had not been forced to eat.

"That is the mistake I made with my first child. We had a battle royal every mealtime. In the end, I lost. She is still a finicky eater. I am not going to make the same mistake with this baby. His appetite has slowed down, and I am just letting him eat what he wants the way he wants to."

■   ■

That is a good way to respond to his changing appetite. Parents also have to remember that a child who normally has a good appetite may have a meal or two (or even a day or two) when he is not hungry, just as there are certain meals when adults are not as hungry as at others.

"I know that and I try to remember it; but it always seems to happen just the day I think I've made something that he should eat and enjoy, such as scrambled eggs or chopped steak. Then I find I urge a little too much. He refuses, and before I know it, we've started a small war."

We have to remember that children's appetites can be very variable, especially in the second year. We also need to recognize that our children may not now care for the foods we like or think are best for them. Later, they may develop a taste for the very thing they turn down now.

Children Do Not Need Varied Menus

"But what does one do about a child who eats no variety at all? He'll only eat one cereal—Rice Krispies, which he picks up with his fingers—hamburgers, carrots, and apple sauce. Very rarely will he eat chicken or anything else, except his milk."

Children do not need the large variety of foods we offer. Your child's tastes will change in time. Some children have an innate feeling for the foods that agree with them and may be upset by the other foods a parent thinks they must have. This is often true of children with allergies. They seem to have a sense of what agrees with them. The child's preferences should be respected. Food should not be forced on a child.

Eating Patterns

"One of the things that upsets us is that the baby won't sit and finish a meal. He'll have one part of it, then get up and play a little. Then he is ready for his fruit and he'll sit for that. Then he wants more play. It seems to us he is eating at short intervals all day instead of having full meals. That bothers us, and we try to make him sit still and finish the whole meal. But it's a battle, and then he usually won't eat as well."

Part of the problem is that your child—and this is true of many children—can't eat what we consider a full meal because he does not have the capacity to consume that much food at one time. The parent should not take it personally and feel that her culinary efforts are being spurned. The child simply cannot eat so much and cannot sit still for a whole meal, either.

We are accustomed to the idea that one has to have three square meals a day. That's really for adults. This eating schedule was convenient for work. It is better for your digestive system, however, to have a small amount of food more frequently than to have three big meals. More recently, industry has discovered that productivity of the work force increases if there are additional breaks for nourishment. That is how coffee breaks came about. Our children also need several "coffee breaks" a day as well as regular small meals. Gradually, as they get older and become more socialized, the children will want to participate in the family mealtimes. You need not feel upset now if children do not eat a meal from start to finish with the family. If there is recognition and approval when they do sit down at the table, rather than a scolding when they don't, they may learn to eat with you sooner.

So for now, it is better to put very little on the child's plate in order that the child will be able to finish it and ask for more. When he finishes, even if it is very little, he should receive positive recognition so he will have a sense of accomplishment and a good feeling about mealtimes. The parent, too, will not feel so frustrated.

"I have no problem with my baby's eating. It's just that when he finishes his food and I'm not close by, he throws his empty plate on the floor."

These actions can be anticipated. When the child seems to have had enough, ask him to hand the cup or the plate to you and say "All gone." He can be rewarded by your approval when he hands you the cup or plate. Such anticipation can turn a frustrating and messy situation into a happy learning situation.

Of course, we must also remember that children have to do some experimenting. They are really scientists in their way of trying to find out about the world they live in. They have to learn that tipping a cup over spills the contents; they have to have a chance to find that out. Some parents prefer this experimentation in the bathtub. However, if a small amount of liquid is placed in the cup in the first place, not too much will be left to spill. When the baby finishes her milk and does not spill it, the mother can smile and say, "Good, you finished your milk." If she says it with some enthusiasm, the baby will feel that she did something well and is approved of.

Avoiding Conflicts About Getting Dressed

Another area in which the child's need for autonomy often manifests itself at an early age is dressing. For many months children may have been "helping" in their own dressing by bending an arm when they see the sweater sleeve approaching or by lifting a leg to step into pants. Some will continue to do that for some time to come; others will suddenly refuse. Often this behavior develops because the child does not want to stop the play activity in which he or she is engaged. Getting dressed is a signal that another event is going to take place, perhaps even as welcome as going out to the park or as unwelcome as mother's leaving for work. In any case, the child does not want to be dressed, and a battle for control of the situation can easily develop between parent and child. It is often helpful if children are given some warning that "in a few minutes" it will be time to get dressed. Or you can indicate that when the child gets dressed, there will be play. Because the process is slow, the parent can become very impatient. Parents need to use a lot of tact in such situations, saying, "Let me give you a little help with that shirt, and then you can put on your pants." Approval of whatever part of the dressing process the child can accomplish will give the child a sense of achievement and pride. Again, it is important to allow enough time so that the child does not become rushed. Perhaps you are interrupting play or an activity the child wants to continue, just as an adult absorbed in an activity may wish not to be disturbed.

"You are talking about my biggest problem. My daughter refuses to let me put a sweater on her. It's too cold outside to let her go without one. I get furious and she screams."

In cases where the child is striving for autonomy but is not really ready, it helps sometimes to give the child a less frustrating way of exercising her independence. Perhaps the next time you can show her two sweaters and ask her which one she would like to put on. She then has the choice of the red one or the blue one, but she does not have the choice of whether she will wear a sweater.

Confrontations over dressing do not have consequences as serious as confrontations over eating; but if they become part of a daily pattern between parent and child, they are not healthy. Understanding what is going on in the child's mind may help you to be more patient and think of better ways of handling difficult situations.

Sleep Patterns and Bedtime Routines

How are you managing in getting your babies to sleep now? Have you been able to establish a good bedtime routine and pattern, or is it still unstable?

"Now we do very well getting the baby to sleep, but we have trouble with him waking once or twice a night. Sometimes it's just for one night, or maybe for a few nights in a row—and then he is back to sleeping through the night. It always worries us, because we think: here we go again, back to the old days of being up half the night. Will this continue?"

Sleep Patterns

You know, we all sleep in cycles. We have periods of deeper sleep alternating with lighter sleep. If during one of the periods of light sleep, the baby should be aware of some sensation in her stomach caused by gas, or if she bites down on a sore gum when she is teething, or if she hears a loud noise in the street, she may wake up. Some babies cry out momentarily and then go off to sleep by themselves. Occasionally, they may need comforting for a few minutes before they go back to sleep. This does occur from time to time and should not be a cause for alarm. As adults, we are often awakened by something, turn over, and go back to sleep. Few people sleep all night without waking at all.

"Our baby sleeps well, except when she is teething. Then she may be up for a while several times during the night until we find a way of soothing her gums by rubbing them with our fingers or bits of ice, or by giving her something to bite on. Sometimes she needs a bottle. It's miserable on the nights when it happens; but as soon as the tooth comes in, she is fine again."

"We have a different situation. Whenever we expect company at night, our baby seems to sense it; and then it takes forever to get him to go to sleep. How do they know? I try to do everything the same way, and he just knows."

Perhaps you think you are doing everything the same way. But you may be communicating some tension, hurrying things a bit, just enough to alert the baby to a feeling that something is different.

"What is so awful if your baby isn't asleep when the company comes and stays up a little while and sees them? Then you can put the baby to bed."

There is nothing wrong if you are comfortable with that and can put the baby to bed more easily later. It depends on what is the most comfortable way for you and for your baby. Some babies get overstimulated by visitors before bedtime and then have difficulty going to sleep. If that is your experience, perhaps it is best to invite the company for a later time when you know the baby will be asleep.

"If I am having company, my system is to start preparing several days ahead after the baby is in bed. On the day, I try to keep the same order of things, just doing everything a little earlier, so I'll be sure he is in bed and asleep. It usually works out all right."

That is a fine arrangement if your child can respond to that system. Some children's biological clocks can't be manipulated that easily. Many of us see that when we have time changes and the clocks are put ahead or back one hour. The children do not change their rhythm all at once; and so, in order to make the changes in time coincide with daily routines, parents have to alter the schedule by ten to fifteen minutes every few days until they have overcome the hour change.

"You know, I never realized that until we went back to standard time. My baby used to get up at seven in the morning and when the time changed he was getting up at six. That upset me, but he was really getting up at the time he was accustomed to."

That's true; but by shifting ten to fifteen minutes a day, most babies gradually get into the new time sequence. Have any of you observed that?

■   ■

"That's what I tried, but it took about two weeks to really get him settled into the new time."

"Our baby is a good sleeper except when he is sick. If he gets a cold he may fall asleep, but he wakes many times during the night. When he is well, it takes a few days to get him back to sleeping all through the night. I may have to go in to soothe him once or twice a night for a few nights. My mother says I should not do that, that I may get him into the habit of waking."

Disruptions to Sleep Patterns

If your baby wakes a few times after an illness, it may mean that he isn't quite over it, or that maybe he is experiencing some of the unpleasant sensations of his illness in his dreams. In any case, he should be comforted. He will not make a "habit" of it if he has no need to wake. If he was a good sleeper before the illness, he will return to his usual routine. It is important, however, not to let the moments of comforting in the night become playtime. Responding to the child's cry should be brief and low-key, with as little extra light and stimulation as possible.

"Our baby also is usually a good sleeper. But to go to bed, he has to have everything done in the same way each night: the same song on the music box, the same teddy bear in the corner of his crib. Last weekend we visited friends for the weekend. We took the Portacrib, blanket, and teddy but forgot the music box. We had a terrible time. He finally went to sleep when I patted him and sang the same song for him. That made us wonder if we had done the right thing by getting him so used to the same routine. Wouldn't it have been better if he had gotten to bed with a different pattern every night? You see some children who can go to sleep anytime."

There are some children who are very relaxed and easygoing, who sleep whenever they are sleepy, anywhere they happen to be. However, that is not the case with most children. Most feel insecure in strange surroundings and need the support of a familiar routine and familiar things in order to fall asleep. It sounds as though you responded appropriately to your child's needs for security. When he becomes more accustomed to traveling, he will be more able to fall asleep in strange places. It is a matter of maturity and endowment. Parents have to respond according to each child's individual needs.

Importance of Relaxed Bedtime Routines

"We used to have a good bedtime routine with our baby. My husband would play with her and look at a favorite book with her, and then we would put her to bed with her ba-ba (blanket). Now my husband's schedule is changed and he gets home later. He is hungry and wants to eat; she's tired but won't go to sleep. Suddenly we find she's up until ten o'clock and very cranky."

■   ■

Changes like that in a parent's schedule can be upsetting to the whole family. Some thinking needs to be done on the best way to reintroduce a playtime with daddy and a bedtime that is comfortable all around. Perhaps, since it's important for the baby to see her father, she could nap a little longer in the afternoon. Then she would not become overtired so early. Perhaps father could have a small snack when he first gets home and then play with the baby. Then you and your husband can have a later, more relaxed dinner. Another solution is for you to serve dinner right away, letting the baby sit with you or play near you. In this case, you will have to expect that she will demand attention and be very unsatisfied if you talk to each other and ignore her. After dinner, your husband can play with her for a while. The important thing is for the child to feel that the evening playtime and bedtime routine are pleasant and unhurried. Children are very sensitive to particular tensions and the parents' desire to rush. It is our experience that an hour of undivided, loving attention works better in the long run than the begrudged twenty minutes that don't satisfy the child's need and that can therefore stretch into *hours* of crankiness and crying.

"That sounds great for the baby. But what about me? I've been home all day and I'd like to talk to an adult. My husband and I rarely get to talk alone."

It is hard when the needs of family members seem to be in conflict. The child needs to be with her father, and you and your husband need time together. You have to satisfy everyone as best you can and recognize that this stage won't last forever. Soon your child will be able to play a little more by herself and you and your husband will be able to talk more. It is important for parents to plan times alone, without the baby, on a regular basis to satisfy their own needs.

"My problem is similar. My husband and I both get home from work late. We want to play with the baby, but we are both tired. She is a bundle of energy."

Again, each family must make its own plans on how to handle these situations. The child doesn't have to play with both of you at once. One parent can play while the other relaxes or prepares dinner. One parent can go through the bedtime routines while the other washes up. The important thing—to get back to good sleep patterns—is to establish a bedtime routine that is as unvaried every night as possible. This helps the child feel secure and relaxed: a state of being that is important for relaxed sleep. It is also a good idea not to let play activities in the evening become too stimulating, because the child then takes longer to wind down.

"Are there babies who are naturally poor sleepers and never overcome this?"

■   ■

We know that there are adults who for some reason require little sleep and manage very well this way. In the same way, there is a great variation in how much sleep children need. Some need to sleep a great deal; others need much less. There are some children who wake at night to play in their cribs, and then go back to sleep. That is their pattern. Others wake and cry and need to be comforted and helped to relax and fall asleep again. The majority finally develop a pattern of sleeping through the night. Sometimes this may not become fully settled until they are two or three; but it does finally come.

Crankiness and Its Causes

Do you think you are getting to understand your child's personality? Do you seem to be able to get along with each other comfortably, or are there times of frustration?

"I think I understand my baby most of the time, but there are times when she is very cranky and I don't seem to know what to do. What is the explanation for it? And what should I do?"

Fatigue

There are many things that can make a child cranky; and most children are cranky at one time or another. One of the most frequent reasons a child is cranky is that he or she is overtired. Some children tire very quickly from stimulating play, a shopping trip, or visiting. Others seem to have a greater tolerance for these activities.

"My baby fits into the first category. If we stay at home and keep to a routine, she is fine. A short shopping trip or just stopping in a small shop for a minute or two is okay, but shopping for a week's supply in the supermarket—forget it! She ends up having a tantrum and screaming. So now my husband or I do it alone. That way we aren't upset and angry with the baby, and actually we get it done faster, too."

That shows you have tuned in to the baby's capabilities and are dealing with them comfortably.

Illness and Teething

Sometimes, children are cranky at the onset of an illness, often before there are any overt signs such as fever, cough, vomiting, diarrhea, rash, or runny nose. Crankiness is a warning signal in a child who is usually quite contented.

Another common cause of crankiness at this age is teething. The gums are sore and make the child very irritable. Most of you recognize this. You see the drooling and the chewing of the fingers and toys, often accompanied by a decrease in appetite and waking at night.

■   ■

"Of course, we know about those things. Even so, they seem to come unexpectedly and always jolt me. The other day, the baby was so fussy when we were in the park that I came home a little annoyed. As I was undressing her I noticed she was quite warm, so I took her temperature. It was 102 degrees. I felt so guilty for being cross with her."

To be annoyed when you don't realize that there is a problem is a very usual response. Perhaps one of the reasons you are annoyed with the children at this stage is that you expected easier sailing after the difficulties of infancy. This crankiness frightens you a little unconsciously and you are feeling, "No, not that again." But it's only for a short time, until you've found the cause and can cope with it.

"Teething is the one that is bothering me. Does every tooth that comes in cause so much pain and crying?"

It varies with each child. Some have thick gums and do have a hard time with each tooth; other children have pain only with certain teeth. Some have no problem at all: the parent simply discovers that a tooth is there by the click of the spoon on a new tooth.

There are some remedies that work for some children, such as rubbing the gum, applying something cold like a chip of ice, or using a refrigerated teething ring. There are also medications to rub on the gums, which your physician may prescribe if he or she thinks it is advisable.

Inconsistent Routines

There are other causes of crankiness. Sometimes, now that the children are older, we may not be as consistent in our dealing with them. Baths, play, and feeding routines may not be followed in their usual order, and this may bother them. You've begun to do things one way one day and another the next, and the children don't know quite what to expect. This, too, can be upsetting and make them cranky. They are not yet verbal, so they can't say, "Isn't it time to go for a ride in the stroller?" or, "I'm ready for my nap now," or, "I'm hungry. Isn't it lunchtime?" We have to recognize that they are not as flexible as we think they should be at this age.

Growth Spurts

There is another situation that seems to make children irritable, which we've mentioned before. Children often display irritability just preceding a growth spurt or change in level of development. When they are reaching to a new level of achievement, they have a feeling of disequilibrium that expresses itself in irritability. No amount of comforting seems to resolve it until a day or two has passed and they suddenly seem to have arrived at the new level of achievement. These changing levels may range from crawling to walking or from babbling to saying some words. Then all is serene again. It may help parents tolerate the irritability to look for signs of new development.

Whining and crankiness are especially irritating to parents, because this behavior often occurs when the parents are overtired or preoccupied with other things themselves. Many parents are fatigued by long trips to the supermarket or by visiting; so just when the most patience is needed, the parent is least able to give it. As we've noted many times before, children are very sensitive to their parents' moods and tensions.

The worst time for parents comes when they plan some excursion or activity especially for the child and the child becomes irritable and cranky. What you have planned as a nice treat becomes a nightmare all around. Your feelings of disappointment and frustration are understandable. It is important, however, not to blame the child—he or she is *not* purposely trying to irritate you. The child may be tired or sick or in a state of developmental disequilibrium—and unable to enjoy the treat you planned. Or perhaps the activity—a puppet show or a library story-telling—is too advanced for the child's level of development. At this age the child cannot say in words, "I don't understand this." All he or she can do is become restless and irritable. Better understanding of the child's level of development and what activities are appropriate helps parents to avoid situations like these.

More on Socialization: How to Handle Biting and Screaming

Biting

Many parents are bothered because their children are biting them or other children. Nursing mothers are somethings bitten, and this has often been a signal to begin weaning. Some babies never bite the breast, even when they have teeth. Sometimes biting is a way of showing anger. Often it is a sign of frustration in the nonverbal child who cannot express what he wants. Sometimes biting is the child's way of showing affection.

From a purely physical point of view, biting may signify the discomfort caused by emerging teeth. The baby bites for relief of discomfort and may bite anything! If the biting is due to teething, the proper response is to soothe the gum by giving a teething ring or teething biscuit, or by rubbing the gums with a chip of ice—or even with an analgesic medication prescribed by your doctor.

The parent's first response should be to try to discover the cause of the biting. This is not always easy, since the child cannot express himself or herself verbally. The answer may be reached only by trial and error. In the past, one could soothe the baby by diverting him, even if one didn't discover the cause. A toy or food or some attention was all that was needed to stop the biting. But now that the children are older and are beginning to be verbal, the parent should show displeasure, firmly saying,

"We don't bite Mommy (or Susie or Johnny); we bite on this." Then, give the child something appropriate to bite on. You may also say, "Biting hurts Mommy."

Showing your displeasure by hitting the child is only more anger-producing and may intensify and perpetuate the behavior, so that it becomes the usual way of showing anger. When parents hit a child, the child's response is often to hit back or to hit a younger sibling or pet. This can be avoided by dealing with the situation calmly and appropriately from the start.

Biting is not always an expression of anger. It can also be an attempt to express affection. This may be the baby's attempt to kiss the parent or other child, and it is mishandled due to the child's lack of experience. In that case, the baby has to be shown how to pat or kiss. Showing affection by biting does, however, have a certain place in our culture as evidenced by the expression "I love you so much I could just eat you up."

"When my baby bites me, I get very upset because it hurts. Someone told me to bite him back so he would see how it feels and that would stop him."

That is a very common suggestion. Biting may frighten him and make him stop. It may also make him more angry and give him the sanction to repeat the biting: if a parent does it he can do it, too. The same applies to hitting. It has been noted that children who are hit or spanked tend to hit others. To teach by frightening the child is not a solution we advocate. To teach by good example is more productive and doesn't undermine the child-parent relationship.

"When my baby hit another child who was visiting us, I think he did it as a way of making contact. But I was so embarrassed I slapped his mouth. I wanted to show the other mother that I really didn't approve of it. He cried and didn't seem to know what to make of it."

When toddlers are playing together, parents have to anticipate their activities and separate them before they bite, if possible. If the parent is too late, she should show her disapproval by saying firmly, "We don't bite," and show the child how to stroke the other child and say, "Nice." In that way, you can teach your child what to do while showing the other parent that you do not approve of the behavior. Then get the children started on some other activity.

"How long does this biting last?"

It disappears more rapidly when appropriate alternative activities are substituted and when verbal communication is stimulated. It is quite common in the preverbal stage, but it passes when the child can express himself or herself in other ways. Teaching by parents and maturation both help in this process. The important thing to remember is that this is a phase; it will pass. The parent needs to be a teacher, and not a lion tamer with a whip!

■   ■

Screaming

We have been noticing that in the children's play here some of them are beginning to run back and forth screaming. Are they doing this at home? How does it affect you.

"Have I noticed it! My little girl runs around screaming like a wild Indian, especially when we open the door of the apartment and let her run down the hall. She scares all the neighbors with her screaming."

"I don't allow it. When my child screams, I just put my hand over her mouth and say 'Stop it' or 'Shshsh,' and she stops for the time being, anyway."

They all go through a stage of screaming when they are learning how to use their voices and how to modulate them. They are making discoveries. This is perfectly normal and should not be limited all the time. There are times, of course, when one must limit screaming. If someone in the house is asleep or ill, the child should not scream. The best way to stop it is to get the child interested in another, quieter activity.

"I'm very upset when my little girl screams. She used to scream so loud when she was an infant and was hungry and wet. Now that she is beginning to understand more, I thought we were over the screaming."

You thought it was just a continuation of the same pattern. Certainly, children may still scream if they are frightened, hurt, or frustrated. But the screaming we are talking about now is more like the vocalizing they used when they first discovered their own voices. Now they are screaming with a sense of achievement, and also as a way of letting off excess energy. It is a form of play and exploration. When it gets to be too much for you, start another activity. Look at a book, play some music, or take a walk in the park. You can begin to say, "Not in the apartment (house). Let's go out." Children need to let off steam.

"I have a different worry. I am haunted by a friend's three-year-old. When he does not get his way, he stands there and just screams. And of course, the more his mother says, 'Stop that,' the more he screams. He is obnoxious. I don't want my child to become like that."

It is very risky to make a judgment about a child's behavior when one does not know the whole situation. From past experience, I would hazard a guess that the boy you describe may not have had his needs met in the appropriate manner. It seems to me that you should not worry that your child will behave in the same way as your friend's child, because your approach has been different.

"Well, I guess there are different screaming situations and no two are alike. We have to distinguish between them, just as we had to learn to understand the different cries when they were infants."

Children do have different screams, as you say. We have to remember that children aren't the only ones who scream. Sometimes mothers scream. If

■   ■

a child is about to pull something down over himself that is hot, or runs away toward the street, a parent screams out in fright. That occasionally happens and can't be helped; it's a spontaneous response. However, when parents use screaming consciously as a means of setting limits, then it is not appropriate or useful. In fact, it may be counterproductive. It may serve as a model for the child on how to relate to others, who will then find the child "obnoxious." Finally, the child may begin to ignore parental screaming and just tune out the parent. Children do not like to be screamed at any more than adults like to hear children screaming.

"I can remember to this day how my mother always screamed, and I hated it. But I find that I do it sometimes, too. I guess it's ingrained. I hate myself when I catch myself doing it, because I had resolved not to do it to my children if I ever had any."

Perhaps you are unconsciously modeling yourself after your mother. When you are aware of it, you can control it. That happens to all of us. Some parental models were very good, and we want to emulate those; some others, it is better not to follow. It is good that you are beginning to understand which models are beneficial to good growth and good parent-child relations and which are not.

Recognizing the Challenge and Responsibility of Parenting: Baby's Needs Versus Parents' Needs

Parents' Feelings About Responsibility of Child Rearing

How are you feeling now in your role as parents? Do you have more time for yourselves? Do you still feel that you are a "hostage" to the child?

"At first, I had that feeling a good deal of the time. I felt, here I am so young sitting at home all day with the baby. I don't know yet exactly who I am, and I'm responsible for a baby. What should I do? I can't complain; he is a good baby. Sometimes it is fun. But it's not like playing with a doll. There is so much responsibility."

You sound a little overwhelmed by the responsibility and perhaps feel that you should not have to be responsible. You miss your freedom to come and go, those carefree days when you could read a book or go to the movies on a last-minute whim. That is natural and understandable. Everyone goes through those things. Accepting responsibility is part of growing up—and sometimes we would rather not grow up. But there is satisfaction in discharging a responsibility well. That's what maturing is all about: learning to manage life's experiences to the best of one's ability. Raising your child is part of growing up and a part of maturing that has to take place. Some parents naturally take on the responsibility of child rearing and become more mature and parental. They had good parenting models themselves and they carry them on. There are other parents who did not have this kind of model and feel frustrated all the time and angry at their children.

"What if a mother feels this way and is cross and angry a lot? Don't the children get used to it?"

The result of a continuing battle between parent and child may often be seen in the personality the child develops—one that is angry and irritable, too. This is not a personality structure that makes for success or happiness for the child or the parent. That is why it is important to recognize how one feels and acts and the consequences of persistent anger or frustration.

Learning to assume responsibility and to enjoy discharging it successfully is important in any endeavor—whether one is a dress designer, a mechanic, an office worker, or a doctor. Each situation requires the assumption of responsibility, and we mature as we work at it. It is true of parenting, too.

"But when a mother devotes herself to child rearing, she must give up so much if she has had a career."

"I used to think that, too, but I see now what it means to be a mother. I am learning so much about personality development and how a child grows to be a person that I really feel that when I go back to work I'll be more valuable. It's worth it to me to take time off from my career to see my child develop well."

"As you know, I decided not to give up my job. I really could not afford to, financially or professionally. My child seems to be adjusted to being cared for by us and by my mother, who helps us. I agree that I may have to advance more slowly, because I do not accept overtime assignments. I want to have time with the baby, but it is tiring. I am often cross."

"I refuse to settle for advancing slower. I take on all assignments. In my firm, it is 'up or out.' Fortunately, my husband is settled in a more nine-to-five job. He is more the 'mommy' in our family—and truthfully, we both resent that sometimes."

These issues are of prime concern these days, and parents, especially mothers, are under tremendous pressure, whether they are staying home with their children or working outside the home. Right now, we are discussing how you feel about your responsibilities. Certainly, holding down a job in addition to caring for a child (or children) increases the responsibilities and, often, the feelings of being overburdened. Whether you are at home or at an office, there are times when you "want out." We understand that, and we want to help you slow up and take stock. You don't have to be superwoman or superman.

"The problem with mothering is the long hours: it's never over. I have so little time for myself."

It you think back to what it was like when the children were infants, you will realize that you have come a long way. You have developed successful patterns for yourselves and for your children's days. Learning how to do it is all part of the maturing experience. Now that the children are older, you are expecting more time and you are frustrated that at this toddler stage the children are putting demands on you in a new way. But you are becoming more experienced, and soon your lives will begin to assume more of the characteristics they had before the children came.

"When we first talked about this, I could not believe I would adjust. I just 'wanted out,' as they say. As my baby learned to sleep, I began to enjoy the situation more and more, and now it's a real satisfaction for me. Of course, I'll go back to my firm when my children are older. My profession will still be there. I may need to brush up and make new contacts, but this is for the future. Now it's my children's time."

"My mother always went to business. I resented her being away so much and I hated the people who took care of me. I vowed I'd stay home if I had a child. Well, I am staying home, but I find I'm angry about it. It surprises and worries me. I realize now I did not have a good model for being a mother. I will have to try to work at it, because I really do want to be a good mother."

Parents want to be good parents. They come to parenting with different past experiences, so for some it is harder than for others.

Part of the reason you feel burdened by child care *now* is that you expected the children to play on their own without as much parental involvement.

Child's Need for Parents' Company and Attention

"I find my child wants me with him as much as ever. He pulls me to his toys, says 'Sit,' and then he can concentrate and play for quite a while. But I must be there in the room."

This is still part of the separation struggle. It is important to be available to them when you are there—not to just sit in the house, but to be there and to be involved with them. That is what you are complaining about. Right now, in order to keep you there they try to keep you involved. It is a way of reassuring themselves that you are really there. If you are involved with them, you can't possibly go away. That's one of the reasons why they want you to play with them all the time. When they feel secure, they will gradually do a little more on their own. Of course, playing with you is also more fun and stimulating.

"That's all well and good, if you have time to do that. What if you have to make the bed, or fix a meal? Then what do you do?"

In that case, you take the toys the child is playing with and say, "Let's play in the bedroom or kitchen," and arrange a place for the child to play beside you while you work. He is with you and you can talk to each other. The child will feel included in your activities. You can get involved momentarily in the play and then continue your work. Both can be satisfied; no conflict need arise.

"That works for me most of the time, and I feel I have a good relationship with my child. Once in a while she is resistant and we have a little crying."

Sometimes that happens when the child is very absorbed and doesn't want to be disturbed. Then one has to give a little time and say, "As soon as you finish this, we'll play some more in the kitchen (or whatever room you need to be in)." Children can't always switch their interest to another area quickly and need a little time to adjust. Remember, they do not yet have a smoothly working nervous system. It's still immature and does not respond instantaneously, as adults would like it to do.

"Whenever I try to visit with other people she wants me to be with her. Even if we are home and she has been playing with her toys all on her own, the minute someone walks in she is right there and wants me to play and pulls me. Should I allow it? It makes me angry, and I know my friends think there is something wrong with the way I am trying to bring her up."

She doesn't want you to be monopolized by someone else. To her, that means that she is excluded and that you are, in fact, "taken away" from her. If you recognize this, you can pick her up, put her in your lap, and include her in the conversation. Let her get acquainted with the visitor. When she feels secure and included, she will interest herself in her toys. She may make frequent trips back to you to assure herself of your attention to be sure you are still there.

Child's Need to Feel Included

"It is not so bad when we are at home. It's just when we go visiting that it is a problem."

Children need to feel included when they go visiting; they often feel excluded. They can't tolerate exclusion. If you put them on your lap while you talk, and talk and play with them too, you help them feel included. In this way, they are also helped to socialize.

"My biggest problem is when I'm doing something in the house and he just wants to be with me."

Getting housework done is a problem. It has to be patterned into the daily routine just the way you patterned the bath, the feeding, playing, and other activities. You say, "I've got to do the dishes. Now, it's Mommy's dishes time," and you do the dishes. Say it firmly, not as though you were asking, "Will you let Mommy do it?" but as a fact: "This is what we are going to do." Then make a habit of saying it that way, so that he knows this is "dishes time," "cleaning time," or "cooking time." Children learn that when you are cleaning or cooking, you are still around. They will come in and out of the room. This gets to be a habit; it gets to be something that's expected, a part of their life experience. If you are cooking, talk about it and show what you are doing. Give the baby a spoon to play with or a taste of something you are stirring once in a while.

"Suppose the child doesn't respond by getting interested in what you are doing?"

Then you have to find some other activity the child can engage in near you while you work. It certainly may not work the first time. It has to be repeated until it becomes an accepted part of the baby's life, too. You have to say, "Mommy has to do this; this is Mommy's job." When you are finished say, "Mommy is finished. We can play now."

"I have two old pails with pieces of cloth in them. When I am doing dishes, I give her some plastic shapes—it doesn't matter what it is—and she does dishes too."

That's fine. If you set it up like that you can get your work done. However, there are some mothers who prefer not to involve the baby in their work and wait until the baby is having a nap. That is when they do their work. Are some of you managing that way?

"I prefer to do my cooking when she naps in the morning or afternoon. I really enjoy cooking, and it is relaxing not to be interrupted all the time."

"Well, I don't do any housework during my child's naptime. That's my time for myself, to relax and read or wash my hair. That refreshes me and I feel better."

Mothers do need that little bit of relaxation and time for themselves. There is no one, not a doctor or a secretary or a businessman, who does not need a few minutes for a rest break at some time during the day. A mother should program some relaxation into her job, too. Some mothers may even find they need to nap for a little while themselves.

As in every other profession, parents must try to have some balance between work on the job and relaxation. As they learn more about child development and the child's changing needs, parents learn to make adjustments so that the child's needs—and theirs—can be satisfied. Bringing up children *is* a big responsibility, but it can also be a lot of fun.

Integrating Child into Family's Social Life; Parents' Need for Time as a Couple

Most children are ready for more socialization. Are you able to participate in more social activities now with your children than you were before?

■   ■

Taking Children Visiting

"I take my baby almost everywhere with me now. What bothers me is that some older women make remarks about it. I take my baby in her carriage when I shop in a department store. I've had some older women be very rude about the fact that her carriage takes up a lot of elevator space, which is true, but I just don't say anything."

Older generations were used to keeping babies at home. That was the time when there were extended families or hired help with whom to leave the babies at home. In this day and age, a mother would be totally isolated if she could not take her baby with her. You are quite right not to become involved in arguing with people who are simply not in tune with the times.

"I feel very uptight about taking the baby to somebody else's house where there are no children. We've been married about six years, and most of our friends either have children in their teens or none at all. Our baby is over his shyness of new places and he is into everything. He wants to look at and touch absolutely everything. Also, sometimes he screams with delight. It can be nerve-racking if you are not used to it."

Some adults do believe that children should be seen and not heard and that a quiet baby is a good baby. They do not know that screaming is one form of expression before children learn to talk. As for the exploratory behavior that you describe, that is perfectly natural at this age and it does make visiting difficult if your friends are not used to this stage of children's development.

"We have the best time now, visiting relatives or friends with somewhat older children. They love playing with the baby and he loves it, too. I feel comfortable because he can walk by himself and I don't have to worry about their dropping him anymore. It's really great; I recommend it to everyone."

That does sound like a very good arrangement for all concerned, including your friends' children, who enjoy the responsibility of looking after the baby.

"We are trying to begin to entertain a little, but we have a problem getting the baby to go to sleep. She just seems to want to stay up with the company. Is it wrong to let her stay up past her regular bedtime?"

You have to experiment and see how disturbing it is to her sleep pattern and whether it's better to get her off to sleep before the company comes. Children really have social aspirations; they want to be part of the family's activities. Formerly, in large families, the baby was wherever the rest of the family was; the attitude that "it's six o'clock and the baby has to be in bed" is a modern concept. Different cultures have different patterns. Each family has to establish the pattern that suits its style of life. What is important is to keep that pattern consistent. However, occasional devia-

■   ■

tions can usually be tolerated, provided the parents recognize that they need to make patient effort to get the baby's schedule back to its usual form in the next day or two. Maybe the next night the baby will take a little longer to go to sleep. Or she may be a little cranky the next day because of lack of sleep. None of this is serious. If the parents understand what is happening, they can be patient with the baby when necessary but continue the social life they enjoy. It usually works best when parents integrate the baby gradually into the kind of social life they want to have.

"We take our baby everywhere we go—shopping, visiting relatives, or to the museum. It works well, but we have to accommodate, as you say, to her tolerance level. Sometimes I wish we could just go by ourselves. I'm tired of short visits and seeing half an exhibition."

"I agree with you. We tried to go to an adult restaurant and it was a disaster. Now we eat at McDonald's and other places that are good for kids."

That is a compromise that is appropriate now. When you go out for dinner without the baby, you can go to a restaurant of *your* choice.

Parents Need Time as a Couple

You are also raising another important issue. Now that it is becoming a little easier to include the children in your social activities, at least at a certain level, you find that they are always with you. Not only do you need to see the whole exhibition or finish a whole conversation, you also need time by yourselves as a couple. You need time to find out how you are thinking about yourselves as the individuals you were before you had the child—and as the couple you were. Sometimes a father feels neglected and thinks the mother cares more about the child than about him. Some mothers feel quite isolated from the adult world; they haven't had time to hear much about the father's work outside the home or to keep up with their usual interest. If both parents work, they have spent most of their nonworking hours caring for the baby. They haven't had much time to talk to each other; except for the baby, their lives seem quite separate. This is not very good for the marriage.

"My husband was just saying that. We both work, and he said, 'You know, I think I come last in your life, after the baby and your job.' It gave me quite a shock. I'm still thinking about it; he may be right."

"My husband is complaining that we never go out without the baby. Personally, I like it that way. I don't want to leave her with a sitter. I have no relatives nearby."

"In our family, I'm the one who is complaining. My husband loves to play with the baby. He hardly talks to me anymore. I feel like the third wheel."

It is important for all of you to make an effort every once in a while to go out together by yourselves—and do something that you enjoyed doing together before the baby arrived. While we have always stressed being considerate of the child's needs for security, we do not think that you should never leave your child. It is healthy for you to pursue your own interests, and it is important for the child to learn to separate from you and to feel comfortable with at least one other caretaker. If a child has no sense of your leaving and returning, an emergency situation in which you have to leave would be all the harder for the child to tolerate.

"My mother left me with baby-sitters I hated. I was terrified of them. I decided never *to leave my child."*

Often, the way we were raised carries over into our own child-rearing patterns, either as similarities or as opposites. Sometimes we go to extremes to spare our children the discomforts we felt. This is understandable. However, we need to be aware of our own maturation and assess whether our response is appropriate. While it is a good idea to be with the baby as much as possible, the baby does need to be able to trust and relate to other people, at least one other adult besides the parents.

Separation Anxiety: A Resurgence of Clinging

Have you noticed that the children are going through a period in which they find it more difficult to separate from you and stay closer to you physically—actually clinging to you sometimes?

"My child is doing that just when I thought she was getting to be more self-sufficient."

"My son was so independent when he started to walk. Now his constant clinging makes me want to get away from him."

Resurgence of Dependence

Parents are disappointed when their children seem to become more, rather than less, dependent. When they first learned to walk, the children were so exhilarated and pleased with their new mobility that they didn't notice when they strayed far. They didn't even notice the bumps and bruises when they fell. Often, you were anxious and ran after them. Now they are bigger and older, and you think they should be more independent. But when they move away from you now, they discover that the world is pretty big and they have much more comprehension of how far away from you they are. They come running back and cling to you for support. It is a stage when they need reassurance that you are *there* for them; that you are not trying to run *away from them.* When you try to get away from them, they cling even more. If you try to hurry independence, you defeat what you really want to accomplish: the child's development into a self-sufficient, independent individual.

"Does that mean that during this stage mothers should never go away and leave them? That I must give up my afternoon off? That throws me into a panic, because I look forward all week to that time away."

No one is saying that mothers should not have some time off. Mothers need time for themselves in order to be able to cope with their job of child rearing. Child rearing is a very hard job, and parents have to have relief. Nobody works twenty-four hours a day, every day of the week.

"My son used to like our baby-sitter and was glad to see her; but now the minute I put on my things to leave, he begins to cling to me and cry a little. Should I stay with him longer, or not go? The minute I'm out of sight, he stops and begins to play as if nothing has happened."

He has to protest; he has to show that he is attached to you. It wouldn't be good or healthy if he didn't notice that you were leaving. He has a sense of attachment to you and he makes that attachment known. A child of this age should notice your leaving. If he did not protest, it might mean that he was not sufficiently attached. Of course, it would be more understandable if he could say, "Please don't go. I'll miss you." You have to understand that is what he is saying when he cries when you leave. It is important to say "good-bye" and that you will be back soon. Talk about the things he will be doing and tell him when you will be home—for example, after his nap or before his bath. He can understand that. Then when you return, make the greeting happy and let the child rejoice that you are back.

"Should I promise to bring him something if he is a good boy and lets me go?"

That is a bribe. A child will get into the habit of expecting something material in exchange for your going. The present that a parent brings back each time is herself or himself. A toy can be given to the child occasionally when you find something appropriate and want him to have it—but not as a bribe.

"Since I have begun to go out more often now that I have a good caretaker, the baby does not go to sleep as easily. He needs me to be with him until he falls asleep. He seems afraid to let me go. Should I sit with him?"

It often works out better, if children are very anxious, for you to sit with them until they are asleep. When they know that you are going to be there, that you are not going away, the time that you have to sit with them gets less and less. This new clinging is a transitory stage, and they will get over it. They are working out their separation from you; it is not an easy task for them, and they need help. They need to establish the habit of preparing for bed and sleep with a special story, record, or song the parent sings.

During this period, children need more parental support. If you go to the door or phone, they are right after you. As they cling more, you in turn get angry and feel more confined. You feel you can't do anything that *you* want to do. But you must remember that it is only a transitory phase. If you can reassure them during changes that cause anxiety—when a new caretaker comes to your house or one of the parents is ill—they will gradually stop clinging. Most parents don't expect this resurgence of clinging; that is why you are asking about it. This is something that has been well understood only recently. In the past, parents often dealt with it by slapping the children, putting them to bed, and letting them cry. And it seemed to work. The children did become quiet, but some needed psycho-therapy later to overcome their insecurities.

If you go through the inconvenience now—and it is inconvenient and does make your life miserable for a while—your patience and attention will be rewarded by a child with greater self-confidence.

"I have no problem putting my son to bed for his nap, but at night I have to give him his bottle and hold him till he's sound asleep; otherwise he just clings to me and doesn't want to let me leave. I was wondering why only at night. Is it because his father comes home for dinner and then leaves for another job? Is he afraid that at night I will leave him, too?"

That sounds like a very good interpretation of his behavior. He is clinging because he doesn't understand that his daddy has to go to work but that you will be there. When he is older and understands more, the clinging will end.

Separation Problems at Bedtime

Difficulty in separating at bedtime is a very common situation. All children need special attention at bedtime: stories, a special song, and sometimes a drink of water. Children do not like going to bed because it separates them from the family. Some children play very hard and get very tired; they fall asleep the minute their heads touch the pillow. There are others who do not. That doesn't mean they are "bad" children; each has a different pattern. Some may not separate easily at bedtime until they are three; others may do it at one and a half or two. Everybody envies the parent whose child goes off to sleep easily. With understanding and patience, all children do it eventually. One hastens the process not by force, but by allowing the child to deal with it on his or her own maturational timetable.

"My problem was different. I went back to work for five days and left my son with his grandmother, who often stays with us. I worked from 8:30 A.M. to noon; I never had trouble when I left. But Saturday morning he would not let go of me; Sunday, the same thing. Then, on Monday when he saw his father getting dressed, he would not take his eyes off of me. When he saw that I wasn't getting dressed, he was satisfied that I wasn't going out, too. The minute he was satisfied, he went to his room to play. But for three days he followed me everywhere like a little puppy. I thought he was beyond that stage; his behavior made me kind of angry. Now I'll know what to expect."

When you know what to expect and understand what the behavior means, then it is easier to deal with.

The children are now getting to the age when they can relate to more people than Mommy and Daddy. They can relate to others now because they have learned to trust their parents. That is why it's very important in the beginning to establish a good relationship with the parents. When children feel secure with their parents, they are able to feel secure with other people. But they still do not like to separate from you, and they show you they don't like it. You have to continue to reassure them.

"When I go away, she cries a lot because I once left her with a person she didn't know. She cried from the moment I went out until I got back. I will never do that again. She never behaved that way when I left her with someone she knew. Now it is hard to leave her."

It sounds as though you have to reestablish her sense of trust. She must relearn that you will come back and that you will not leave her unless she is comfortable with the person who is taking care of her. Just one unfortunate episode can undo so much effort in helping them separate. Parents often find this hard to understand.

Sneaking Out Causes Problems

Do some of you find it so upsetting to your baby when you leave that you sneak out?

"Well, I used to do that. But as we learned here, it just upsets the baby more. When I came home he cried and stayed glued to me. I realized that he thought I might disappear again. It's hard to make them understand that you won't go away again—that day, anyway."

That is indeed the problem. Once you have sneaked out, then the child no longer trusts you. He or she does not know that you won't disappear from the bathroom or from the kitchen, even if you are in the middle of cooking. It is exceedingly important to say—and mean it, "Mommy is home." When you really practice this, the child will gradually regain trust and feel secure that you will stay, that you are still home—even if you are in the next room. Gradually, he will not be so anxious when you leave the room or go to the door to answer the bell. Then, when you do have to go out again, you tell the child before you go and reassure him that you will return. When this pattern is established between parent and child, there is a mutual sense of trust. The child will feel secure that he knows what is going to happen to him.

Children do not like surprises; they like to be able to prepare for what is going to happen to them. They feel very vulnerable and they constantly need reassurance that someone, preferably the parent, will be with them, that they will not be abandoned. Just because you tell them that you are going out and will be back does not mean that they will not fuss when you leave. They may, indeed, fuss or cry; the important thing to remember, however, is that these tears do not mean broken trust. They simply mean that the child is sad to be left behind; they mean the child would rather be with you than with the substitute caretaker. This behavior shows appropriate attachment.

■   ■

"I have noticed that sometimes when I come home the baby turns away from me. Does that mean he did not miss me or recognize me?"

How Children Show They Have Missed Their Parents

Sometimes when they have really missed you a lot, they won't come to you when you return. That is one of their ways of saying, "Look, you left me and I'm angry." You will not be as disappointed when this happens if you understand what it means. They have felt abandoned. It is hard for them to suddenly change their mood when you return.

"It's hard to take. I come home ready to hug and kiss the baby, and he turns away. I have noticed that in a few minutes he comes over and won't stir from my side. Now it's clear to me what it all means."

"I have a dilemma just now. I had a separation problem when I had to spend time in the hospital with my father. My daughter had to stay at my parents' house with a sitter and was upset for months. Afterward we finally reestablished her sense of trust in us, and I would hate to undermine it now. However, my husband is getting a two-week vacation; he hasn't had one in two years, and we would like to go away together. I've made plans for my parents to come and stay for a week before we leave so she can get used to them. It's making me very uncomfortable and I don't know what to do. It seems to me she knows my neighbor better than she knows my parents and would be happier with her, but I can't ask for such a favor."

It sounds as though your parents were quite willing to try to get to know their granddaughter better. In the week while you are at home, you can leave her with them for short periods of time and see how they get along. Remember, she is older now. She will be in her own home, not in a strange place. She will have her own bed and toys and the playmate next door. Her grandparents can carry out her daily routine in the same way you do. Everything will probably go very well, and she will learn to trust her grandparents, too.

"But what if she doesn't take to them?"

You will be able to determine this before you leave. Then you can decide what is best to do. No matter how well they get along, you have to be prepared for signs that she missed you. She may cling for several days or she may be a little bit cranky when you return. As long as you understand, you can try to meet her needs without feeling guilty or angry.

"Don't you think making this effort and possibly changing your vacation plans is catering to the baby too much?"

It is not a matter of "catering." It is a matter of understanding the baby's needs. In this case, there has already been an initial unintentional trauma. It shows a great deal of understanding and sensitivity on the parents' part to understand this and to want to avoid a repetition. Most parents will not really enjoy their vacation too much if they feel that the child is suffering. Everyone needs time off; parents of young children certainly need time off as much as—or more

■   ■

than—most. This is a case, however, in which a little extra thought and planning by the parents can avoid problems later. Understanding and consideration for the child's needs sometimes takes more time initially but can make life easier and more pleasant in the long run.

Comforting: What Is Appropriate Now?

How are you comforting your children now when they cry and need soothing?

Oral Comforting

"I find a bottle or a cookie works surely and quickly. I guess that is why I offer those first."

"When my baby stumbles and falls, I go and pick him up and hold him; but that is not enough now. I have to talk to him and say, 'It's okay. Mama's here.' Sometimes he will run and get his bottle himself if it is nearby."

That certainly indicates that he still finds the bottle the best form of comfort. That is what we are concerned about: that there may be too much dependence on bottles or food for comfort. Gradually the parent has to begin to substitute other forms of comfort so that later in life drinking or eating are not the main sources of comfort. There may be some connection between too much dependence on oral comforting in early childhood and overeating, alcoholism, and smoking as ways of overcoming trouble later in life. These oral satisfactions may become the way of allaying anxiety or distress in adult life.

"What about a pacifier instead of a bottle?"

A pacifier may give immediate comfort; one sees many older children still sucking on pacifiers. As we discussed when the children were babies (see *The First Year of Life*), pacifiers should be used only to provide additional sucking for a baby who takes bottle feedings too quickly and has insufficient sucking. The problem with both the pacifier and feeding as automatic comforting devices is that they tend literally to plug up the child's feelings. When the child is sucking on a bottle or pacifier or chewing on a cookie, he cannot express himself verbally. Children often cry now because they cannot express themselves in any other way. But if we hold them and calm them down, we can try to ask them what the problem is. At this age, they may be able only to point or say one word, but the parent may be able to understand what the problem is. If another child has taken a toy and we have not seen it happen, the child may point to it if we take the time to ask. Getting the toy back is, in this case, more appropriate comforting than being handed a cookie. In another case, the child may cry because he cannot do something he wants to do. Help in mastering the activity is more beneficial to the child than any oral comforting. In a few months, the children will be more verbal and it will be even more important to try to communicate with them about what is upsetting them. Always handing a child a pacifier or cookie—"peace at any price"—turns off the child's natural inclination to communicate his feelings and concerns.

Just as we learned to listen to different cries and tried to understand them, we must now learn to *listen* to words. Such a pattern will lead to good parent-child relations and open communication, without which both parent and child may feel misunderstood.

"It takes a lot of ingenuity sometimes to find what is making the baby unhappy and just what will comfort him."

Yes, to be a parent requires a lot of ingenuity and versatility. That's why we keep repeating that being a parent is an important job that requires knowledge, understanding, patience, and a dedication that puts it into a category of profession—not just a job to be done somehow or other.

Other Forms of Comforting

"My husband is more adept at diverting the baby than I am. I catch on when she is wet or hungry, but he seems to know just when to tickle her, or jog her on his knee, or show her pictures in a book."

"My best bet is to turn on some music; sometimes just my singing does it! Of course, it's nice for me, too, because we all like music."

"Are you saying that we should never console them with a cookie?"

No, that is not our intention. We are saying that comforting by putting something into the mouth is no longer the appropriate form of comforting. Furthermore, used as the sole form of comforting, it may lead later in life to unpleasant consequences. At present, the child should experience a whole variety of comforting mechanisms and interchanges with the parent that can enrich the relationship between parent and child. The emphasis at this age should be on establishing an open communication pattern.

One must always make the distinction as well between oral comforting and satisfying a child's hunger. Often children will cry and become fussy when they are tired and hungry. Sometimes a child will tell the parent he is hungry, but many children still cannot tell you at this age. The parent must then guess, by knowing the child's schedule and recent food intake, whether the child needs food or another form of comforting. If the child is really hungry, then the bottle is more appropriate than a cookie from a nutritional point of view.

The main point is that parents' styles of comforting need to progress in keeping with the child's new development capabilities. Only oral comforting is no longer age-appropriate.

Rivalry with Siblings and Other Children; Children's Need for Attention and Inability to Share

Sibling Rivalry

Most parents are generally aware of the potential for sibling rivalry, and most parents try to plan for the older child when a new baby comes into the family.

They recognize that the older child should not feel left out. They may also not realize that their child feels left out if another child, outside the family, gets too much of their attention, even briefly. Have any of you been noticing your child's need for attention?

"Yes, our child seems in constant rivalry with her baby brother. Although I take primary care of her *and our maid does almost everything for* him, *I still have to give him* some *attention. He is my baby, too. It is very disturbing."*

It's very hard for a mother to apportion her time and attention to satisfy more than one child at a time. The closer the children are in age, the more difficult it is, especially if the parents do not understand that it is natural and normal for the older child to want as much attention as the younger one receives. Parents often feel that the older one should understand that it's the younger one's turn. They think the older one is selfish and that he should relinquish his mother's attention for the baby's good. This is an expectation that is in no way realistic. The older one may not yet be mature enough to understand sharing his parents' attention. He still requires a great deal of recognition of his needs, and his emotional needs are much greater than parents anticipate. No matter how bright the child may be, his emotional development and experience are only at the level of his chronological age.

"I know what you say is true, but it is so hard to live through the situation. My son is even upset if I pay some attention to the dog. He comes running over to get into the act!"

Yes, that's just it. Children need to feel "in the act," as you say. There seems to be an inborn quality in the child that makes exclusion of any kind impossible to tolerate.

We have been talking about sibling rivalry, but children can also be jealous of parents' attention to each other. When parents embrace, the child comes right over and wants to be part of it, too.

"Does that mean parents should not embrace in front of the child?"

Not at all. It is good for the child to be aware of the loving relationship between her parents. It is a good example for the child; but the child should be included in the demonstration of affection if she seems to desire it. She should be included in all greetings to family and friends. She is part of the family, and this needs to be recognized. Some children are more insistent about this than others. Parents should not become angry and feel this is an intrusion, considering the child's actions out of place. The child is behaving as a child. The problem is with us adults. We want children to grow up faster than they can.

Rivalry with Other Children

Have you also noticed how your children behave if you hold another child on your lap or pay attention to another child?

"As a matter of fact, I have found it quite embarrassing when my child raises a rumpus if I pick up another child, especially if he falls and I am nearer than his own mother."

It is considerate to pick up the other child if you are nearer, but do not expect your child to like it. For her, you have become unavailable when you tend to another child. The hurt child needs his *own* mother's comforting. Mothers really have to console their own children. If for any reason you have to care momentarily for another child, it is best to step aside as soon as the mother arrives. Then pick up your own child, assuring her that you are there for her, and get her interested in some activity with you.

"I have noticed that even at home. My baby can be playing and concentrating on his play, but if he sees out of the corner of his eye that I am going toward another child, or even to our pet dog, he comes running right over. In a way I find it funny, but also embarrassing, because it seems to me that he is developing into a selfish person."

At this age, it is not selfishness but an age-appropriate and primitive need to be assured that he is not going to be separated from you by anyone else. The parent needs to give the child that assurance.

"If we do what you suggest, aren't we catering to this behavior? Won't it encourage the children to demand attention and condone jealousy?"

We want to help you avoid reinforcing this behavior. Parents invite this kind of behavior by ignoring the child's needs and causing him or her to be more demanding. Children whose needs are not met become very demanding. This may continue into adult life. Some adults are still trying to get their primitive needs satisifed. We are trying to help you meet your child's needs for attention and to understand how upsetting attention to another child can be at this age. When your children are older and more verbal, they will be able to tolerate your attention to others better.

"You are right. My older son is quite tolerant of the baby now. But he got quite clinging recently while he was sick. This baby is much more dependent on me, and she was terribly jealous. Every time I went to my son, she wanted to be right with me, too. The hardest time was when his fever was really high, and he wanted me to stay with him."

Couldn't you get someone to help you with her, to give her the attention that she needed?

"No, she wanted only me. There was one day that was really rough. That was the next day, when he felt better but was still very demanding and cranky from being sick. It was really impossible."

That's a good day for grandma to come and help. Sometimes you really do need help, because you have only two hands. When one of the children is sick, you can't be close to both of them together.

■   ■

"I would try to explain to her and kind of pat her head and say I knew she wanted me to hold her, too, and things like that. But it didn't really work."

One way to try to ease the situation is to give her attention before she has to ask for it. If you give her attention *only* when she asks for it, then she has to keep asking for it. For instance, perhaps when your son was sleeping, you could have given her some attention, even though she did not ask. It is very hard. But if you understand what is going on, then you don't get so angry at your child.

Understanding Child's Need for Attention

"But don't they become spoiled 'nags' if you always try to do what they want? That is what my husband and his parents seem to think."

That attitude is a misunderstanding of a child's needs. If you understand what is going on, and you try to give the child a little bit of attention when she is not asking for it, that keeps her from thinking that she gets attention only when she demands it. A "nag" is a child who continues to ask until he or she is satisfied. If the child is responded to promptly most of the time, and even has some needs anticipated, he or she develops a sense of security and trust and does not become a "nag."

"I have a problem when we have visitors. When my son is on somebody else's territory, he is a perfect gentleman. But if somebody is here, he even takes toys away from small babies. He pushes other children around. He is bratty on his territory."

It is his turf, and he has a feeling that the other children will take his things away from him. He may have already experienced that. In order to be polite to a visiting child, you may have inadvertently offered her one of your child's favorite toys. So he is now expecting the worst when someone comes.

Children of this age are now just coming into the "I, my, mine" stage *(see pages 136–38 for more discussion on this)*. They are just discovering who they are and what is theirs. You must assure your child that the toys are his. Ask him which one the visitor can play with for a few minutes and explain that his toys will not be taken away.

It's a good idea also for children to take one or two of their own toys with them when they go visiting, so that there will be less conflict with the host child. In addition, their play will have to be supervised by the parents.

"I find the most rivalry is over toys in the park. My child seems to want whatever the other child has. If he picks up another child's toy and the other child wants it, what should I do?"

First, it is important to bring some of your child's toys to the park. When this situation occurs, give back the other child's toy. Then give your child his own toy and say, "This is yours," and begin to play with him. You may have to move away from the other child to another part of the playground.

■   ■

"But what should I do if the situation is the opposite—the other child takes my child's toy? If I take it back from him, the other child's mother thinks I'm mean."

That is not your primary concern. You help your child retrieve his toy, if he wants it, and say, "I'm sorry." Try to find something to give to the other child and explain that he or she may have a turn with the toy later.

"You don't think they should be left to fight it out themselves?"

They are too young for that kind of negotiation. They are still nonverbal. They know what they want, but they can't express their feelings verbally. All they can do is cry, kick, bite, and scream. If this physical way of handling a situation is allowed to continue, it becomes the pattern for social contact. It encourages physical violence rather than verbal resolution of arguments. That is the making of a "brat" and a "bully." What we are doing is setting an example of appropriate negotiation. This procedure takes patience, but it works and avoids fights and bad feelings between both adults and children.

"How long does it take for them to get over this need to be included all the time? I can't even talk on the phone without having her cry, crawl to my lap, and pull on the phone."

That depends on the kind of relationship you have established with your child and his emotional development: how far along the child is in his ability to separate from you; how verbal he is; how long he can concentrate on an activity of his own; how secure he feels.

More on Discipline: A Positive Approach

Now that the children are more active, do you find it more difficult to set limits? What are your concerns now?

"My big problem is at the park: my son runs out the gate of the playground. The minute the gate is open, he runs for it and gets out. I have to be on the watch all the time and stop him before he gets out. Sometimes I'm too late. I have to chase him, and he just loves it. For him, it's a game!"

"I have the same problem. My daughter knows she is not supposed to go out the gate. She goes to the gate and looks back to see if I am looking at her. I look at her and say 'No,' and then usually she just runs back. Sometimes she does run out and I run after her. But she knows she is not to do it."

She is looking at you to say "No." She still does not have the ability to limit herself. You remember what we have discussed (see *The First Year of Life*) about learning limitations: that the baby would go up to an ashtray, and you would say "No" to her and give her something else to do. After several weeks or months, she would go up to it and say "No" to herself but still pick it up. Then finally she would say "No" and would not pick it up. It may take a little more time before she goes over to the gate, hears you say "No, don't go out,"

■   ■

and comes back herself. Learning self-control follows much the same process in each case, but running away is even more tempting than touching an ashtray. There is such a sense of mastery in being able to run. We must recognize that. Our problem is to teach the limits of where children can safely run. That's the hard part. If we are consistent in our limits and don't permit them to become a game, the lesson is finally learned.

Children Don't Yet Understand the Consequences of Their Actions

"In the park, I have a different problem. My baby likes to play in the sandbox. He picks up the sand in his fingers and lets it drop; sometimes it blows in his or another child's face. Other mothers accuse him of throwing sand. Usually, it isn't really on purpose, but other mothers don't understand that. So I've stopped going to that part of the park, although he enjoys it, because I don't know how to handle him there."

You are right; he doesn't understand the consequences of throwing sand. He needs to learn how to play appropriately in the sand. *You* should be with him and show him how to shovel and build in the sand. Children of this age should be watched in a sandbox.

"Last summer they were all eating sand, but that has passed. Now they are in the running stage. How does one take a child this age to the beach?"

You can take her for a walk on the beach holding her hand. You can help her make sand castles and dig holes into which the water can come. You can keep her busy doing things such as playing with a beach ball or other sand toys. When she loses interest, you can go for a walk with her again or collect shells. Often, she will be interested in playing beside another child. Then you can enjoy talking with the other mother as long as the children are near you. Children of this age should never be out of your sight at the beach.

One of the things you have to stress is that the child cannot go into the water without you. You approve all the safe things that the child can do at the beach: how much fun it is when the sand dumps out and makes a pie; how nice it is to make a little trough for the water to run into. What fun it is to run *with mommy* down the beach. If the child runs away, you have to say "No" firmly and bring him back, just as you would in the park. The danger in the park is running into the street. At the beach the danger is running into the water alone. No child should be permitted near the water without a life jacket. That should be standard equipment at all times, but parents must still watch closely.

"I do all of these things and I actually enjoy being there. Sometimes some of my friends are there with their children, and that makes it very nice, too. But the other adults seem to think I spend too much time with my child and should let him occupy himself."

Again, we find that the adults without children are making parents who are giving their children appropriate attention feel uncomfortable. It is true that children should be allowed to occupy themselves, but that comes at a later stage. At the beach, children of this age need close attention and supervision.

We have been talking about the kinds of activities that require new limitations. We have not yet spoken about whether you feel you are saying "No" about more things, or whether you are saying "No" too much.

"I find I am doing that. Whether we are in the house or outside, my child seems to be doing something she shouldn't: putting dirty paper in her mouth or jumping on the sofa or running out of the playground."

Positive Approach to Teaching Discipline

Instead of saying "No" all the time, it is good to use a positive approach whenever you can. When the child is about to put paper from the floor in her mouth, say, "Paper goes in the basket," and get her to throw it there. Then you give her a cracker and say, "The cracker is to eat; paper goes in the basket." She has an impulse to put the paper in her mouth, but it can be diverted to the appropriate action of putting it in the basket. This approach enables you to be more positive. Do you ever try that?

"I try to. I try to be positive, but he goes right back to whatever I tell him not to. So I end up saying 'No' more times than I'd like."

One of the reasons we have trouble is that we were brought up with "No." Unconsciously, our first impulse is to say "No" because it was said to us. We treat our children that way because that is how we were treated. It may take a while to change that pattern, so you mustn't be disappointed with yourselves if you don't always respond more positively. The important thing is that you understand the concept and try as often as you can to say something other than "No," which should be saved for the hot stove, crossing the streets, pulling down the lamp—things that are dangerous. Try saying, "The cup is for drinking; the ball is for throwing." When the children accept the appropriate action, then give them recognition for their achievement.

"I know. I find that when he does things I approve of, he will come back and do the same thing again, even the next day. When we go out on the terrace to play with his toys, he puts any papers that are lying around into the basket. That has become part of his routine each day. He knows I approve."

Now you see that it works. You can continue that kind of experience. It gives the children a great feeling when they are doing many things that you can approve of. It is very important for them to get the message that what they are doing is good. Then, they can approve of themselves; the approval doesn't always have to come from somebody else. Many people never experience this educational process of learning to recognize when their efforts are good. These are the people in therapy who are afraid of others finding fault with them and who are never sure that what they do is right. These feelings come from very early lack of positive recognition. We want each child to feel, "Yes, I am okay. I am doing right. I can do things and I am an achiever."

Development of Self-confidence

"Won't it make a child 'stuck up' to feel that he is approved of and to think well of himself? Doesn't that make a conceited grown-up?"

To be aware of one's ability and to have a sense of self-confidence are characteristics of a healthy, mature adult. A person whom we refer to as "stuck up" is usually a person whose sense of security is fragile, who did not develop a realistic sense of his own ability and needs to reassure himself by bragging about his actions to others. We are aiming for the early healthy development of a sense of achievement in our children, to enhance their motivation to achieve in school. Motivation for school achievement continues in children who feel confident about achieving by their own efforts. Early recognition of children's achievement enhances these feelings.

"I wish my parents had known this. I was always trying to please and I never got any response from my parents except disapproval. It's funny; they continue it even now. I think I could have gone to college if I had had the least encouragement."

"I think my husband's family must have been like that, too. He feels he made it in spite of his parents. He often thinks I'm coddling our child."

It is a good idea to talk these ideas over with the other parent (and the caretaker). As we've said before, it is important for the child to receive similar approval and limitation from all of his or her caretakers. It is confusing to the child to receive different limitations from each parent. Perhaps you can help your spouses (and caretakers) to use this more positive approach to discipline.

We believe parents sincerely want to see their children achieve. They have the mistaken idea that pointing out all the negative aspects of behavior will help their children overcome them. They do not realize that this approach is counterproductive and discourages the children from trying because they become afraid to fail. Instead, parents need to emphasize their approval and recognition so that the children develop self-confidence and a sense of self-worth.

The Child's Ability to Delay Gratification and Respond to Parental Requests

Children's Inability to Wait

Are you finding that these toddlers still need to have instant satisfaction of their needs? Or have you noticed the beginning of some tolerance for delay?

"This is a subject I discuss with my husband all the time. He thinks that at this age our son should be able to wait for anything. It bothers him most when we have to stop the car for a red light and the baby begins to fidget and cry, saying 'Ca, go.' My husband thinks there is something wrong with the baby."

■   ■

That is a very common situation. It is a good opportunity to say to your son, "Soon the light will be green. Red is stop. Green is go." Tell him that now is *their* turn to go; soon it will be *ours*. You may have to do this for weeks until the idea of stopping, waiting, and going becomes familiar to him. It can be a game as well as a chance to understand the new associations of red for stop, green for go. It will help him cope with a situation in which delay cannot be avoided. It may also help him begin to accept delay in other situations as well.

"We have tried to play the 'stop and go game' in traffic because our daughter hates to wait. My husband added to the game by counting the passing cars and, although she can't count, it seems to help her wait."

"Trying to get my son to wait affects me a little differently. He wants me to come and play with him 'right now!' I can't stop instantly whatever I'm doing; yet I want to, because I'm worried that he will feel I'm rejecting him."

If you didn't ever stop to play with your child when he asked, he might get the feeling of rejection. At this age, most children can wait a little while without feeling rejected. When babies are very young, they cannot wait. You have all been through that. When they were hungry, they needed feeding pretty quickly. When they got a little older and began to know that the sounds you were making in the kitchen meant you were preparing the bottle, their cries were less insistent. They were able to wait a little while. Now that they are beginning to be verbal, it is possible to say, "I'm coming in a minute (soon)," or, "Just a second," and then go to them. Now they are able to tolerate a little more delay. As they get older, the delay can gradually be increased. That is one of the ways to help your children develop the ability to delay. The ability to postpone gratification of one's needs or wishes for an appropriate time is a measure of maturity. Children who are not verbal cannot be expected to respond to "Just a minute." They have to learn by patient repetition of the situation what "Just a minute," "I am coming soon," or "Wait for Mommy," means.

Helping Children Learn to Wait

We have talked about the importance of daily routines—of sequencing the events in a child's day so that he or she knows what is coming next. In addition to establishing a sense of security and trust, knowing what to expect also helps the child to wait. If the child begins to understand that a certain activity usually happens next, she can tolerate a little delay more calmly. She learns that this is the time for eating, sees the preparation of food, and *knows* that food is coming. This growing ability to delay develops more quickly and with less fussing from the child if we are patient and don't exploit the child's acceptance of some delay. For instance, if the phone rings as you are preparing dinner and, because the child is quiet, you think you can talk for a while, the child's tolerance limit may be surpassed. Often we expect too much of children too soon. Sometimes we even expect them to understand *our* needs and to delay gratification until we are ready to serve them. Then we get impatient when they fuss.

"Something that I find takes patience is giving my son medicine. He won't take any kind of pill or medicine without a fight."

Never rush him. And never urge him to take the medicine "for Mommy."

"I used to have that problem. But now I say, 'Tell me when you are ready,' and she turns right around and takes it."

That is something we can all learn. Saying "When you are ready" or "Tell me when" often works with children. If you want them to come to the table to eat and they resist, you may say, "Your dinner is here. When you are ready, you can come." Often, in just a few seconds, they turn around and sit down. But if you say, "Sit down right now and eat your supper," you are not allowing the child any autonomy. Remember, this is the age of beginning independence, and children balk when they feel too dominated. Many of us were brought up with "Sit down right now" and feel that our children should be, too. Often one parent holds this view and the other doesn't. Do you find that you are having disagreements about what to expect from your children?

"Not from my husband, because we discuss these topics when I get home. Some of our relatives are critical; they think we cater to the baby."

Appropriate Responses

As we have said before, meeting the child's needs at his or her level is not catering. In the same way that we expect children to wait longer than they can, we often expect them to respond more quickly than they can to our requests or demands. At this age, the children's central nervous systems are not sufficiently developed for immediate responses to our requests. It is unrealistic to ask them to "come right away" or "sit right down." The message has to travel to the brain, register, and travel out again to generate the appropriate activity. Children cannot make quick transitions from one activity to another. If they are playing, they also may not want to stop suddenly to get dressed or to eat. If we look honestly at our own behavior as adults, we will recognize a similar attitude in ourselves. How many times has a child—or another adult—asked us to do something and our reaction is, "Just a minute. Let me finish this chapter (or this phone call)?" Children of this age are not verbal enough or socialized enough to say to you, "Just a minute," but they have similar feelings. Demanding immediate response from a child leads most of the time to a confrontation between parent and child. We, as adults, must be patient. We must understand that children are *unable* to respond quickly. Often they are also *unwilling;* but with a little forewarning and patience, they can be encouraged to do what needs to be done.

Understanding the child's inability in these areas as *immaturity* and *lack of experience* will help us to be more realistic in our expectations and more patient. This understanding will help us avoid unnecessary frustrations.

■   ■

Family Differences in Child-Rearing Attitudes

Do you find that your ways of being parents are very different from your own parents' and friends' ways of parenting? If so, how are you managing?

Responding Is Not Spoiling

"I have a lot of trouble not only with my relatives but sometimes with my husband, because he is so influenced by them. They all think I'm spoiling the baby when I respond to his cries."

We have talked before about how different cultures and different generations view the question of spoiling. Introducing new ways of child rearing is often threatening and upsetting to people who have reared children themselves. It is really very difficult. It takes persistence and patience—you do have to be patient teachers. If you get angry at the advice and just seethe inwardly when your relatives don't view things your way, you don't accomplish much and may hurt your relationships. It may help to say something like "I respect your point of view; I know you've had a lot of experience. Let me try to explain why I am doing it a little differently. I think this way is working out; if it is not successful, then I may try your way."

Intimidation by Family

"My family says, 'You and your special methods! You think your child is something special.' And I have to admit I do. I tell them he is something special and remind them that they must have felt the same way about their children."

"It's very hard for me to speak out like that. I have an aunt who has three grown children, and all are in psychotherapy. All have had a real bad life, so to speak, right? And she was scolding me unmercifully for letting my little girl hug me. I felt like saying to her, 'Well, if you did more of that with your children, they wouldn't be where they are today.' I had to use my self-control to keep quiet."

It is easier to keep quiet. You might be able to handle her by saying, "You know, Auntie, everybody has her own way of bringing up her children. You brought up your children your way, the best way you knew; and I am trying to bring up my child the best way I know."

"It is very easy when we are talking about it here; but when I am there and she is literally screaming at me, and that is exactly her method—screaming—I just go to pieces. My husband just laughs. He says that as soon as I know she is coming, I get nervous. I open the door and I am a different person. I can't control the feeling. She made me feel that way when I used to visit her when I was little, too."

Her behavior to you revives your whole childhood experience. She's still doing just what she did to her own children and to you. You are responding automatically to your emotions and not using your head or your professional expertise as a psychiatric nurse. It is very hard to escape from your childhood role when it is forced on you. That is one of the reasons that we talk so much about helping our children to establish self-confidence. Now you see why it is so important. If they develop self-confidence early, it will be easier for them to cope in such situations.

"My father has the same ability to put me in a state of total panic."

Yes, and then it's hard for you to remember that you are a grown-up. You are an adult and you are really on a par with him now. You are a parent. He has a great deal of interest in you. He has a right to have an opinion and to express it, but he really has no right to direct you. It is perfectly all right to listen to him and then say, "Yes, I see you would have liked that better."

"It is so easy to say it here but so difficult at home."

That is why we repeatedly talk about these issues here—so that after a while, you will learn how to make use of what seems helpful. It is very, very hard. It is like a music lesson. It seems so easy when your teacher explains it. The hard part is to go home and use what you learned. It is much the same for you. Practice makes it easier each time.

"I have trouble with my older brothers. My son often wants to be carried after we've walked a short distance outside. Sometimes he is tired; and sometimes I think the traffic frightens him, so I pick him up. They say, 'Put him down. Do you want him to be a mama's boy?' I get upset. What makes me so insecure that I listen to them?"

It is not a sign of your feeling insecure as a mother. You know what to do as a mother. But your behavior suggests that your original relationship to your brothers is continuing. Did they always make you feel they knew better in regard to your schoolwork, clothes, or boyfriends as you were growing up?

"They were always telling me what to do, and I was always intimidated by them."

They are still doing that to you. You know very well what you expect of your child and how you want to bring him up. You are not reacting to them as your child's mother. You are reacting to them as the little sister. They are putting you back in the mold of little sister, and not allowing you to emerge into your role as mother.

It is not a conflict that is being induced so much by differences in the ways of child rearing as it is the difficulty in recognizing that you have grown up to be a parent. If you deal with the situation maturely, your relatives may soon respond with less of an authoritarian attitude. In any case, you can hold your ground with more sense of security. There are conflicts, however, that do arise over different attitudes toward child rearing. We spoke earlier of spoiling. Are there other areas that cause disagreement?

■   ■

Permitting Exploration

"Yes, I'm in trouble with my mother most of the time, now that the baby is getting around on her own, especially if she tries to climb up into a chair or even run down the hall. She is always saying, 'Be careful.'"

This anxiety may carry over to the child. If the anxious adult is present often enough, it can influence the child's development. This is another instance in which the parent has to stand up firmly for the child's freedom to explore. It is not easy, but one has to assure the anxious relative patiently that the child is capable of climbing or walking. Stand by and show the grandmother how well the child does and overtly recognize the child's achievement. Say that you know children do fall and that you watch to see that the child does not injure himself.

"You know, I try to do that with an aunt who just dotes on the baby, but I find myself getting angry at her. She acts as though I'm not aware or don't care— that only she has the baby's interest at heart."

That is a tough situation to handle. Try to stay calm and collected and don't compete with her to demonstrate who cares more for the child. Show her calmly what the baby can do now. She may then be able to appreciate the baby's achievement, too, instead of worrying everyone about it. This will diminish some of your tenseness.

Allowing Normal Activity and Noise

"My father-in-law thinks children should be seen and not heard. He expects them to sit still and be quiet, even at this age. He keeps saying, 'Shhh, shhh,' with his finger to his lips whenever the baby begins to make a sound. Now, whenever he comes, the baby just clings to me and won't go to him at all."

It is very inhibiting for a child to be told to be quiet all the time. Children need to be free to express themselves. Older people often think the quiet child is the good child. Such constant disapproval is not a good way to build the child's self-esteem. Perhaps you can explain some of this to your father-in-law. Someday he might go out with you to the park, so that your baby can run around and make noise without disturbing his grandfather. Then, when you come back inside, perhaps the baby will be ready to look at a book quietly with his grandfather.

"When my parents come to look after the baby, they skip her bath and let her stay up an hour later. Then she seems cranky the next day. When I suggest that they follow my routine, they say, 'Oh, it won't hurt her every once in a while.' It makes me not want to have them again."

Life is much easier when parents, grandparents, and baby-sitters all follow about the same routines with a child. It can be upsetting all around when things are changed. On the other hand, if it is only occasionally and the child really enjoys her grandparents, it may not be so bad. Having a good time with

■   ■

the grandparents is very important in building a relationship with them. Parents should try not to be disapproving of the grandparents' care. Within reasonable limits, children can accommodate to some variations in their routines. If the baby gets back to her schedule after a day or two, it's probably all right. If it takes longer, then you must explain that to your parents. They may be skipping the bath because they do not feel secure in handling that. We stress the security that children get from following a routine, but we do not want you to become inflexible about it.

Favorite Toys and Security Blankets

Have some of you noticed that your children are becoming attached to certain toys or other objects that they need to take with them wherever they go?

"She mothers her bear all the time; she puts it to bed, gives it a bottle, and sleeps with it. I look on it as a little playmate for her. My mother says, 'Oh, what a dirty bear. Does she have to take it everywhere?' I say, 'She really likes that bear. So why shouldn't she take it?' Then I think to myself: have I really failed her somewhere?"

At this age, most children are attached to such objects. So you shouldn't be affected by the comments that other people make. If she really wants to take her bear, and it makes her feel secure, then she should have it. When a child has this need, it indicates that his or her sense of security and ability to separate from home are not yet well established, and that is perfectly normal at this age. Removing the toy only intensifies the feeling of insecurity; it does not help to deprive the child of this object. Doing so may satisfy the adult's sense of control, but that is not the goal in this situation.

"My baby has a favorite blanket, which he clutches and rubs against his face when he goes to sleep. He likes it best, it seems to me, when it gets smelly and dirty. When I wash it, I have to return it at once to his bed. He won't accept a substitute that looks just like it. Is that normal?"

This is a very common situation. The blanket represents a comfort that the child has found for himself. Some children relinquish these early comfort mechanisms and move on to others as they get older; others cling to them for a very long time. In some cases, it becomes a symptom that requires special intervention, but in most cases this attachment to an object disappears as the child matures. It is interesting that you mention your baby likes the blanket best when it is smelly. Certainly the sense of smell is important to children in the early months. The smell of mother distinguishes her from others. The freshly washed blanket smells of detergent, not the familiar body smells permeating the unwashed blanket.

"My sister's child is five years old. He had a favorite blanket that is now in shreds. He still carries one of those shreds around with him when he seems a

little unsure of what's in store for him. My sister and her husband are very upset. They scold him and hide the piece of blanket, but he always finds it."

Fortunately, they have been sensitive enough not to throw it out. This need to carry around a blanket is so common that a cartoonist has used it for a popular cartoon character, Linus. You may have seen it. Linus always carries around his blanket. In fact, many people refer to the child's blanket or toy as his "Linus blanket." In any case, such objects should not be taken away before children are ready to relinquish them or find their own substitutes.

"One little girl I know had a knitted afghan that she gradually unraveled. For years she carried this ball of yarn around in her pocket. It became dirty and raveled, but she had to have it. Finally she outgrew it. Her parents understood she needed it and never embarrassed her with unkind comments."

There are many instances of that sort. However, there are more in which the parents interfere and take away the blanket. Then the child may become irritable and even depressed. A pattern for depressive responses to separation or change can sometimes be traced, in later years, to what seemed like such innocent episodes in the child's early life.

Think about the college student who takes pictures, blankets, books, and other items from home to decorate a college room. It's considered appropriate to give the room a "homelike look." Yet this may be a later stage of the same need that was not sufficiently gratified by the blanket in very early childhood. There are adults who never leave home without special items from their dressing table or desk, even for a short visit. We call this sentimental, but it, too, may be a vestige of the "Linus blanket" or transitional object syndrome.

We tolerate many things that adults do, but we often give small children a hard time when they are only behaving appropriately for their age.

"Well, that gives me a new perspective. I was getting a little ashamed of having my baby drag around his battered, dirty, stuffed dog Spot and I was on the verge of throwing it out. Now I know better and I'll be prepared to protect him from others who are critical."

There are a lot of pressures on parents these days. Our society has become very complex. We are often surrounded by conflicting demands and tensions. These tensions are very quickly felt by our children, no matter how hard we try to protect them. Perhaps this is one reason that "Linus blankets" have become so prevalent. We must recognize our children's needs for comforting, especially when we are not able to be with them all the time.

This tangible bit of security is the child's way of coping with feelings of anxiety. By taking the object away, we only increase the anxiety, which may then be manifested in other ways that the parents may find even more annoying.

In the normal course of development, such objects are used by children in making the transition from complete dependence on others (parents) for security to more independence and self-reliance. Children should therefore be allowed to keep the object while they are making this transition and not be forced to relinquish it before they are ready. Once again, this is a passing stage. It helps the parents to be more tolerant and patient when they understand the meaning of this behavior.

The Child's Sexual Identity

What are your feelings about this issue? Do you think that boys and girls should be brought up differently? Do you see differences in the way boys and girls behave?

"You know, I've been wondering about that. We went to visit some friends who have a little girl about my little boy's age. She has a baby doll. My son has no doll, and he seemed so intrigued with hers. When we were going home and he had to put the doll down, he began to cry. My husband seemed upset at the time and when I suggested that we ought to give our son a doll to play with, he had a fit. He said, 'Do you want to make a sissy of our boy?' Was he right? Would playing with a doll at this age make him less masculine?"

The question boils down to this: how much is an individual's identity as a boy or girl determined by biology or endowment at birth, and how much does the way society treats each sex determine sexual identity?

Are Girls and Boys Born Different?

"That's just what I want to know. Are boys naturally more athletic and aggressive than girls, and are girls naturally more gentle and 'motherly' than boys?"

A recent review of the literature on sex differences seems to point to only four real differences. Boys seem to be more aggressive both physically and emotionally, excel at visual spatial tasks, and are better at math. Girls are superior in verbal ability. There seems to be no difference in how boys and girls are endowed in other areas such as ability to learn, to achieve and analyze situations, or in self-awareness or response to social pressure. The question remains whether these differences are psychobiologically or environmentally produced. We know from the research that small differences in infant behavior can subtly influence the parent's response. For example, infant boys are more muscular than infant girls; they are neurologically less mature at birth and startle more. Mothers (statistically) comfort infant boys more by holding them close, while they comfort infant girls more by smiling and talking. One may well ask, therefore, whether the verbal superiority of girls is *caused* by this differential parental treatment or whether innate, subtle sex differences *cause* different parental responses. Many child development specialists are working to find the answers to this question, for there is much about the relationship between biological endowment and environmental influence (nature versus nurture) that is still not known.

■   ■

"You were saying that aside from those four areas, a girl and a boy aren't very different. So how come we see so much difference in the way they behave?"

Your children are about eighteen months old. By this time, we have consciously or unconsciously given them cues on how we expect them to behave. Even though we usually dress boys and girls in overalls, we do at times dress a little girl in a dainty dress and let her know we admire her femininity. Many people are consciously or unconsciously more gentle in their approach to a baby girl. With a boy, we show approval of evidences of his masculinity. We say, "What a big boy you are!" or "My little man!"

"We do that all the time with our little boy. He just beams and, of course, so does his father. I guess I would say different things if I had a girl."

"Well, I have a girl and a boy. There certainly is a difference in the way I treat them. I guess a great deal of it is caused by the difference in sex. I always wanted her to look pretty and be neat as a pin. I never gave her cars or trucks to play with. With my boy, I'm just not so fussy about his clothes. Now he has cars and trucks and my daughter plays with them, too. It surprised me that she was so interested. Sometimes she acts as tough as he does, and sometimes he is very gentle with a doll. I find I like that."

Should Boys and Girls Be Treated Differently?

The issue you are raising now is really more important than what toys are appropriate per se. Do we expect only girls to be gentle? Is it wrong for boys to be gentle, tender, and considerate? Should these characteristics be feminine only? To be rough and tough has been considered appropriate for a boy; but if a girl is like that, some think she is not fulfilling her role. Many people believe that boys should not cry, that only girls may cry.

"My husband made a strange remark yesterday when he came in. He said, 'Is he still all boy?' I wonder what he means by 'all boy.' Does he mean rough and ready? I think that he has the feeling that he must be ready to meet the world outside—the hard man's world."

That's a very common attitude. But treating a little boy in a tough manner before it is appropriate may have the opposite effect. It may undermine his trust in adults as advocates for his welfare and make him timid and distrustful or extremely aggressive. At the same time, following the opposite attitude for girls by sheltering them all the time may have the ultimate result of making them helpless. These are the stereotypes of masculine and feminine roles that have been traditional in our society. We know from our own observations, as well as from the research, that many differences in girls' and boys' behavior and aptitude develop because of differential parental treatment. We see that boys' aggressive behavior is often overlooked, or even encouraged with a paternal smile and a shrugging "Boys will be boys," or, "That's my tough guy." Boys are more often encouraged, "Hit back; don't be a sissy." Girls are encouraged to settle their differences verbally. Similarly, girls have traditionally been rewarded for quiet, compliant behavior, while quiet boys cause concern, particularly to their fathers. Such sex-role expectations and taboos have led to many differences in how children have been treated and in how they come to view themselves. The question is: Do we as parents want this to persist? If we can influence our children's development, what is best?

"I agree with the earlier comment that it's a man's world—and therefore I want my daughter to be as tough as possible."

"I want my daughter to grow up able to cope on a par with men, but I don't want her to be masculine and lose her identity as a female. Women need to be considered equal to men, but they don't have to copy men."

"I would want my son to be able to compete in the world. But I would still like him to be kind and loving to his family, and not be so 'macho' that he couldn't help in the house or take care of his children."

I think you are expressing new expectations for male and female roles. You want children who become assertive *and* kind, self-reliant *and* sensitive, competent *and* compassionate.

"But how can we, as parents, achieve that? Do you think the way we act to them now makes a difference?"

"My husband tends to comfort our son less when he hurts himself than he does our daughter, although she is older. Is that one of the ways we encourage an inappropriate difference?"

Yes, I believe so. When a small child is hurt, that child needs attention appropriate to the extent of the injury and age of the child. The child's sex is not the issue. The issue is the child's need to be comforted. We comfort babies with holding, rocking, feeding, and singing. We comfort older children by helping them up, rubbing the sore spot, talking to them in a reassuring way, and then getting them interested in some other activity. It's the question of level of development, not the sex of the child.

Parents Are Sex-Role Models

Another way we influence children is by the model we set as parents. Each of us has been influenced by the models in our own families, some of which were more traditional than others. If the father, in addition to his work outside the home, also helps in child care, cooking, and housework, he sets that kind of model of masculinity for his children, both sons and daughters. If the mother engages in some athletic activity, has a job, or engages in volunteer work as well as cooking and housework, she sets that feminine model for her sons and daughters. These children will see a father who does things that were once considered only suitable for a woman and a mother who does things that were considered appropriate for a man.

That brings us back to the question with which we began this discussion. Should a little boy play with dolls? If we want him to become a father who can take care of babies, the answer is "Yes." Playing with dolls is practice for child care; he is not learning to be a girl. Later, still without learning to be a girl, he may be a baby-sitter. By the same token, a girl can play with cars and trucks or throw a ball because she is learning to be a more versatile woman. She isn't learning to be a boy. In addition, we must remember that children of this age are learning by doing—by acting on the objects around them. The greater the range of objects they have to interact with, the greater their range of experiential learning. When children play with dolls, they have an opportunity for imaginative, creative role-playing as well as for imitating real life. As in their play with many other kinds of objects, they are learning about classification, size, and relationships. The exercise of putting on and taking off a doll's clothes is as valuable for increasing manual dexterity in boys as in girls. In other words, some of what children learn from objects has nothing to do with sex roles assigned to those objects by adults.

"That makes me feel much better and gives me a good, sensible explanation for my father-in-law."

"But what about the girl who is a complete tomboy or a boy who just wants to play house and dolls?"

Such situations arise for girls when they have only brothers or boy neighbors to play with. The same is true for boys who live in a household of females and have only girls to play with. If children play with others of both sexes, then such a concentration on one type of play is usually transitory. To return to what we were saying earlier, it is best for children to have a wide variety of experiences. We should try to encourage our children to develop many interests. To do this, boys and girls need to play with dolls *and* trucks, blocks *and* crayons, books *and* baseballs.

We must be aware that in speaking of the differences found between boys and girls in the literature, we mean the statistical differences between large numbers of boys and girls. That a greater percentage of boys are superior in mathematics does not mean that there aren't large numbers of girls with superior mathematical ability. Each child is an individual with his or her own endowments. Parents themselves vary in their interests and endowments. In some families, it may be the mother who tends to the athletic development of the children while the father encourages the arts and music, even though the opposite may be considered more common. Parents provide role models for their children. As people play different roles in our changing society, these models are changing. What children of both sexes need is to have the opportunity to have both male and female role models.

"What about single parents? They can't supply both models?"

That is true, and it is one of the difficulties of being a single parent. I would hope that friends, relatives, or teachers could provide the child with the other model. Such models may be hard to find, with the high incidence of divorce in our country; but single parents have a great need for help so that their children can have this experience. We are now in a transitional period, and our society must explore ways to meet this need.

"This is a very complicated problem. I think I've taken too many myths about sex characteristics for granted. At the same time, I want my son to be clear that he's a boy."

You are raising a concern of many parents. Even though they may not like sexual stereotypes, they are also very interested in having their children develop healthy heterosexual orientations. A woman who is satisfied with being a woman—even if she yearns for greater fulfillment—communicates this satisfaction to her daughters and sons. A little girl then finds satisfaction in being a girl "like Mommy." If the father values the mother and the daughters as individuals and women, this satisfaction is enhanced. The daughter must be loved *as a girl,* not only as an individual, by the father. If he is disappointed that he didn't have a boy and this is communicated to the daughter, she may deprecate all that is feminine. In our opinion, that is not healthy. Similarly, a boy finds satisfaction in being a boy "like Daddy" when his father is confident of his own masculinity and his masculinity is valued by the mother. The mother who constantly denigrates the father does much to place her son's heterosexuality at risk. Once again, therefore, parents' feelings about themselves serve as conscious or unconscious models for the child's developing sexual identity.

As all of you are well aware, we are now in the midst of a sex-role—and sexual—revolution. The answers are not easy or simple, and we will be talking about the implications for child rearing again.

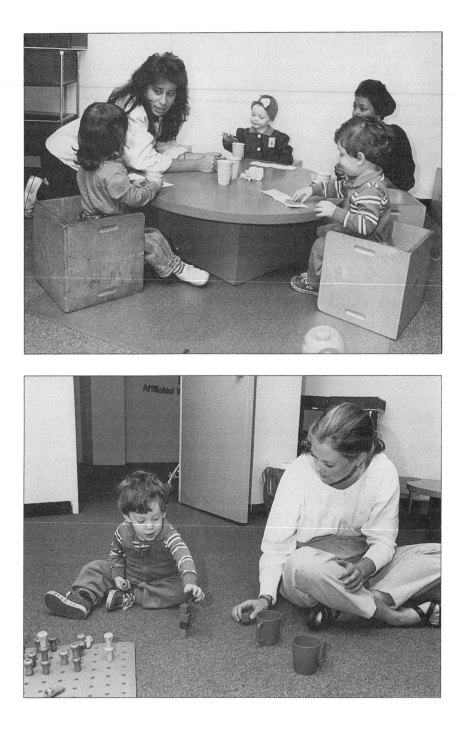

Highlights of Development—Eighteen Months

Most children are walking well now and seldom falling. Many may also have begun to run, although a little stiffly. Most children can climb stairs with one hand held. They can seat themselves in a child's chair and climb into an adult chair. They can throw a small ball and walk over to a large ball placed on the floor, preliminary to the skill of kicking.

Children of this age can make a tower of three or four blocks and can put ten blocks in a cup. They can get a marble out of a small jar by dumping it out (instead of trying to reach in) and can put it back in. When given paper and a crayon, most children take the crayon at once and scribble spontaneously; they can also imitate a single line drawn by the parent.

Most children enjoy puzzles and can place the round piece and often several others in the puzzle board. They can turn the pages of a book, usually two or three at a time rather than singly.

While looking at a book, the children may point to the pictures and name one; some may only point or look selectively at familiar objects.

 Most children now have a vocabulary of about ten words and should be able to name at least one object on request.

When feeding themselves, the children may hand the empty dish to the parents. If the parents' responses are not quick enough, however, some children push the dish off the high-chair tray or table. Children can now feed themselves with some spilling. When playing, children are able to pull a toy along the floor after them. They like to carry and hug a doll or stuffed animal.

Changes in Sleeping and Eating Patterns

Sleeping Patterns

Are you finding that just when you felt you had the child's routines stabilized, the children are changing waking times and eating habits—that many changes are taking place?

"There has been a great change in my son's waking routine. He used to wake, take the bottle, and go back to sleep until 7:00 or 8:00 A.M. Now he wakes at 6:00, drinks an ounce of milk, and then wants to get up. He keeps coming into our bedroom and wants us to get up, too. We keep saying: 'No, we are not going to get up now. Go in your room and play.' Should we get a gate for his room and make him stay in there?"

Can you go back to sleep, knowing that he is up and moving around? Would he stay happily in his room behind the gate?

"Well, it is not so much sleeping; it's just that I want to stay in bed. Now that you mention it, he probably would scream if he couldn't come out."

Could he play in your room, then, while you were in bed? Sometimes children will bring some toys and play in the parents' room or on their bed.

"He brings his ball and giraffe in and says, 'Daddy go,' and 'Mommy come here.' He doesn't leave us alone."

He has had a good night's sleep; he's all rested and ready for action. It might be better if you took turns getting up while one stays in bed, instead of both of you getting agitated about it.

"Sometimes my husband does get up and goes into his room and lies down on the daybed. This seems to satisfy our son—he doesn't want to be in his room by himself."

I think he wants to be sure that you are available; he has that need. It is a stage of the separation issue. When he wakes up, he needs to know one of you is available.

"We have been having the same trouble. All of a sudden, our little girl is waking at 6:00 A.M. I don't want to get up, so I take her into our bed. We talk or sing songs. I can't go back to sleep, but I rest."

A lot of parents seem to resolve the problem of children's waking early in this way. It keeps the child quiet and in view and enables the parents and child to get a little more rest.

"I thought that it was bad to take the child into bed with you—that it was a bad pattern to establish."

■   ■

Letting the child spend a little time in bed with you in the morning to have a short period of quiet conversation or play is quite different from letting the child sleep with you all night. This period is not a sleep time; it's a quiet playtime. It is probably good to say to the child, "Come in and talk with Mommy." Emphasize that it's quiet playtime before the day begins. It is only a good idea to do this if you will be getting up soon. If it is the middle of the night, say, "It is still nighttime; we sleep in our own beds at night. In the morning, you can come in for a few minutes."

"Does it help to put the child to bed later so he will wake up later?"

Sometimes putting children to bed later works if it happens to meet their biological needs. Some children get a second wind; others get overtired and do not go to bed as easily. Many continue to wake early. Most of your children will begin to sleep later in the morning. One day, you'll find you are complaining that you can't wake them up in time for school. You are all laughing now, but the time really will come!

"I think my daughter is in a transition state. Sometimes she'll wake up at 6:00, and the past two weeks she has been getting up at 7:30. She seems to switch back and forth."

This is an example of what we were saying. These changes occur for most children but at different times, in keeping with each child's rate of development.

"What are the causes of these changes?"

One of the reasons is that their growth and metabolic rates are changing. Some are teething. Some are experiencing changes in eating habits as well. They may not have been hungry at suppertime and didn't eat well; then they get hungry earlier and wake earlier in the morning. Some need less sleep than they used to. If they are continuing with long naps, they may wake earlier. Sometimes this change suits the family. Sometimes there is a misfit between an early-rising child and a late-sleeping parent. The parents are night people; they stay up late and want to sleep late. The child's schedule is different. He goes to bed early and wakes up early—at the right time for him, but too early for his parents, especially on weekends. But even now, there are some children who have become accustomed to being quieter on weekend mornings.

"I think our baby is beginning to notice that we sleep later on weekends. Either we don't hear her, or she is really sleeping later."

Some children adjust early to differing family tempos. You are lucky if that is happening.

"Our child was doing fine until the time changed. Now she wakes at 5:00 A.M."

■   ■

Of course, there are always external reasons such as time changes, family trips, or vacations that cause disruptions in children's routines.

"I'm glad you mentioned vacations. We are going on a vacation and are a little concerned because even at home she has sleep problems. I know I should take her blanket and her teddy bear, but is there anything else? There is going to be a crib there."

Are there any other things that she especially likes?

"A musical pillow that I always play when she goes to sleep."

It is always a good idea to take along all the baby's favorite sleep toys as well as other toys, blankets, and pillows, so that the child has familiar things to help her make the transition to the new setting. Then the new place will not seem so strange or threatening. In addition, I would follow the same bedtime routines as at home.

"We've noticed a different kind of change. Our daughter has been waking early lately because she seems to be getting much wetter. The last few nights she has awakened at 5:00 A.M. with her whole bed so wet that even her face and hands are wet. Is there any way to prevent this? I know it is hot and she is drinking a lot."

If you are having problems with very wet beds, it is a good idea to place a second soak-proof pad and sheet on the bed. Then, when the bed gets wet, you will need only to strip off the top sheet and pad, leaving another dry sheet underneath. This takes less time than making up a fresh bed in the middle of the night and is less disturbing to the child.

"We have had the experience of our baby waking wet, too. After he's changed we go through his whole bedtime routine again and it works well. The last thing before he goes to bed he switches off the light. He loves to do that. So when he wakes, we turn on the lights and change him. Then we tell him to turn off the light. He does it happily and goes right off to sleep without any hassle."

You have apparently set up a good routine for him. That's a nice example of how it can work. For some children, just putting them back in their favorite sleeping positions with their bedtime toys is sufficient. Each family needs to tune in to their own child and follow the appropriate routine consistently and patiently. It's hard in the middle of the night, but it's the most productive way to do it. Once the child senses irritation and impatience on the part of the parent, he becomes tense and irritable and harder to get to sleep.

Eating Patterns

"I find changing him isn't enough. He needs a bottle. He takes all of it most of the time. So I think hunger is what wakes him. Is it normal to be waking for a feeding at this age?"

■   ■

It depends on the child's metabolism and biological clock. Perhaps he is having his last feeding too early and is getting hungry during the night.

"He eats at about 6:30 but he doesn't finish his milk then. Is there some way to get him over that?"

It may be that your child is a little overtired at the time you feed him. It might improve the situation if you were to give him his supper a little earlier. Then he might not be overtired and might be able to take more. Or just before bed he may need a small bottle or cup of milk so he won't get hungry during the night.

Many children seem to wake because they are thirsty. They don't need a feeding, just some water. Have any of you had that experience?

"Yes, my son was eating a good supper and was still waking up at night. At first, I gave him a bottle and he took most of it; but I didn't want him to be too fat. I spoke to my pediatrician, and he advised water instead of a bottle. That's what I give him now and it works fine. He takes it and goes right back to sleep."

"We are having a different problem. It's a change in eating. Our daughter used to gobble down her breakfast, but now she is not a good eater in the morning. I go through all the trouble of making a really good breakfast, such as cinnamon toast or pancakes, and she won't eat."

I wouldn't go to all that trouble. I'd sit down and eat my breakfast in front of her and say, "Mmmm, this is good." She'll see that mother is enjoying her breakfast and she'll want some. If you make something especially for her, she may not want it. There are some children who don't want to have their breakfast when they first get up; they don't get up feeling hungry. If you have that kind of child, there is no point in struggling with her or forcing her to eat. We have talked about the importance of not making eating a battleground. It is very common in the second year for the child's appetite to slacken off, even in the best eaters. It is a natural stage of development, and knowing this should help you resist getting into battles over eating. For some mothers this is very hard to resist, because they worry that there will be malnutrition and a decline in health. Many of these changes in eating patterns will be transitory if the parents don't make too much of an issue over them.

The Beginnings of Self-control

Temper Tantrums and Crying Fits

Are you finding that you are having more difficulty with enforcing limits, with your child crying and having temper tantrums just when you thought the children were understanding more and should be able to do what you ask? Do you find they are suddenly bursting into tears?

"Exactly. Often, when I look up at my daughter, she runs away and lies down on the bedroom floor and cries."

"My son did that yesterday. He was perfectly fine, sitting in his high chair having dinner, and then all of a sudden he started to cry and struggle to get down. When I took him down, he ran away."

Sometimes there are physical reasons for such outbursts. If it happens while the child is eating, he may have bitten down on a sore gum or on his tongue or cheek. This happens frequently and causes the child a sudden, sometimes sharp pain. There are also emotional reasons. The child may have spilled his milk and be concerned that he will receive a scolding. Or he may want to pour out his milk—something he knows will earn him parental disapproval.

"But why do they try to run away from you when they start to cry?"

Children may run away because they think they will be scolded. Sometimes they run away and cry because they know they've done something they shouldn't have.

"But how do you know what the real problem is when they suddenly cry?"

Sometimes it is very hard to tell. Often, if the child bites his tongue or cheek, he will cry very hard and put his hand to his cheek or mouth. He will appear to be in pain. If the cup is nearby and there have been problems about cup throwing, the parent may guess that this is the problem. Again, it is a question of each parent's tuning in to his or her child's particular behavior and needs.

"If they are afraid of being scolded and run away, why do they do it?"

The temptation to carry out their impulses will win out most of the time for quite a while. First, control has to come from the parents, control from without. Later, after patient teaching, control from within—self-control— is established. At this age children still need to be prevented from touching a hot stove, or putting their fingers in light sockets, or running across the street. The parent must exercise these controls for a long time before the child can control himself or herself. At first, you say "No" and find an alternative for the child. Later, the child stops momentarily and looks back at the parent. Finally, he will say "No" and have enough self-control not to do it. That is the story of how self-control develops. Children don't learn self-control until we have consistently helped them with control from the outside. Most parents expect children to achieve self-control sooner than it can possibly come.

Helping Children Learn Self-control

Helping children to learn self-control is one of the big jobs that parents have. Teaching this begins at home and is continued in nursery and elementary school. Children learn self-control bit by bit. For instance, you tell your son not to touch a plant; after a while, he doesn't touch it anymore. He has developed that bit of self-control—and you don't have to say "No" for that anymore. Gradually, he will add other areas that he can control, but not everything. The parents will think, "Well, he stopped doing that; why can't he stop doing this?" For each child, this process takes a different length of time. It depends on the individual child's maturational timetable, combined with the parents' consistent and patient help.

"Are there some children who are not able to develop this inner control?"

There are some children for whom it is much more difficult. They have trouble accepting "outer" control as well as developing "inner" control. Children of this type either don't have intact central nervous systems or they have never had anybody patiently help them achieve self-control. The latter cases are in the majority. Children born with injured central nervous systems, or those who do not develop properly, are relatively rare.

"Is there anything that can be done for these children?"

When such cases are detected early, procedures can be instituted that will be helpful. What concerns us most here is much more commonplace. More often, parents haven't been consistent and expect too much, too soon. By being too demanding and impatient, the parents can create discipline problems. Learning self-control takes time and is very variable. Children may get the concept of what is appropriate in one area, and in another area they may not get the idea at all. Parents have to be very consistent, and this is hard. Have you been experiencing that.

"My daughter pushes her baby brother roughly and grabs his rattle or teddy bear. I keep saying, 'No, no, you love the baby.' But she does it again."

And are you very angry about it?

"No, I don't get angry. I understand that having a baby brother is very hard for her. I don't think she would really hurt him, but I let her know I don't want her to hurt him."

She really doesn't care if the baby gets hurt; and she certainly doesn't love the baby right now. You can accept that and be understanding of her feelings, but you *cannot* accept the possibility of her hurting the baby. She doesn't understand what she could do, the possible harm she could cause the baby. But she can understand that you are very displeased—and even angry at her. She needs to learn that what she has done does not meet with your approval.

"You mean I should say, 'Mommy does not like that; that makes Mommy angry'?"

■   ■

Yes, and you should be pretty emphatic and dramatic about it, and say sternly, "No, we don't do that." Then give her something to do that you can approve of. You apparently are not emphatic enough; you are too objective and not emotional enough. You recognize that she is experiencing jealousy toward the baby and you feel a little guilty about causing her this pain. But she could very easily harm the baby, and he deserves your protection. He cannot protect himself. Children need to understand that you have strong feelings about certain things that they do.

"When she goes near the stove, I just say 'No' once, and she runs off."

Her getting near the stove really frightens you, so you are very emphatic about that. When you say "No," you mean it and she knows it. You must do the same thing about the baby. Then, immediately give her something else that she can do. Or say, "Let's play with the baby; look at him smile at you when you give him his rattle." Then be very approving. She will need help in having a pleasant encounter with the baby. Give her approval when she is nice to the baby, not just attention when she is not so nice.

"I had that problem with my son. It's better now that he's three. It usually happens when I'm not in the room. He usually knows enough to be nice to his sister when I'm around."

Your son is making progress. He has learned what you expect and what you approve of, but he cannot control himself all of the time. Children under three or so should not be left to play unsupervised. If you need to leave the room, take one of them with you. This is a stage that will pass. If parents are constantly in conflict with one child because of the other, sibling relations will be difficult. If you can separate them sometimes, the problem situations are fewer and the relations between parents and children will be easier and more pleasant.

External Control Before Inner Control

"I have a good friend with a child the same age. Sometimes they play well together and sometimes there's a lot of pushing and grabbing toys. Once my daughter was bitten."

A good deal of the difficulty between children of this age is that they are not yet verbal enough to say, "Give me back my ball," or, "Mommy, Lori took my doll." They can't explain the problem. The only thing they know how to do is to bite, pull the toy away, or hit—these are the only weapons that they have to defend themselves. And they have not learned to control these impulses yet. They will need parental control in most areas, including play with other children. The areas where they can exert their own inner control are still few. Parents have to be patient and consistent in helping children to develop these inner controls.

The children are torn between carrying out their impulses and seeking parental approval. This conflict causes frustration, which is then released by screaming and kicking, because they cannot express themselves adequately in words. Parents often escalate the number of tantrums by concentrating too much on limitations and behavior of which they disapprove. It is important for children to receive attention and approval for the things they are doing right. If children get attention only when they are doing something the parents don't like, they tend to do those things more often.

It does help us to feel better about our role as parents if we "take stock" every once in a while and recognize how much the children have learned from our patient teaching—and from their own increased understanding of the world around them. Self-control develops little by little with parental assistance, and we are seeing the beginnings now.

Obedience: Parents' Desire for Instant Response

As the children grow older, parents are expecting more mature behavior, particularly in the area of obedience. Are you beginning to feel that these toddlers should be responding more quickly to your requests? Do you think they should be able to "obey" more quickly now?

"It seems to me my son never does what I want him to when I want him to. I have to tell him over and over. It makes me angry. When do they begin to respond? I don't want him to be a brat. I want him to behave."

Children's Inability to Respond Immediately

We understand that you do not want your child to be a brat, but no child of this age is neurologically able to respond instantaneously. Most parents do not understand the very complicated process involved in an individual's response to another's request. First, one hears the message, which goes to the brain for registration and decoding *(understanding)*. Then the reply *(words* or *actions)* must be formulated and the responding message must be sent to the body. Finally, the body responds to the message. The pathways on which these messages travel—the pathways of nerves—are not fully established at birth. Gradually, the nerve pathways develop and messages travel along them. At this age, the messages are moving slowly along the pathways of the central nervous system.

If a child is about to bang on the coffee table with a block, he is following the impulse to do that. This activity cannot be stopped instantaneously. The parent needs, instead, to give the child another outlet for the impulse. Point to the floor and say, "Bang the block on the floor." Children of this age cannot respond instantaneously; neither can children who are considerably older. You hear the parent of a three- or four-year-old say, "You stop, and you stop this minute." But the child can't stop; he goes right on doing what he started because a message has gone up to the

■   ■

brain and needs an outlet. If you haven't given him another way to finish that message by giving him a substitute activity, he will go on with the act. Even when an alternate response is offered, the child may not be able to act on it at once (no matter how much he may want to), because his nervous system is slow in responding. The system simply does not have the facility for quick changes until its pathways have had a great deal of practice.

"Is that why my child can't stop and I can't make her hurry? When I try to make her hurry, she gets all upset and can't do the simplest thing, such as putting down a toy to get her hand into a sleeve."

It's the same reason. Her nervous system can't stop or speed up on short notice. As a matter of fact, the circuits seem to get jammed, and it seems as though the child becomes paralyzed and can't act at all. When we understand the level of maturity of their nervous systems, we can be more patient. We can give them some warning about the need to do something. We can say, "In a little while we are going to get dressed . . . take a bath." We can give them a little time to respond.

"That procedure drives my husband crazy. He says our child has got to learn to obey—immediately."

Your husband may be reenacting his own childhood. This may be the only model of parenting that he has. He needs to understand the level of development of the child's central nervous system and that the child cannot respond instantaneously.

"But what about safety? What about when they may run in front of a car?"

That is a very good question to ask right now. You cannot depend at all on a child's stopping in time to avoid being hit because you yell "Stop!" You must keep the child close enough to you to stop the child yourself. There are many things that we expect from children that they cannot do yet.

"But when can we expect instant response—for safety's safe?"

We really cannot expect an instantaneous response until children are between eight and ten years old, depending on each child's development.

"Is it too much to expect my little girl to stop pulling my hair when I tell her to? Sometimes she also pulls the hair of a child while playing. She seems to enjoy touching hair, but it soon becomes pulling. The last time, I slapped her, and she hit me. It made me more angry."

You have a twofold problem now. First, you need to understand why she is pulling hair. From your comment, it sounds as though she enjoys the sensation of touching and exploring the texture of hair. Pulling, then, is another related activity. She is not doing it to inflict pain; she doesn't know how hard she is pulling. You have to indicate that she can pat your hair, but that you don't like her to pull it—that it hurts. You can take her hand and show her how you like to have it done. You may need to do this many times until she gets the message and derives satisfaction from the approval you give her when she does it correctly—that is, without causing pain. This impulse to touch your hair might also be diverted into brushing your hair or her own hair. The second part of the situation you described is the hitting. You have set the example by hitting her.

Hitting and Slapping

"You mean she hit me because I hit her in punishment?"

Yes, you gave her the example. She doesn't know that in your view only grown-ups are supposed to hit. A child doesn't understand that. Whom would she learn that from? Children imitate everything we do. That is how they learn. When we realize this, we may want to consider carefully what we are, in fact, teaching. Do we want them to learn that there are things, such as slapping and spanking, that adults can do but children cannot do? Children may, indeed, learn this lesson but reshape it to the concept that if you are bigger you can hit smaller people. One finds children who then hit younger and smaller children. We believe it is better to teach what is accepted and what is not—what is right and wrong—*without hitting*. With understanding of their levels of development and provision of substitute activities, we can teach them to behave in appropriate ways. If we understand that instant obedience is not possible, we will be more patient and think of more constructive ways to get our children to do what needs to be done. In this way, we will avoid angry confrontations and punishment.

Patience and understanding on our part are also better ways of eliciting the *desire* to do what we ask. Angry confrontations usually dispel any desire the child might have had to willingly do what we ask. If we adults are given ultimatums, we usually respond negatively. If someone tells us to "type this report" or "cook dinner right now" while we are doing something else, we become annoyed. Our need to manage our own lives is threatened by such demands. Our children feel much the same. They are just now starting on the path toward autonomy. They don't like being told what to do. If they are given the opportunity to respond at their own speed to our *requests,* and are given approval when they do, children willingly begin to behave the way we wish. They do not become brats from being treated with consideration for their level of development. Children become brats, or "spoiled," when they are treated inconsistently and when inappropriate demands are made on them. Because parents often do not understand this aspect of child development, conflict between parent and child develops, causing poor parent-child relationships and the kind of behavior that has been labeled "the terrible twos."

■   ■

How to Handle Temper Tantrums

Are you beginning to think that your children are hard to control, that they cry and kick and scream when you want them to stop doing something or do something they don't want to do? How do you handle these situations?

"I've been troubled with that lately. My little girl was so easy to handle. I only had to call to her and she would come. I could stop her from doing something that I didn't want her to do and give her a substitute, and she would accept it. But now, she has a mind of her own. If I take something away from her, she has a fit. She cries and gets so red and stamps her feet, I stand there shocked at times; sometimes I get just as mad and want to hit her."

"When I have to take something away from my son that is dangerous or breakable or when I have to stop him from banging on a table, he lies on the floor and kicks and screams."

Temper Tantrums Are a Signal

Temper tantrums are one of the ways children have of telling you something is wrong in their world. They are still unable to modulate their reactions—to make a small protest for a small thing and a proportionately larger protest for a more important thing. Children always give such protests all of their energy. The uproar is upsetting to parents. They are frightened and annoyed, too, because no one likes to have a screaming child. Most of us have said, "I'll never let my child kick and scream and become a brat." Then you see this behavior and you are afraid it is happening to you. You wonder what you have done wrong.

When a child acts like this, the most important thing that a parent can do is to keep calm. The next step is to recognize that the outburst is a *communication* that would probably not be as upsetting if it could be converted to language. It would be different if the child could say, "Mother, I want to play longer. I don't want to go home yet"; or, "I am upset with myself because I can't make this toy work"; or, "I want to push my *own* stroller."

So the next step is to try calmly to understand what the communication means. You must ask yourself whether the child is overtired or overstimulated, frustrated, unable to understand your request, not ready to make the transition from one place to another, or trying to get your attention. Depending on your assessment of the situation, you will respond in different ways. The overtired child may need soothing and gentle reassurance and then a bottle quietly on your lap. The frustrated child may need your quiet assistance in making the offending toy work. Once the parent has handled the current outburst, it is important to keep in mind the situation that brought it about and try to avoid the repetition of

■   ■

that situation in the future. For example, some parents leave the children in their pajamas playing after breakfast. Then, when it is time to dress to go out, the children make a fuss because they don't want to stop playing. This rebellion might be avoided if the children were dressed as soon as they got up. That kind of rescheduling to avoid conflict situations is one way to cut down on the number of tantrums. If you think about your own situation, you may be able to apply it to your way of doing things.

"Well, I know most of our tantrums come when he is overtired. Sometimes it takes us too long to get home from a visit. We're having too good a time and we don't leave early enough. I guess it's up to us to adapt to his needs if we want to avoid problems. Just recognizing the situation and knowing how to avoid it will really help me. I won't feel that I have a rotten, spoiled child—just a tired one—and I won't get so angry."

"Suppose you haven't been able to avoid the situation, or you just don't understand how the tantrum came about. Then what do you do?"

If the tantrum develops in spite of your efforts to avoid it or you do not understand the cause, the first thing, as we said before, is to remain calm and not to scream louder than the child. This is often the way parents respond, and it's easy to understand their anger. However, it's the least productive and most harmful way to respond, because it only makes a bad situation worse.

Different Approach for Each Child

"I agree that's a bad way, but I can't seem to do anything else. That's what my mother did to me. What can I do?"

Each child may need a different approach. You have to experiment and see which way is most helpful to the child. Some children should not be given too much attention. Others respond best if you sit quietly near them— available to them but not intruding on "their space." Some children respond best if they are held and soothed and told that the parent understands they are upset and will try to help them.

"Well, isn't that catering to a child? Won't it encourage them to always respond that way?"

Most children will not continue to have tantrums if the parent's response is appropriate; responding to a child's needs is not catering.

"What about the child who always makes a fuss to get his way?"

The child who *always* makes a fuss is usually the one who hasn't been able to get an appropriate response, the child whose communication is not understood or who hasn't been heard unless he makes a fuss. Getting attention in this way becomes the pattern for the way he and his parents relate to each other. We call it the "angry alliance." This child is often referred to as a brat. It is important to understand that he was not born a brat—he became a brat.

The Problems with Spanking

"Don't some children need to be spanked to make them behave? My parents spanked all of us?"

We do not believe that children need to be spanked to be taught what is acceptable behavior and what is not. If the relationship between parent and child has been one of trust, with consistent limitation and approval from the parent, the child learns what is acceptable and what is not acceptable. Spanking is a dangerous form of discipline, because it sets a bad example and can lead to child abuse when carried to an extreme. We do not believe that teaching discipline needs to depend on causing pain. If spanking is the usual form of discipline, it may cause loss of trust in the parents and make children hostile and irritable, fearful and inhibited, or compliant and ingratiating. Discipline should come from the parents' desire to *teach* rather than to *punish.* Punishment is unfortunately ingrained in the upbringing of many of us. We are struggling here to overcome that legacy.

"Well, in between spanking and comforting the child, are there other ways of overcoming a tantrum?"

Yes, there are. They all take thought and ingenuity and an understanding of your child's behavior. Sometimes, when a child is having a tantrum and is lying on the floor kicking and screaming, a parent can sit beside him and quietly begin playing with a toy. The parent does not pay attention to the child, but just makes remarks about the toy, such as, "My, this car goes fast," or, "I am building a very high tower." In a short time, the child's attention is attracted and he joins in the play without "losing face."

A recent research study has shown that praising the child's acceptable behavior rather than concentrating on bad behavior dramatically reduces the frequency and length of violent temper outbursts.

"Sometimes I have done something like that or just left him alone, and the tantrum passed. Now I do it regularly, and it seems to me the tantrums are fewer and shorter."

"I used that method and I felt it was working. But one day my mother was over. She said I was doing it wrong—that I should put my child in his room and close the door until he stopped. Is that a better method?"

At this stage of development, isolation may cause fear and an even greater sense that the child can't communicate. When he is verbal, the child may understand and appreciate the request to go to his room until he feels calmer and like talking about his problem. But that is not an appropriate response for this age.

■   ▩

Take Time to Assess Child's Request

One last piece of advice on how to avoid tantrums: avoid unnecessary confrontation by carefully assessing the child's requests before saying "No." We often find ourselves in conflict with our children because we have said "No" too quickly to a request that, upon reflection, is fairly reasonable, or at least not worth fighting over. Then we are in the uncomfortable position of "rewarding" the child's outburst by backing down, or of sticking to a position that we wish we were not in. When a child asks for something, there is no harm in saying, "Let me think about that a minute." Then use the time to decide whether you will stick to your position if the child fusses. If you are ultimately going to back down, it is better all around to say "Yes" in the first place. You avoid a confrontation and your child learns that a less frequent "No" really means "No."

We believe that if you respond now in a manner that suits the child's temperament and level of development, he or she will be better able to cope in the future with limitation, frustration, or changes in developmental equilibrium. The stage of temper tantrums does come to an end with appropriate handling by the parents and maturation by the child.

Appropriate Response to the Child: Meeting Needs or Spoiling?

The underlying theme of most of the discussion topics in this book is the importance of parents' knowing the level of their own child's development and the responses appropriate at each given age. Many of the topics have touched tangentially on the issue of "coddling" or "spoiling." Parents sometimes feel that what we recommend as appropriate at a given age looks like coddling to others, if not to themselves. Is that still an issue, and if so, how do you cope with it?

"I get that all the time from my family—not from my husband, but from my father and mother and aunts. They are European and think children should be seen and not heard. If my little girl wants something while I'm talking to one of them, they think she should wait till they are finished. I'm told I'm catering too much to her if I pick her up and attend to her. When they leave, I'm a wreck, because they have been telling me in no uncertain terms that I don't know how to bring up my child and that's not the way they brought me up. I can't tell them it's just because I remember that upbringing that I want to treat my child differently."

There is certainly a cultural clash in your family. What you are doing is appropriate. Your daughter comes to you because she needs something or because she does not want to be excluded from the family conversation.

You have a right to bring her up in a way that you feel is correct. It is hard to stand up for your viewpoint against a continual barrage from your

■   ■

family. If you and your husband agree on your method of rearing your child, that is all that is necessary. You may still be trying to get the approval of your family that you did not get as a child and you would like them to recognize now how well you are dealing with your child. It is difficult for them to recognize now how well you are dealing with your child. It is difficult for them to show approval because it is not their way. In time, they will begin to notice what a secure and friendly child she is. You can listen to them and then do as you see fit. Only you and your husband need to agree on what is right. Part of the tension for you is brought on by your need for your family's approval. You need to approve of yourself and your way of doing things.

"My husband and his family think I am making a mommy's boy of our son because I pick him up when he wants to be carried, or because I stop doing something and play with him for a few minutes if he wants me to. They say he won't get this attention all his life, and since he won't get it, he may as well get used to it now. It's a hard world, especially for a black child, so he might as well learn it now."

Gradual Delay of Gratification

There certainly is a time for learning that one cannot have instant gratification. We begin teaching this by delaying gratification in small doses as the children get older, according to their developmental level. Now we also deny them the things they cannot have, either because they are dangerous to the child or too fragile for the child to handle. We introduce an alternate activity. There is a time and way to teach a child limits and delay according to each child's developmental level without destroying a child's basic trust, security, and self-image. That is what we are trying to do without introducing harshness into the child's life when he or she can't cope with it. By making children secure now, they will have the self-reliance to cope later when they are ready. And if the black child's world is more difficult, all the more reason for the parents to help their children establish basic trust and a good self-image early, so that they can succeed in the world.

"My husband has the same attitude. He thinks I coddle our son and that he's going to be a sissy."

We have recently talked about expectations that parents often have for their children, based on the child's sex rather than on the child's level of development and needs. Your husband's attitude stems partly from wanting to make sure that his son becomes manly and partly from not wanting him to be a "spoiled brat." What he needs to understand is that the child must have his *needs* met in order to feel a sense of security and trust in people. How can a child trust those closest to him if he feels that something that he needs is denied? Children need to feel capable of evoking appropriate responses from people. By learning that they have this capability, they develop self-confidence and a good self-image and better coping

■   ■

mechanisms for the hazards of later life. Think of your own lives. If one rarely succeeds in getting what one needs, one develops a sense of powerlessness. We don't want that for ourselves or for our children. We want to see our children become competent, self-reliant individuals with a drive to achieve without hurting others.

"Do you mean we should give our children everything they want—to develop self-confidence? We can't deny them anything?"

Emotional Needs Versus Material Wants

We believe children should always be given what they *need*. In other words, when they express hunger, they should be fed; when they feel insecure or express fear, they should be reassured; when they hurt themselves and cry, they should be comforted; when they feel excluded, they should be given attention. These are some of the needs that parents should satisfy. At the same time, we have to distinguish between emotional *needs* and material *wants*. We should not—often we cannot—give children everything they *want*. We believe that children who express excessive wants are really in *need* of something else. For example, a child who wants every toy he sees and has a tantrum when he doesn't get it probably desperately needs more consistent, loving human attention. A child who wants her parents to watch everything she does and looks for approval all the time probably needs more attention and time with her parents—and more approval *before* she asks for it. One often sees behavior like this in children after the arrival of a baby brother or sister. Children cannot say, "I need your attention." Instead, they are clinging and demanding and perhaps say, "Mommy play," or, "I want that and this" in a very command-ing way. This often irritates parents who feel that they are catering to a lot of demands. One must step back from such situations and try to analyze what the reasons might be for such behavior. More often than not, one will find that some basic need is not being met. Now is the appropriate time to meet such needs.

"But won't that make a child expect it for the rest of his life?"

On the contrary, meeting a child's needs at this age builds self-confidence and the child's feeling that he or she can obtain what he or she needs. The person whose needs are not met *now* will continue to try to find such satisfaction throughout life. Often such people are never satisfied—no matter how outwardly successful. You can probably recognize this person-ality structure in some of the people you know.

"But some kids really are spoiled brats. How do they get that way?"

We believe such children have been "spoiled" by their parents' inconsistent handling of them. These children have low self-esteem and low self-confidence. To make up for these bad feelings about themselves, they often become aggressive and unruly or whining. They have found that bad behavior earns them more attention than good behavior. They do become brats; they are not pleasant to be with—and yet, one must feel very sorry for them. Their legitimate needs for approval and attention and satisfaction have not been met consistently and appropriately. They are not learning how to cope appropriately in the family and will probably have trouble entering the larger world of school and community.

Sharing: The "I, My, Mine" Stage

Are you worried because your children are having difficulty in sharing toys when they have visitors or are playing in the sandbox at the park?

"Oh, yes. It's a battle every day when we go to the park. I almost hate to go, but I can't keep him inside in such nice weather. No sooner is my son in the sandbox than some child comes up and wants his shovel and may take it. If my son cries, I go and get him something else to play with, but I'm upset by what the other mothers think because my child won't share his shovel or any other toy."

You seem to be more concerned about what the other mothers may be thinking than about how your child is feeling. When a parent allows other children to take her child's things and intervenes only if he protests—and then does not retrieve his toy but gives him a substitute, the child may get the feeling that he has no right to his toys. He comes to see the other children as a menace to his toys. He feels helpless when his toys are taken. If his parent doesn't help him retrieve the toy, his self-confidence and sense of self are undermined. This can create difficulty in his social relations; he may withdraw and not want to play with other children. If he is more assertive, he will hang on to his toys and not let the other child have them. In that case, he is considered selfish.

"Well, isn't that selfish?"

Beginning of Sense of Self

This behavior needs to be regarded from another point of view: the maturational level of the child and what he is ready for in the way of social relations. At this age, he is just beginning to establish who he is, where he belongs, what belongs to him—the "I, my, mine" stage. He has to learn that certain toys are his and that he has a right to keep them. He has to learn that other toys belong to other children and that they have a right to keep them.

Children do not know this automatically. They have to learn it. Parents' intervention and patient teaching are essential in this learning process. They must reassure their child by retrieving toys that are taken from him and by giving a substitute to the other child, saying, "Johnny wants to play with *his* truck now; you may play with this car." In the same way, when your child takes another's toy, you should return it and give your own child a substitute.

Gradually, the child learns that what belongs to her *is* hers and that she has a right to it. She also learns that other children and Daddy and Mommy have a right to their things. She gains confidence that she may keep her toys because her parents have helped her achieve this sense of possession by helping her retrieve her things. She may then have the confidence to let other children play with something that belongs to her when she is not playing with it. She learns she can play with another's toy when he doesn't want it. This is the beginning of learning to take turns— and the beginning of sharing.

"I have a girlfriend who has two kids, one three and one a year and a half, and they both share. She says, 'Oh, when my son was alone, he was spoiled like that, too.'"

Being possessive of one's things at this age is not being spoiled. That is simply a stage the children are going through—not being ready to share yet. Your friend may be making her one-and-a-half-year-old child share earlier than she is ready to. Actually, the child may be giving up—she may not understand that anything is hers. She may think everything belongs to her brother.

Parental Help in Social Situations

"I have another question about this. When I see my son fighting over a toy and it belongs to somebody else, I get my son's toy and say, 'This is yours, and that is the other little boy's.' Is that helping him? My husband thinks the kids should settle it themselves."

At this age, the parents must intervene. The children are not ready to settle it themselves in a way that is beneficial to both. The stronger child will keep the toy and learn that "might makes right." The less assertive child will be the "loser" and may then tend to want to withdraw from contact with other children. Children need help in learning to socialize and interact with others. They are too young to "settle" such situations by themselves.

"It's not so much the other children as the other mothers who concern me by saying I'm teaching my son to be selfish."

Then you have to explain to them that he is in the "I, my, mine" stage and that you are teaching him to take turns. Explain that you are teaching this by allowing the child who has the toy first, or who owns it, to keep it and by giving the one who grabbed the toy an alternate. One of the mothers who comes to the Center was able to teach the mothers in her playground this technique. They found it works, and now they all have a similar attitude. If you think this is a good idea, share it. It may make it easier for everyone.

Genital Play: Self-discovery

Have you noticed that your babies are beginning to touch their genitals? How do you deal with it?

"I am so glad you brought this up, because it has been bothering me. Lately, every time I change my son's diaper, he puts his hand on his penis and pulls on it before I can get him changed. I try to change him as quickly as possible so he won't get a chance to do it, but he is faster than I am!"

Why do you think this worries you so much?

"Well, I think he may harm himself because he doesn't know what he is doing. That's my reason; that's why I get him diapered as fast as I possibly can."

"When my son does it, I just take his hand away and then I hurry and dress him. Why do such young children touch themselves?"

Normal Exploration

Children touch themselves because they are exploring their bodies. The genital area is another part of themselves with which to get acquainted. They put their fingers on their eyes; sometimes they even poke them in. When they find it uncomfortable, they remove their fingers, or we stop them. They explore their noses by putting their fingers in their nostrils; they explore their ears in the same way. When sitting on our laps, they may explore our eyes and noses as well as our mouths, hair, and ears. We seem to understand and tolerate this exploration, except when they become too vigorous and hurt us. Then we inhibit them. As a matter of fact, as they touch these body parts we name them. Then we are pleased when the baby learns the names and can point to them. However, the genital area is different. We are disturbed by that; it is taboo, somehow.

"Well, isn't touching the genitals the beginning of masturbation? My mother says it is. She told me to pull his hand away as soon as he reaches for that area, or else he will become a masturbator. She says this is very unhealthy."

"My mother isn't nearby, but she doesn't need to be. I remember what she used to do to me. She made me feel so bad if I even put my hand to my panties to scratch! I'm determined not to make my child feel like that, but the whole thing makes me uncomfortable. I'm surprised at myself."

You have raised an interesting issue. Many of us were made to feel anxious and guilty about our developing sexuality. Intellectually, we understand that it was not a healthy way to deal with sex, and yet we find those old

■   ■

feelings and fears coming back to us as we raise our children. It may help all of you to express those feelings and to understand that your anxieties are natural, given your own upbringing. Some of you will be able to cope more naturally with your children about this issue than others.

"It isn't only little boys who do it. My little girl reaches for her labia when her diapers are off. What should I do?"

The simplest thing to do if that bothers you is to finish dressing the baby as quickly as possible. Pulling the child's hand away repeatedly seems only to intensify the need to touch. If you want to limit this activity, give the baby something else to occupy her hands while the diaper is being changed, without frustrating the child by pulling the exploring hand away.

Good Feelings About One's Body

Although this diversionary tactic may be a more comfortable procedure for parents at this stage, one needs to remember that masturbation is a normal phase of sexual development and should not be regarded as a disease or crime. Touching the genitals creates a pleasurable sensation for children, as it does for adults. Having good feelings about one's body is an important aspect of the child's developing sense of self-worth. Therefore, we must try not to interfere with the child's discovery of, and pleasure in, his or her body. Parents do need to teach their children, as part of their growing social sense, that masturbation is a private act. Most children will only need a few kindly parental reminders to that effect; but it will be important not to convey disapproval of the act itself.

"Rationally I agree with you, but I find I get emotional about it. Isn't there a danger that children will spend too much time giving themselves pleasure?"

If children do not receive any other kind of pleasure, they can become overly engrossed in this kind of self-initiated pleasure. But this will not happen if children are properly attended to and their needs for stimulation and love are met.

"You say it is important to teach them without conveying disapproval. I don't quite see how we will do that."

Now, while the children are still in diapers and are still not verbal, it is premature to think of doing that. For now, as they show interest in touching and exploring their bodies, it is important to be as matter-of-fact as you can while you are changing diapers or bathing the children.

"Then would you suggest that when the baby touches the genital area you name it and say, 'That's your penis' or 'That is your vagina,' just as we say eye or nose or mouth?"

Yes, that is the correct terminology and should be used as we would for any other part of the anatomy. One does not have to either emphasize the genital area or avoid mentioning it.

"Is it important to use the correct anatomical name? I've always referred to that part as the 'wee wee.' Is that wrong?"

It's a matter of family feeling and custom. Some families use "penis" and "vagina"; others use "wee wee" or "tinkle" or some other term with which they are more comfortable. It's really not the word that matters; it is the attitude of the parents—and whether it conveys information or prohibition. "Wee wee" and "tinkle" are nursery language and easier for children to imitate. That may be why these words are so commonly used, especially at this age. Often parents begin with these words and then switch to the correct anatomical names when the children are more verbal. Some families may find the nursery words less threatening and may continue using them.

Honesty About Sex Is Important

The most important thing is to try to deal naturally and honestly with this issue. As we said earlier, interest in the genitals at this age is largely a part of children's natural exploration of their bodies and the world around them. The more matter-of-factly parents handle this exploration, the easier it will be for children to gain a healthy attitude toward sex as a normal part of life that has its proper place and time, just as other aspects of life have. Of course, sexual satisfaction in adult life depends on more than this, but honesty about sex is an important beginning.

Fathers' Expectations of Their Children and Wives

Differing Feelings of Parents

Mothers and fathers may, however, have different expectations and feelings about their child's development and their parenting roles; and it is healthy to discuss them.

The children have changed a good deal in the last few months. What have the fathers been observing? What strikes you as the most important developments?

"To me it's the development of the personality that is beginning to emerge. At first, the baby seemed like an undifferentiated blob to me, really. I mean that. But as she begins to develop she is becoming somebody."

"I keep wondering how much of the change is due to our influence and how much they would be as they are, anyway?"

The child's genetic endowment comes first; then comes the influence of society. You are the child's first contact with society. The child is born with a certain potential—sometimes greater, sometimes lesser. Some have potential in certain areas and not in others. The job of the parents and grandparents and society is to help them develop that potential to its maximum.

"That's certainly true, and I agree with that. But there are times when what children do is so hard to figure out: what things upset them, how much they understand, and that sort of thing."

It is a puzzle at times, and at times we don't get it right, but by spending time with the child we get more experience and understand his frame of reference. It then becomes easier and more fun.

"I'm afraid I have certain fixed ideas. At least, my wife says I have and that I expect my child to behave in a certain way—that I'm expecting immediate responses from him that he is not able to give. We argue about that because I think I was that way—or brought up that way—and I'd like him to be that way, too."

Do you think that you are trying to make him respond as you think you did at nineteen or twenty months? Is it possible that you are remembering yourself at a later age? Most studies show that few of us remember much before we are three or four. But even if your memory is correct, or refreshed by what you have heard about yourself, would it be fair to expect an exact replica of yourself?

"You may be right. Perhaps I am trying to push him into a preconceived notion that I had."

Perhaps you are. That is not unusual, but it is not a good idea to try to mold a child into something he wasn't meant to be. All of us can probably think of examples of this kind of parental pressure. There is the parent who wants the child to be a musician, and the child wants to be a baseball player. The child's natural capacity doesn't suit him for a musical career. Another example is that of a child who is a bookworm and the athletic father who wants him to be a football player. That doesn't work, either. So you have to go along with what the child's potential is, allowing and encouraging the child to reach that potential. Parents really need to understand the messages children give them. They need to let children tell them what their special needs are and what their special talents are. Parents have to listen to their children and watch their development and behavior. Children give off cues all the time about their interests and preferences.

"I remember as a child always being lectured by my parents and being told what to do. I know I hated it, but I've since figured it was for my good. Is that out of fashion?"

It's not that it is out of fashion, but that we understand more about personality development. We understand now that the parent is a model, and the child will often follow what the parent does much more readily than what the parent tells the child to do. It's the unspoken word, the model that the parent sets, that is more effective than a lecture. If the parent is the kind who is very angry and short-tempered, the child models that. If the parent always speaks in a very gentle voice, the child will then have that model in mind. If the child grows up in a family where the means of communication is always shouting, that will be natural to her—unless her own endowment is such that it intimidates her, and then she may be inhibited. You see, it's the interplay of endowment and environment that determines the person's development. We are trying to help you combine these factors in the most effective way for each child.

Thus far, we have been talking about the need to understand our children and their changes in development. Since the child has come into the home, there may have been a change in the relations between spouses. Fathers have certain expectations of their wives, and vice versa. Sometimes it is hard to adjust to a wife when she has taken on the new role of mother. Most of the mothers have worked up to the time of the child's birth. They were fairly independent and enjoyed their contacts with the other people involved in their work, as well as the socializing they did with their husbands and friends. Some of the mothers decided to go back to their jobs, and a caretaker stays with the child. Others have temporarily given up their jobs to be at home with the child. In either situation, they have a number of adjustments to make. Though many fathers do help with child rearing, many may have little idea of how time-consuming child care can be. They may expect that the household will continue to function as it did before the child's arrival, or that it should be returning to normal now that the children are getting older. Perhaps we can talk a little about the fathers' expectations. It is very important that these expectations be appropriate and realistic for the well-being of the entire family.

Need to Share Feelings

"I must say I was completely unprepared for the change in our life. Before the baby came my wife was everything to me, and I thought I was to her. It never occurred to me how much of her time and attention would be given to the baby. We wanted the baby and had him when we were ready—or so we thought. When I come home now, she barely greets me. She says, 'Why don't you play this or that with Sammy?' Then she dashes off to get our dinner ready. I thought we would share more, having the baby, but instead he seems a wedge between us. That's not true all the time, but just at times."

This happens often, but it is not a situation that cannot be changed. A husband can communicate to his wife how he feels. She may actually be having similar feelings. She may feel that all he wants is his dinner ready and the child in bed. He may want to share playing with the baby, and she may want that, too. It has to be verbalized and worked out. It doesn't happen automatically.

"I'm not disturbed by the attention our child requires. What bothers me is that my wife doesn't seem to have any control over him. For instance, if he wants to drink his milk rather than eat his food, she lets him. When I feed him, I won't let him do that. I just look sternly at him, and he doesn't ask for his milk."

You are saying that your wife should be more insistent. Does the baby eat as well when you are feeding him?

"I don't know about that. I just know he doesn't ask for his milk first. His mother lets him have a drink first, and then he gets the food in between sips. I think that's wrong."

It sounds as though eating might become a battle for all of you. That is not an issue that should be a battleground. It may eventually make eating a problem.

Parents should agree on a consistent attitude toward, and routine for, their child. The pattern of the day—the order in which things will be done; what things a child may play with, which are forbidden; bedtimes and playtimes—are all things parents should agree on. We have talked before about the importance of consistent limitations and how inconsistency creates the spoiled child. The child also needs consistency in order to feel secure about her environment and her place in that world.

"Is it too much for a man to expect his wife to have a little time for him after she takes care of the kids? Some days she is so pooped that she goes to bed at seven when the kids go to bed. Her going to bed at that hour is a bone of contention between us."

Maybe you think that she could get some rest during the day so that she would have more time to spend with you?

"Yes, that's just it; I do think so."

That's a very common feeling with fathers: that their wives should save some energy for them. Many husbands do not realize how tiring a day with young children can be. But if it is a constant pattern, then one can understand that a husband would be a little upset.

"It isn't a constant pattern; I don't mean to say that. Sometimes, of course, I come from work tired, too."

Having two children so close in age is very demanding. Maybe what your wife really needs is someone to come in for an hour or two and relieve her during the day. Then she would not be so tired in the evening. Sometimes husbands are not aware of how their wives feel, and wives are not aware of how their husbands feel, about certain situations. While you are complaining about not seeing your wife enough in the evening, she may be thinking, "Do I have to drop dead before he realizes how much I need help?" Husbands and wives need to talk honestly about how they feel. It helps to try to approach the problem from the other's point of view. What do you suppose would happen if the husband, instead of complaining about being neglected, said, "I am sorry you are so tired. What can I do to help you out? I miss talking with you in the evening." When husbands and wives face these situations together, solutions can usually be found.

Sometimes a very small reorganization, such as having a high school girl in to play with the children for an hour or two or take them out for a walk so the mother can do something else or take a nap, makes a lot of difference.

"We have had our moments, but I think my wife is doing a nice job. I realize it's hard for her; she's given up her career temporarily for the baby's sake. I really appreciate that. I try to help her and give her some time off. I try to let her know what a great job she's doing."

It is important to let each other know our good feelings, not only the bad ones. Many husbands feel that they lost their wives after the babies were born, that the wives are spending all their time and their whole effort on the baby. These husbands don't look at the situation from the wives' point of view. They don't realize how much the wives miss their freedom and how much they might like a little help.

"I guess I felt that I'd lost my wife at first, but not anymore. I try to help now. I don't think I'm overtired in the evening, and my wife tries to rest during the day. So we both arrange to have some energy left for each other when the children are asleep."

"I take care of the kids one day on the weekend, and I do other things: washing and cleaning, occasionally."

Do some fathers feel that they work for a living and then work more at home? Do they feel they do so much and get nothing in return?

"No, I don't think that now, but at first I sometimes had that feeling. We talked it over and divided up the responsibilities as we thought we needed to."

"In our case, I work late, so I can't help at home; but I do all the food shopping and other errands. It's easier for me to do it. She, in turn, does all the housekeeping and baby care."

"Our situation is different, because my wife has returned to her full-time job. We have a good housekeeper, so things are pretty well organized in the evenings as far as housework goes. But the baby is exceedingly demanding now. We have very little time—and no energy—left for each other. Sometimes I feel as though I've lost my wife; her responsibilities as a mother always seem to come first. Our romance is over."

"We have a problem, since we both work. We were getting so far apart we decided that we had to do something about it. Now we try to have lunch together once a week."

■   ■

That is a good idea that we would certainly recommend to all working couples whose locations of work make it feasible. Your baby will thrive best in a home where the parents are close and happy. It would therefore be good for you as a couple and for your child if you could regain your former closeness. Your child will ultimately benefit from the opportunity to live in a family with two parents committed to each other (as well as to the baby).

It sounds as if there have been times when all of you—whether the mother has gone back to her job or not—have experienced the children as an interference in your lives. Because of the various accommodations that you are learning to make, this feeling of the children's being an interference is beginning to pass and your marriages are beginning to come together again. Children should be part of the family, and not blocks between mother and father. Most of you sound as though you are working on ways for this to happen, and this is a positive approach; but it requires effort, patience, and understanding.

Mothers' Expectations of Fathers

How do mothers feel that a child affects your relationship and social life? Do you think it has affected you and your husbands differently?

"I guess after the first few months I expected that there would be more time and that I would have more energy to entertain and go places with my husband. I thought it would be easier to leave the baby with a sitter as he grew older. Instead, I find that as he grows older he needs more experienced sitters and I am more anxious about whom I leave him with and how he relates to my substitute—because that is what a sitter really is. My husband thinks I'm too fussy."

Who Has Primary Responsibility for Child Care?

Usually mothers make the decisions about sitters, but it is important for the fathers to know that these are sometimes difficult decisions. They relate to the management of your life and to the healthy development of your child. To fathers these decisions may not seem like difficult or large problems, because they are not home with the child all the time. Child care is not their total responsibility; they have largely delegated this responsibility to the mothers. Concerns about getting sitters or the need for relief from child care have not been part of their experience, so they have difficulty understanding the problems. Mothers should explain how they feel about this issue.

"It is always a surprise to me how little notion my husband has of how hard it is for me to get the housework done and tend to the baby. He thinks the baby plays a lot while I take care of things or read the paper. When did I last do that?"

■   ■

Many men have no notion of what really goes on at home. Fathers need to learn what it is like to care for a child all the time and why and when the mother needs help and relief.

"My husband is helpful with our son. He used to help me more with the cleaning, but he really doesn't have the time for that now. I'd rather he spend the time with the baby. I do the cleaning when I can! I just don't clean that much anymore."

All that is really needed is to have things in their place and relatively clean. The fixation on having a spotless house seems to be the wrong emphasis. Spending time with the children and sparing yourself so that you, as a person, can relate to your husband and your children is much more important.

"My husband minds when he comes home and finds toys strewn around in every room, wherever the baby happened to leave them. He says, 'What have you been doing all day? The place is a mess.' I couldn't care less at that point. What I'm concerned with is getting our dinner and getting the baby ready for bed."

If you know that this kind of thing bothers your husband, it is a perfectly good technique to let the child know that cleanup time just precedes Daddy's coming home. The child learns to participate in "putting away" time. Of course, the mother may do most of it at first, but as children get older they will do more and more if their effort is recognized. Then, when your husband comes home, you can say, "Johnny is learning to put his toys away." Sometimes, if you are behind schedule, your husband might help. In some families, the father doesn't mind the job of putting all the toys into a box himself. Each family has its own way of settling this kind of thing.

Mother's Viewpoint

We have been discussing how you feel about the father's expectations of the mother's role and how his home life is managed. Now, perhaps, we can talk about what mothers expect of fathers.

"I'm glad we are going to talk about that. I think we are drifting further and further apart because my husband doesn't concern himself at all with what is going on in the house, what the baby is doing, what I'm doing, or how I feel. What makes me so mad is that he comes home in such a pleasant mood and says 'How are you, dear?' then kisses us. Asks, 'Need any help?' And before I can answer, he is off to the bedroom, showers, changes, turns on the TV, and waits for dinner while I get it ready and put the baby to bed. When I ask him why he never helps, he says he would be glad to but there doesn't seem to be anything for him to do—that I have it all in hand."

Are you that efficient? Perhaps you are so efficient that you appear critical of what he does to help you, so he may have given up.

■   ■

"You may have something there, because I do want things done in a certain way. The baby is used to a certain routine, and my husband does things differently."

The baby can get used to daddy's way of doing things. In fact, children should have the opportunity to experience the father's care. They can get used to each parent's style of caretaking.

"Well, my husband isn't much for helping in the house, and I don't expect much: just taking the garbage out and once in a while shopping on his way home. If I ask too often, he acts imposed upon. You see, he thinks that is not his job; marketing is my job."

"In my family, it is just the opposite. My husband does all the marketing on his way home. He prefers it that way. He can see where the money is spent, and he sometimes gets just what he likes, too. It suits me fine and relieves me of having to shop in the supermarket with the baby. It is really a big help."

Husbands do have different views of what is their job and what is the wife's. Some of it depends on the home they came from and what examples their parents have set. If they were accustomed to having the mother assume all the responsibility for the house and care of the children, as well as catering to dad's needs, then they expect this from their wives. If it was a household in which the parents shared chores and child care, then it is easy for them to do the same. If it was one in which the mother played the helpless role and the father assumed major responsibility, that is what a husband will expect and he may be a little uneasy if his wife is too efficient. All of you have different family patterns to cope with as you build your own families.

"But don't you think wives sometimes need help, even if they are efficient?"

Everyone needs help sometimes. When two people plan to marry, they should talk about how they see each other's roles in the marriage and later when they have children. If they haven't discussed this beforehand, then they haven't talked about some of the important issues that they are going to have to face in their life together. In any job, you sit down and deal with a problem; you discuss what is the best way to solve it. In marriage we should do the same. Problems should not be dealt with emotionally, with recriminations. If you act emotionally in your business and not objectively, then you are not going to make it. Marriage and running a household and raising children are among the most important projects you will ever be involved in; they are not accomplished without thought and effort. You always have to work at it; it isn't something for which you can say, "Now it's done." There are changes taking place all the time, requiring constant effort and adjustment.

■   ■

Need for Parental Adjustments

As with all aspects of life, you have to adjust yourself to the many changes taking place in your marriage and in your children's interests. There are opportunities to make friends and keep friends, there is your individual social life and there is your social life as a couple. There are also all the changing stages that your children go through as they develop. You will get to know the parents of the other children in school; you may prefer these to some of the friends you used to have. Many changes take place, and you have to grow with them. You may move to a new neighborhood. Your husband's job situation may change. You may not have the money to buy a home, or you may have to live in a smaller one. Some changes may be pleasant or challenging; others may be difficult and unpleasant, but all are part of life and growth. Parents grow and change, too, just as the children do.

"We have found that having children has changed our marriage in ways we couldn't have predicted. We did discuss the issue of sharing responsibility financially, socially, and as parents. It has enriched our lives at the same time that it has created problems."

What kind of problems?

"My husband would like to spend more time with me alone. Our child is always with us except when we go out, and we don't go out very often."

This is part of the management of your life that you really have to work at. It is very important to arrange time together.

"Sometimes I get the feeling that my husband and I have drifted apart since we got married."

Do you feel that you had a relationship that you have lost.

"We haven't really lost it; it's still there, but it's more diminished now than it used to be. We used to be such 'lovebirds.' Now we are sometimes so matter-of-fact and cold. At other times we are considerate and loving to each other. It seems to depend on how tired we are and what kind of day we have had and how much time we've had together. When the baby does something cute that I can show my husband, it brings back a lot of the feeling, too, because we can both share that."

Do Fathers Consider Child Care Unmanly?

"The thing that bothers me is going visiting with our child. My husband will sit and visit and expect me to take care of the baby when I would like to participate in some adult conversation, too. It's the same on vacation. I would like to have a division of labor. If he wants to go fishing in the morning, I'll take care of the baby then; but then I want time for my fun in the afternoon. I think that's only fair, but I can't get him to agree to such an arrangement beforehand. He is very old-fashioned in his ideas of what a

■   ■

father should do. If he takes him for a walk, he will come back and say, 'I sure did a lot for the baby today.' I am of the opinion that the father should take some responsibility for the child and not leave it all to the mother. He thinks the father's role is one of providing security. He is a good father in that respect, and I do appreciate that. I guess I can't have everything. It's hard, though, because my own father helped my mother a lot."

It is especially difficult for you because you were brought up with a different model. You will have to be patient, and perhaps your husband will become more helpful as he sees how the other fathers in the group act. Many men are afraid they will appear unmanly if they help too much. What about some of the other fathers? What kind of models did they have for their roles?

"Well, actually, when my husband was growing up, my father-in-law spent a tremendous amount of time at work. He really didn't have time to help. He's now enjoying our baby, which he didn't have time to do with his own son, and he even helps me. My husband is now sharing more and more chores around the home. Come to think of it, he and his father are kind of modeling a new way for each other."

"I am very lucky, I guess. My husband gets involved in everything our daughter does. His father was like that, too."

"My husband is struggling with two jobs, and I don't expect much help. When he does have time, he's very good."

"I have gone along with most of the things my husband doesn't do because he has very demanding work. The baby is work, too, but if I'm awakened during the night, it's not too bad for me because I can get a nap during the day. So I do not bitch about that; I do agree that he has to concentrate on his job. It may be Victorian, but I agree."

That is a wise attitude. Some young men's work *is* very, very demanding. Men are often not able to take as much strain as women. If we look around us, we see that; the life span of the male is shorter than for the female. It appears to be a physiological given; perhaps it is related to the endurance needed for childbearing. Research has actually shown that the life span of the male in this country is shorter than that of the female by about eight years. Perhaps we must recognize that for physiological reasons men need to play golf, or tennis, or swim, or do something relaxing. American men are exposed to quite severe tension, and they do need to have some relaxation. Wives should accept this need and not feel that they are being neglected.

Of course, what many men may not realize is that interacting with a child can be relaxing, because it is such a different activity than what they have been doing in the office. They are tired of their office work, but they are not too tired to do something different. We have found that some fathers love to come home and lie on the floor and play games with their children. This kind of activity takes their minds off their office problems and relaxes them. If the father looks on such activity as a pleasure, it can be. All fathers should be encouraged to try this. Of course, it may not be relaxing for other men; they may need some time by themselves to unwind at the end of the day. You may find that the husband who falls asleep in front of the TV is protecting himself because he has an unconscious physiological need for rest. We can't expect fathers to be supermen, doing everything all the time, any more than we should expect mothers to be superwomen. Just as mothers may have to do some reorganizing so that they can get more rest and relief, fathers may have to do the same.

"You know, a lot depends on attitude. If my husband comes home and compliments me on the job I'm doing, then I don't feel put upon. I can willingly let him have a recuperation period. If he comes home and gripes, then I gripe, too."

"You talked earlier about men's shorter life span and greater vulnerability, and I guess that's true. But with more women working in executive jobs, it seems that they are developing many of the same problems, such as ulcers and heart attacks. Since my husband and I both work, I don't think it's fair for me to shoulder the whole burden at home after working myself."

Parenting Is a Shared Responsibility

As we said, mothers should not try to be superwomen. Ideally, mothers and fathers should share the care and responsibility of child rearing—and many young couples are doing that. Other parents may divide up the responsibilities differently; each family must suit its own needs and situation. The important thing is to talk about each person's needs and to work out the best arrangement you can—for yourselves and for your children.

Many people think that when they get married, it just works by itself. But it doesn't. After you have children, the relationship is different, and it has to be worked at also. You have to work at creating a marriage just as you would if you were creating a painting or a sculpture or solving a mathematical problem. It's a relationship that has to be worked at; it's not static. It can't be static because the outside world is changing, and so is your inside world and the children. The emotional climate that exists between the parents affects the children. That is why we talk about your feelings toward your spouses. Your children are going to be getting more and more aware of your feelings. You are presenting the model for how they will handle relationships when they grow up, so your marital relationship is important not only for yourself but for your children. This is something many people aren't really aware of and should talk about, because the children are taking it in unconsciously all the time. Your smiles and affectionate touches are unconsciously absorbed by the children and become part of the way they are going to be. If you are quarreling and angry, this becomes the child's model for later life. Therefore, to make your own lives and your child's life happier now and in the future, it is important to work out and resolve the problems that cause conflict in the relationship.

Family Excursions and Travel

Now that the children are older, do you go on family outings, or vacations, or to visit distant relatives? How do things go?

"When we go on family outings, everything just seems to go wrong and we end up fighting."

Need for Flexibility in Planning

When adults go out socially, they often expect the children to be interested in the same kind of things they are interested in. They expect children to participate in the same way as they do. At this age, the children get tired, or they sometimes get bored by the things we think will interest them. When this happens, the thing to do is to modify the plans right away. Such changes take a great deal of flexibility and maturity on the part of the parents. No one likes to give up nice activities that have been planned for the family's entertainment. Parents may plan a drive up to the mountains. The child gets tired after the first five miles, wants to stop at a hamburger stand, and then go home. Some parents will be perfectly willing to go home and do not insist on going all the way. Other parents won't see any reason to change their plans. Sometimes it will work out all right, because the child will fall asleep and wake refreshed. At other times, the child will become increasingly cranky and the trip will be spoiled for everyone. Children of this age cannot necessarily tolerate the excursions that we plan. It is best not to make plans that are too elaborate and to be able to make changes if the plans aren't working.

Car Sickness

"My child usually gets carsick. Is there any way to stop that?"

Car sickness is caused by different things. In many cases, it's a disturbance affecting the semicircular canals in the ears. In some, it happens only on long trips if the speed of the car is above a certain level. If children are better on shorter trips, one can take that into account and break up the trip. In other cases, it is best not to give the child liquids such as milk before the trip and only dry foods such as plain crackers during the trip. Some pediatricians may think that an antiemetic medication is needed and will prescribe the appropriate one in the correct dosage for your child. Some children may be sick because of anxiety about travel. In most cases, children outgrow car sickness in time.

"I find that train trips are easier because the baby isn't so confined. Maybe the other passengers are not happy when we walk up and down the aisles,

but it takes up some of the time. Once in a while, we meet a friendly person. If they are unfriendly, we just move on."

"For me, a bottle still soothes my son and keeps him from being too restless when the books and toys get boring. Traveling alone is a lot harder than traveling with my husband or a friend, but it's manageable."

Air Travel

"We're taking a plane trip, and I dread it because it will be for several hours. We hope the baby will sleep part of the time; but if not, how do we amuse her? It's not like car or train travel; there usually isn't anything to point to outside the window except clouds."

Certainly traveling in a plane is difficult for that reason. Also, there are certain times when the child must be confined by a seat belt: at takeoff and landing, and during rough weather. One cannot stop the plane to give the child a chance to run or play. But there are occasional times on a plane when you can walk in the aisles with a child; and children are usually entertained by the serving of food. Sometimes the flight attendant has a children's play kit; and the airlines often give special treatment to families with small children by serving their food first or letting them embark and disembark first.

Another aspect of plane trips that is very different from other kinds of travel is the difficulty caused by altitude. The altitude often causes children's (and adult's) ears to hurt, especially on takeoff or landing, if they have a cold or respiratory infection. Adults often chew gum for relief of this condition, but these toddlers are really too young for gum. Swallowing is the natural method of physiologically relieving the pressure on one's ears. Therefore, it is very important to have a bottle or pacifier handy for children of this age. Children should be offered a bottle or pacifier if they begin to cry suddenly on a plane, because they may feel a change of pressure. The swallowing that results from drinking from a bottle or sucking on a pacifier will relieve the pressure or pain in their ears. Parents must know about this, because these toddlers are usually unable to say that their ears hurt. Much of the unpleasantness of traveling by plane can be avoided if parents are prepared for this occurrence. In fact, if the child—or the adult—has had a cold immediately prior to taking a plane trip, it is a good idea to consult a physician to see whether some medication can be prescribed as well.

Parents must be *prepared* for all eventualities when they are traveling long distances with young children. You never know when there may be a delay. You should always have extra diapers. Some airlines are prepared to help out with extra baby supplies, but you should not count on it.

In general, traveling with children of this age is difficult because they want to be active and can't be absorbed in any one thing for a long time. Every activity works for a while. A cookie works for a while, and a little car or a doll works for a while; nothing distracts them for very long. You have to work out a whole repertoire of activities that you know will engage your child. It is also a good idea to have a toy or two that are new, as well as some old favorites.

Entertaining

Are any of you beginning to entertain at home? How are you managing? When you have company coming to your house, do you arrange it so that your child is asleep and the guests come later? Or do they come during the time that your child is awake?

"There are some people who really don't care to be around children, so we ask them for later; and there are others who come just to see the children—they just love to see them."

"Our friends want our son to be up when they come over because they come to see him, too. After they have spent some time with him, we put him to bed."

"Our children usually go to bed very early. Unless my friends ask specifically to see them, I put them in bed before my friends arrive."

"My children go to bed around seven, so I don't invite anybody to come over until after eight o'clock. By that time, the children are asleep. Sometimes my daughter gets the sense that someone is coming and she won't go to bed until she has visited with them a little. We all just accept this. Sometimes she even has a bite of our refreshments, then goes willingly to bed. I find it's easier if I relax and don't use pressure."

Helping Child to Socialize

You've learned something valuable. Children let you know when they are ready and need to socialize. It's good for them to learn to socialize with other adults. Sometimes children take to this quite naturally, and other times they need some help and reassurance. Sometimes adults need to be guided in relating to your child. They may be too overwhelming in their greeting, or indifferent, so the parent has to be the child's advocate and guide the situation. In any case, it is a valuable experience for the child.

"One of the big hassles with company and the baby is the food. He will want a little bit of this, a taste of that, or he will take a bite of something and leave it on someone's lap. I'm afraid we will alienate our friends!"

As you progress through life, you will notice that many people you thought were your friends are less friendly because they do not like children. You will get to see more and more of the people who are really friends of yours *and* of your children. Some old friendships continue, but many new ones are made.

"We are trying very hard now to renew some of our old friendships. My husband expects me to be able to entertain with silver and candlelight and gourmet food, just as we used to. I'd like to do that, too, but it's just too much. I get worn out and don't enjoy the whole thing as I used to. Then we both feel let down."

Certainly, some of the unnecessary details may have to be omitted. Maybe the silver won't be polished and maybe some of the food will be brought in from outside. In this, your husband can help. Perhaps some of the preparation can be done the night before when the baby is asleep. The menu can be the kind that can be prepared ahead and popped into the oven at the last minute.

"Well, that's what I do. I shop as much as I can when I take the baby out in the carriage; my husband picks up the rest. Then I attend to everything, even to setting the table, the night before. The next day I'm free, and the baby doesn't seem to get in the way as much as some think. Even if he is up when the company comes, we either wait until he goes to bed to eat or sit him beside us and give him a snack."

"We never did entertain formally—never silver or candlesticks; but my husband did expect good pasta or something like that. Now company knows it's potluck. Sometimes they bring most of the food. It's not my husband's style, but he is getting used to it for the time being."

It sounds as though in some cases the wife is worried more about the husband than the guests—how to please him.

"Well, I guess I'm lucky. My husband was always the manager of the preparations, and he still is. He likes to be the host and the cook."

"Before we had the baby, we entertained out at restaurants a lot. Now we don't do that because we want to stay home with the baby. As you know, I still work full time and I just don't have the energy to entertain at home."

If you have continued working, it is important for your baby to be a priority *after work*. Working women should *not* feel that they have to be super-women and do everything. It is important to see your friends occasionally, however, and to plan for some activities with your husband without the baby—or with other adults in a social way. Occasionally, you should go out with your friends; perhaps you even have some friends with a young child who would like to go out with you. Perhaps you can have some kind of food service, such as an Italian or Chinese restaurant, deliver a fully cooked meal so you can entertain at home with a minimum of effort. We say this not because entertaining is important, but because parents need some adult life together with their friends.

It is not healthy to feel isolated from one's friends and trapped by the baby. Couples who never see their friends sometimes develop a sense of martyrdom about parenthood that covers a sense of resentment. This is

■   ■

not a feeling to be encouraged. It is much better to find a way to socialize, no matter how casually.

Moving: How to Reduce the Child's Anxieties

Are any of you thinking of moving?

"Yes, we are about to move. We only have a small bedroom, and there is almost no room for the crib and our bed in the same room. We've begun to pack, and we noticed that the baby seemed confused as we began to put things in boxes in preparation. Do you think she senses something is going on?"

She certainly is aware that something different is going on. For a child, consistency is very important. She needs to see her things in the familiar places. At this age, she can't understand very well what is happening. You may say, "We are going to a new home," or, "You are going to have a nice room," and she probably will understand little of it. However, she may enjoy helping to put, or drop, things into packing boxes. In this way she can be involved in the move in a positive way.

"My friends just moved, and their baby was upset and cranky all during the packing and the first couple of weeks they were in the new apartment. The worst part was the sleeping. He just couldn't get used to his new bed; they bought all new furniture for his room. He just wasn't happy; he just clung to an old blanket and teddy bear. It made my friends miserable."

Maintaining Child's Sense of Security

It is very distressing to parents when they plan something they think will be just fine for the child and the child doesn't respond with joy. Since the child is not verbal, the parents couldn't talk the changes over with him. They would have been much better off to move his old furniture, pictures, and toys to the new home and set up the room as nearly as it had been in the old apartment. Then they could get new furniture later when the child could understand and participate. It is always a temptation to redecorate for the child, but the child may not appreciate that at this age. For the child, it is important to have his familiar things: they help him maintain his sense of security and basic trust.

"For the child, what is the best way to move? Is it best to leave the child at a relative's house and get everything done and then go and get him? Or should the child be included in the move? And what about his toys?"

If you want to arrange to do what is most helpful to the child, take the child to see the new apartment or house several times before the move. Then, in packing, put his toys in at the last minute. All his furniture should be put on the truck last so it will be first off. Then, the child's things can be unpacked first and his room set up as nearly like his old room as

■   ■

possible. It's best to have him with you so that he can see the process and participate with his family. Instead of separating the child from the family, it is better to have a relative or neighbor with you to keep him amused and out of harm. Then he can see what is going on and have the joy of seeing his things unpacked.

Even with the best of plans, he may be a little upset the first night or two. Change in sleep patterns and clinging are signs of the child's anxiety. Sometimes the child is also harder to comfort and gets irritable more easily, or his eating pattern may be disturbed. These signs of anxiety are to be expected, but they will probably be less intense if he is included in the move. In addition, it's a good idea to carry out the child's usual routines as nearly as possible.

Children Need Reassurance During Move

"We have just moved and our baby feels upset. I know that she doesn't get the kind of attention she is used to, because we are busy getting unpacked and settled. To take time just to play with her seems like a waste of time, but I guess you're saying she needs it."

Yes, she needs her regular play, especially because of the strangeness of the place. When she sees her things in place, she will know that this is a place where she can stay and she will get adjusted. You may have to get *your* things unpacked a little more slowly. You will have much more trouble if you try to get her to stop clinging so you can get things done; that only intensifies the clinging. It's best to allow her to be near you as much as possible. Comfort her and play with her; then take her with you as you do things. She may like to help unpack or to play in some of the big packing boxes. You really can't hope to get settled in the efficient way that you would like. Don't try. If it's your expectation that you should do it, that's frustrating to you.

"Well, we have an older child of four and the baby. The older one was able to help a little, and he talked about his new house; but the baby was upset at first, even though we kept her toys out to the last minute."

"Are all children like that? Aren't there some who take it in their stride? Our child adapted easily, but we took our time moving. Each day or so, we took a few things over to the new house and she would play on the floor there. So when we moved it was less of a change for her. We thought about how to make it easier for her and for us. We remembered some of the things from the first year, when she reacted so badly on the weekends that we went to our summer bungalow. Then it was explained to us that the sudden change to a strange setting upset her sense of security."

"Well, then you can't get any work done if there is a baby around."

As we said before, it is better to delay the work than to needlessly undermine the child's sense of security. The work can always be done a little later; putting up curtains or putting the pots away can wait.

■   ■

"We moved a month ago and are going on vacation for a week, which means another new place for her. Do you think this will be unsettling, too? I want her to feel settled, because I go to school again a week after we get back."

Too Much Change Is Unsettling

Sometimes parents plan—or are unable to avoid—too many changes in their lives. These changes are often difficult for adults to cope with, but they are much more difficult for children of this age, because they cannot discuss all the changes. Your baby may certainly show some signs of being unsettled from the move, the vacation, and your return to school. If her behavior seems very strange to you, then you can't deal with it and you become angry. But if you realize that her response to all of these changes is normal for a child of her age, and that what she needs is your reassurance and your presence to help her get adjusted, then you will be able to deal with it. Then you won't get annoyed with her and make matters worse. Understanding the limitations of the child's coping mechanisms will ultimately make it easier for the parents.

"The discussion has been about moving from one apartment to another, but my husband and I are thinking of moving to the suburbs. We moved into a large apartment before the baby came, but we can see that it's very confining. There is a terrace, but I can't really use it for him to play."

"My husband and I had a long discussion weighing the pros and cons of city versus country living. We came to the conclusion that he would spend so much time commuting that the baby would hardly see him. It's bad enough now."

"My husband wants to move, but I don't. I have friends here and plan to work part-time soon. There are few part-time jobs in the suburbs."

Each family will find good reasons *for* and *against* suburban and city living. As in all other situations, each family has to make its decision according to its own priorities. It's wise for parents to carefully consider *together* what their priorities are. We know healthy, happy children have been brought up in *all* surroundings. It is important to consider what will enhance the family's well-being and relationships as a family, as well as what best suits the individual needs of each member. It's hard if one member feels he or she is making a sacrifice for the others. Ultimately, the children will be happy where the parents are happy.

Parental Anger: How to Express It Appropriately

In earlier sessions, we have talked about children's anger and how to handle their tantrums in the most constructive ways. We have also urged you to try to keep calm yourselves and not add your agitation to theirs. We realize that this is often easier said than done. Children can be exceedingly annoying,

■   ■

often just when parents are tired or preoccupied by other problems. All parents lose their tempers at times and yell at their children. Do you find you are doing that more frequently now that the children are older?

Counterproductiveness of Yelling

"I yell a great deal more than I want to. I'm a bug on neatness. When the baby throws things and makes a mess after I've just cleaned up, that gets me and I yell."

Many of us yell when we are angry. We believe the *louder* we yell the more effect it will have on the other person. At the same time, we are unconsciously releasing *our* anger. Yelling is, in fact, more effective as a method of releasing anger than of teaching the child about the behavior we expect. Speaking quietly and firmly is a much more effective way of teaching. Very often, in fact, yelling does the opposite of what we want it to do. It sets the example for the child to yell in return. Or, if the parent yells constantly, the child may simply tune it out and pay no attention. Either response makes the parent more angry and sets up a vicious cycle. We want to help parents avoid such situations in which anger escalates on both sides.

"Must parents be sweet and gentle all the time? Don't they have a right to be angry and show it and shout 'No'?"

Of course that happens, especially when the child is about to do something dangerous. The parent may become excited and shout "No" or "Stop." But, as we have said earlier, shouting gives little guarantee that the child's central nervous system will be able to respond in time.

In addition to times of danger, parents may yell because the child has been exceedingly annoying, doing something the parents do not like at all. We want our children to do the things we approve of and stop doing the things we don't like. The best way to accomplish this is to say "No" quietly and firmly. If the child seems not to understand how serious you are, you may have to add an "Absolutely not," so that he or she knows you mean it. You must let children know *firmly* that you mean what you say. That doesn't mean you need to slap them or yell at them—a firm tone of voice and a stern facial expression are usually enough. You have a right and an obligation to let them know when you do not like what they are doing. And, of course, as we have discussed, each limitation should be accompanied by the offer of a substitute approved activity.

"I've learned that. Otherwise, you get repercussions from it. I get hit, honest. I tell my son 'No' and he knows I mean it; but if I don't give him a substitute right away, he hits me. He needs an alternate outlet."

You are perfectly right. There must be a substitute activity offered, because he has the impulse to do something. The message to act has gone into his immature nervous system, and it can't be turned off by the child at this age.

■   ■

You can help the child by diverting the discharge to an appropriate activity. Accepting alternatives is a sign of maturity—it doesn't come overnight. Parents help children achieve this maturity *not* by yelling at them to stop, but by firmly saying "No" and giving them other outlets. Those children who are forced to stop continually without an alternative outlet build up anger, which they may not express. This can lead to the development of a hostile personality structure that we are trying to help you avoid.

"I can see that yelling is not a good way to discipline. What effect does parents' yelling at each other have on children?"

It sets a model. They get the idea that this is the way to communicate and they yell, too. That is one thing that happens, and another thing is that it usually frightens and upsets them.

"You're right. If we yell at each other, our child looks at us in a frightened way and then smiles a lot and looks as if she wants to be reassured that everything is all right. Or she will just laugh out loud, perhaps to make it lighter, or to stop us."

Sometimes they laugh when they are really ready to cry. They don't know what to do about your yelling and feel very threatened. They laugh, hoping you will stop and laugh, too, because they know you seem pleased when they laugh. Laughter at a time like that is nervous laughter.

"Do you think that our yelling makes children nervous and upset even if they don't understand what is going on?"

Parents' Arguments Frighten Children

Some people have a habit of discussing things in very loud voices and are really not angry, but the children don't understand that. When parents fight in front of children it is very disconcerting to them. Either they will then yell at you that way and yell at their friends, or it frightens them and they don't know what to do about it.

"In my family no one ever did yell, so anger was never really expressed."

You can express anger and you should express anger. You should also express pleasure. It should be clear which is which. It doesn't mean you have to turn off your feelings, or that you always wear a smile. Children will never learn the difference between a pleasant feeling or an unpleasant feeling if you do that. They should learn the difference, but it should be appropriate. If you go into a tremendous outburst because something has spilled and the same outburst when someone is hurt, your anger is not proportionate to the situation or appropriate.

Yelling indicates that you have stored up a lot of anger, perhaps over many different things. It may be mostly against your spouse or another relative or the delivery boy. It is not appropriate, when you have been storing up anger from other incidents, to discharge all of it on the child.

Sometimes people yell when they are frightened. Have you seen that?

■   ■

What Spanking Teaches

"Everyone is talking about yelling at their kids when they are bad. What about a good spanking—that stops them!"

We discussed our concerns about spanking earlier *(see page 132)*. We believe it is better to teach what is acceptable and what is not by saying "No" and offering a substitute. Spanking teaches by inflicting pain. It also sets the example of a physical way of handling differences. In cases of parental anger, physical discipline or spanking can often become excessive and lead to child abuse. No parent wants that to happen. We want to try to help you learn different ways, so that you can avoid that kind of relationship. Besides, neither yelling nor spanking produces the results parents would like.

"Okay, I can understand all that. But how do you keep from yelling or slapping when you are really angry? When I am angry, all my good intentions seem to disappear—I lose my temper and yell. Once or twice, I've even hit the baby; it makes me feel terrible. But how do you handle anger? How do you express anger appropriately, as you say?"

Everyone needs to learn how to handle anger—how to release anger and how to express anger. When you become very angry at your child, especially a child of this age, who may not be able to understand the reason even if you were able to explain it, you should try to control your own actions. If you feel that that is difficult for you, it is best to put him in his crib or in his room and call someone, your husband or a friend, and *tell that person* about your anger. If you are the active physical type, you may have to go into another room and jump up and down, run in place, or pound a pillow in order to release the angry energy that seems to be overwhelming you. Everyone needs to find the best way to maintain self-control and to release angry feelings. There will be many different ways, from counting to ten to going for a brisk walk. The important thing is to try not to let out all your angry feelings onto the child.

Once you have regained your self-control, then you can talk to the child in very simple terms about your anger. You can say, for example, "Pulling the leaves off the plant makes Mommy very angry." Even if the child does not quite understand, you are beginning to set the model for *verbally* expressing angry feelings.

Children need to learn that their actions cause anger, that it is normal to get angry every once in a while—and most important, that anger can be handled by talking about it. This example of how you handle and express your anger will help the child to handle and express his or her anger.

For the moment, the children are a little young to understand this fully. The important thing, however, is for the parents to begin to set this kind of pattern now. Gradually, the children will understand it—and in the meantime you will not have upset their sense of trust and growing self-esteem by overly harsh or frightening displays of anger.

■   ■

Daily Routines: How Much Time to Spend with Children; Time Off for Parents

As the children get older, parents expect to have more free time. Parents are often annoyed to find that although their children are running around, beginning to say a few words, and, at times, even playing by themselves, the children still need a great deal of attention. The parents, especially the mothers, are disappointed not to have gained the freedom they have been looking forward to. In fact, parents with active toddlers often find they have less time and freedom, because the children are taking much shorter naps and seem to be "into everything." Are you finding your daily routines more difficult now?

"We have our day pretty well programmed. My son is used to following me from room to room when I'm straightening up. You can believe it gets a quick going-over. But it's neat. Then we go to the park, where we meet friends. When he naps, sometimes I do, too; or I read or prepare something for dinner. When he is up, we go out again if it's nice—maybe do a little shopping. Then it's home for a bath and supper and Daddy's arrival. When Daddy comes, that is the big moment of the day for him and my chance to cook dinner. It's getting him simmered down afterward so he will sleep that takes a little doing. I enjoy the day with him. It gets a little monotonous sometimes, so I try to vary it a little, but not much, because it upsets the baby."

"Well, you seem to have it all working well. I wish I could say the same. I have a feeling I never get anything done. Maybe I'm not well organized, but I can't get the house neat, the laundry, shopping, and cooking done. The baby won't let me. He just wants me to play with him, or else he is climbing or doing something that takes my attention. Day after day, it's the same—it's frustrating."

"I used to feel that way until I began to involve my little girl in what I was doing. If I'm cooking, I put her in a high chair beside me in the kitchen, which is very small. I give her flour, water, or something so that she can do what I am doing. Sometimes that will keep her happy for quite a while and I get my cooking done."

"I try to do that, too. I involve my son in what I'm doing as much as I can. I put him up on the counter, where he can watch me as I work, and I talk to him. But if I try to watch television or read a book or something like that, he pesters me and wants my attention."

Alternating Play with Parents' Chores

Most of you seem to be having success in keeping your children occupied by involving them in household chores. However, some of you seem annoyed that you can't keep them happy while you are reading or watching television. There is a big difference: in one case, you are involved with the child; in the other you are absorbed in reading or watching TV and the child feels isolated

■　　　　　　　　　　　　　　　　　　　　　　　　　■

and excluded. Children can't stand this feeling. It is understandable and reasonable that you want to relax and read or watch TV for a while. Sometimes you can put the child in your arms and say, "Mama is reading about this," and you can read aloud to him, even though he doesn't understand. Since he does not feel excluded, he may get down after a while and play with a toy. Then you can go on reading, but not for long. In another ten minutes, you may have to pick him up again. Sometimes the child may find something that really intrigues him and he may keep at it, but his attention span is very short. Children of this age are just getting to the stage when they can play alone for a short time. Eventually, they will have a longer attention span and you will be able to read longer. Then you can say, "This is reading time and Mama is reading her book. You have your book." That time will come, but it hasn't come yet for most children. Sometimes, even now, children can look at their books while you read, or they can be involved in turning the pages of their books. This is a good activity to encourage if it brings pleasure, for it leads to the enjoyment of books and reading later in life. If it is a hassle and not a pleasure, it may be counterproductive. If the child feels that reading separates him from his parents, he may come to dislike reading. This may pose problems later in school.

"I have to admit that reading has always been very important to me, and I've been getting annoyed when my little girl interrupts me. I push her away when I'm reading. Then she cries and I can't read. Now I understand why we are both so frustrated. I think she is old enough to play alone, but she is not; she thinks I am neglecting her."

That is precisely the situation. When one does push a child off, it produces a whining, clinging child. This is the situation we all want to avoid.

"This business of the baby's need to be in the kitchen when I'm cooking bothers me. I want to concentrate on what I'm doing and get it over quickly. It takes so much longer with the baby there."

The child's need to be with you is something you have to accept at this age. You can organize the situation and make it consistent by stating, "This is Mother's cooking time to make dinner for us." You may even mention all the things you are going to make. Then give the child something to do in his own space in the kitchen and say, "This is what you can cook." Give him some dough to play with if you are baking or give him a spoon and cup to mix things. The child will feel he is participating in what you are doing. Then you can play a game with him.

Varying Activities Within Basic Routine

"Most of our time is spent going to the park, and I would like to ask about other activities and the daily routine. We go to the park most of his waking hours. I wonder if he will get bored if we spend most of our time that way, but he seems happier there than anywhere else. Have I made it too much of a habit?"

■   ■

Your son is very active and he probably loves the freedom of the park. If you are feeling somewhat confined, it might be a good idea to vary your daily routine. It might be good to try going to a friend's house occasionally. The routine of having an afternoon activity should be continued, but the activity may be varied—going to the park, or visiting, or marketing. The park is good for at least once a day, because that gives your child a place to play with a lot of freedom and a lot of space that he doesn't have at home.

"I wasn't sure whether he was so locked into the routine that we couldn't go anyplace else."

It is probably a good idea to try the other things and see. You certainly could try having a friend come to visit, or you could go visiting.

"I will do that, and maybe we could go for a bus ride."

Yes, a bus ride or a visit to the children's zoo, if you are near one.

"I guess my question is, 'Should I force him in the beginning into doing these things if he doesn't want to?' "

You could give him a chance. If you do it once and he doesn't like it at first, then you can do it again and see—he may like it the second time. You do want to enlarge on the kinds of things that he likes to do. As he gets older and more verbal, you can explain the kind of outing you are going on.

"Is it necessary to be so cautious? My child seems to thrive on new things."

Each parent has to be able to tune in on the level of development of her own child and his or her personality. Some children need repetition of the same routine to feel comfortable and have to be gradually educated to new situations. Other children have more inquisitive personalities and welcome change.

"This discussion makes me realize that I should be talking to my housekeeper about my child's day while I am away at work. I wonder if she is having some trouble now that he is more active?"

It is always a good idea to talk with the substitute caretaker about the child's routines. Sometimes a person who is wonderful with little babies doesn't give enough stimulation to older children. Toddlers, as you all know, can be very tiring. Working mothers do need to take the time to find out how the child's day is changing as he or she gets older. Then there can be some continuity between weekday and weekend activities.

"My husband and I both work full time, but we are finding some of the same difficulties on weekends. Our child seems to be with us every second all weekend long. We have no time for ourselves individually or as a couple."

"I am glad you brought that up, because my husband is complaining that our weekends are totally child-oriented, even though I spend all week at home."

■   ■

Parents' Time Together

We are now talking about how much time the child needs and how much time the parents need together. Certainly, if both parents work full time, the child needs a lot of their time when they are not working. The weekends need to combine activities that will make the child feel like an important part of the family. This means spending considerable time on child-oriented activities— going to the park or playing with the child at home. If there are important family chores that need doing, then our advice is the same as for mothers at home: try to involve the child in as many of your household activities as possible. A trip to the supermarket with mother or father can be a "family time" and a learning experience for the child, as well as getting a chore done. At the market, father (or mother) can say, "We need to buy cereal. Here it is!" Often the child will recognize the package he or she is accustomed to and point it out. Or you can say, "Now we will buy applesauce. Show me the applesauce." Children will often be able to pick out the proper jar. Shopping also gives parents the opportunity to point out boxes and jars, colors such as the red or blue package, and so on. A mundane trip can be turned into a casual but effective learning experience for the child. Of course, making an early stop at the cookie section and allowing the child a choice—and an *immediate* taste—can also help to make the adventure appropriately gratifying to a toddler.

Lastly, all parents, whether working outside the home or not, are saying that the children are taking too much time. Children of this age need a lot of time. However, parents also need time for themselves. Arrangements should be made to have relatives or baby-sitters help out, so that both mothers and fathers have some time for themselves. A little time away from the child enables the parents to return to the job refreshed and invigorated, so we advise parents to arrange regular times away from the responsibilities of child rearing. This can make the difference between considering child rearing a burden or a joy.

More on Language Development

Some of you have been expressing pleasure in your children's ability to communicate, and others seem somewhat disappointed. It is good to talk about your expectations and feelings about your children's learning to talk.

"My son seems to be saying many things and is often annoyed with me because I don't understand him. He seems to have special sounds for certain things that I sometimes understand but often may not, because they are not clear."

That can be very frustrating for both of you. How do you speak to him? The same way you speak to me or to another adult? You may be speaking too rapidly and not enunciating clearly. The child must hear the rhythm and the sounds clearly so that he can imitate them.

■   ■

"Just what do you mean? I don't understand."

Do you say, "Your dinner is now ready; come and eat it while it is hot. Mommy fixed some good hamburger and vegetables"? That's a lot of words, delivered in a quick businesslike way. The child understands the message, but he may have trouble deciding what to repeat out of all that. Instead, you could say, "Here's Joey's dinner," with a rhythm and vocal modulation. It may sound rather singsong to you, but that doesn't bother the child. In fact, he may then be able to say, "Hee, din" (meaning, "Here is dinner") or, "Want din," at some other time. Then you reply, "You want your din-ner?" so that he can hear the words clearly again. This is what I mean by not speaking too rapidly, so a child can try to imitate you. You are his model. When he jumbles words together, it may be because he hasn't been able to hear them separately and clearly.

Encouraging Speech

"Well, I have especially avoided speaking that way because I consider that baby talk. I was given to understand that baby talk retards speech development."

To enunciate clearly in good English, or whatever other language is used in the home, and to speak slowly is *not* baby talk. Clear, well-modulated speech helps the child's language development. Baby talk is the repetition of a child's mispronunciations or private words. Sometimes, such talk is very endearing. When a child says "pizetti" for "spaghetti," we are tempted to repeat it. That is encouraging baby talk and it may impede the development of proper speech. It is better to recognize what the child means and then say, "Yes, you want your spaghetti."

"The way of speaking you suggest sounds so artificial. Doesn't the baby have to get used to our speech just as it is? Before our baby came, I hated so much when I saw my friends with their new babies say, 'My itsy, bitsy, witsy honey' or some such things. I thought it was silly, and I vowed I'd never do that."

Infants respond well to all words that parents use especially for them as terms of endearment. They recognize when a parent's tone is affectionate and when the parent is indifferent or angry. Every baby needs to hear and feel affection through the parent's tone of voice and rhythm of language. Parents have to do what comes naturally to them. If they use special words of endearment for their baby, that's fine. It is also appropriate to repeat the infants' earliest sounds; in that way, they begin to understand that verbal communication is important and valued by the parents. Repeating their sounds was appropriate for children during the first year of life. Now that they are older, it is appropriate to begin to model correct language. The terms of endearment also have to grow with the children and change to suit their levels of development.

"What should our child be saying now, and how much does she understand?"

Most children have vocabularies of about twenty words at twenty-one months. Some of your children have many more words; some don't know quite that many. It depends on their own maturational timetables as well as on how much speech stimulation they have had. It is a combination of the two and varies with each child.

Children of this age comprehend much more than they can express. They understand directions such as "Bring me the teddy bear" and "Where is the light?" Some may even understand a little joke; they find concrete incongruities, such as teddy bear wearing mommy's hat, very funny. They do not understand sarcasm or teasing and are very sensitive to a person's tone of voice for cues to meaning.

"But what should the parents be doing to help the child?"

Parents should talk to their children as much as possible and name things for them. In the house, you can name objects and make simple sentences: "The light is on" and "The light is off." You can name the foods they eat: milk, apple, orange, cookie, meat. You enunciate the word slowly and clearly. Parents can also point to parts of the children's bodies or their own bodies and name them. Whenever the child points to anything, the parent names it for her. Pointing and naming can be a wonderful game for children at this age. In that way their curiosity will be satisfied and stimulated while their vocabularies are being increased. Parents can also point to things and have the children name them; it's an occasion for parents to show pleasure and approval.

"I have tried all that with my little fellow, but he doesn't seem to catch on. I can spend half an hour pointing to the object and say it over and over again. He looks at it but he won't repeat it. It makes me very angry, because we are a verbal family and I am so anxious to have him talk early."

It is not necessary to sit down and have a lesson in speech. Saying the same word over and over can be tedious and boring for him as well as you. He may not be responding because your anxiety makes him anxious and inhibits him; or he may not be ready yet. A child will begin to speak on his own timetable, provided we give him models to follow in an appropriate and natural way, without pressure.

Talking with Toddlers

"It is very hard for me to talk to my baby. I'm not much of a talker. I guess I always thought that a baby didn't understand much at this age and that speech would come on its own when she understood more. Is that why my baby says so little?"

It may be the reason why her expressive speech development has not been as fast as the other children's. Some parents talk less than others—that's their personality. Others don't realize it's important to talk with children. If parents don't speak *with* their children, their speech can be delayed. Many of us speak *to* children. We *tell* them what to do. We say, "Come here," "Stop that," "No," and "Drink your milk," but we don't talk *with* them. Some parents don't realize that "talking with" children means naming things and responding by repeating what they say in correct speech. By this we do not mean correcting their speech. If the child says, "Want pizetti," the parent should not say, "No, say *spaghetti.*" The parent should say, "Yes, I'll give you some spaghetti." In this way, the child knows that the parent has understood and is responding positively to her communication. If one says "No" every time a child mispronounces a word, this discourages speech development and sets up a negative interchange between parent and child.

A good way to talk with children of this age, in addition to the naming game, is to talk about what you are doing and about what the child is doing. For example, as you are fixing dinner you can say, "Mommy is going to cook Susie's supper. She is looking in the refrigerator. She is cooking a hamburger. She is cutting carrots. She is pouring milk into Susie's cup." In the same way, you can talk about the child's actions.

Another game for toddlers that encourages communication skills is the listening game. You can identify sounds you hear from the street: the sirens of fire engines, the honking of cars and trucks, and the sound of airplanes. Then you can encourage the child to listen for such sounds. (This game can become increasingly sophisticated and discriminating as the child gets older.)

Nursery Rhyme Games

"Aren't there some nursery rhyme games that would be good for speech stimulation?"

Yes, one good one is "Here we go round the mulberry bush so early in the morning." This can be infinitely varied with simple language changes: "This is the way we wash our hands, brush our teeth, comb our hair, put on our shoes . . . so early in the morning." Another nursery rhyme game that children may begin to enjoy is "Ring around the rosy, / Pocket full of posy, / Ashes, ashes, / We all fall down." Another opportunity for conversation is while the child is swinging. Instead of standing *behind* the child, push from the front and talk about going "up" and "down," "so high," or about other things you see and hear in the park: birds, airplanes, and the like. When you begin to think of it, there are endless simple ways to engage in appropriate conversations with your children.

Of course, another excellent way to stimulate speech and language development is by looking at books with your child and naming the objects. For this age, books with only several objects on a page, or a simple story line, are best. Too many different objects or a complicated story may be too much for the child's level of concentration. (For a list of appropriate books for the second year of life, see "Suggested Books for Children Twelve to Twenty-four Months.") Listening to records of nursery rhymes and simple songs is also a good way of stimulating language and having fun with your child. Many children's libraries have a record section where you can get ideas for appropriate selections.

We all know that speech is important as the basis for reading and academic achievement. We must not forget that it is important for communication. At this age, children's pronunciation of words will not be perfect, but parents must try to understand and encourage their attempts at communication by constant approval. Your pleasure in their achievements is contagious—the more fun you have together with language, the more the child's language development will be enhanced.

Toilet Training: Signs of Readiness

Now that the children are becoming more competent in using their bodies, are developing speech, and are understanding what is said to them, parents often become more concerned about toilet training.

"I know from our previous discussion and from reading that one should not begin toilet training before the child is ready. But so many of my friends who have children my child's age are beginning training. One little girl is already trained. It makes me a little uneasy. I wonder if I'm being too lax about it."

"That's the attitude my mother has. She says all five of us were potty trained by one year—eighteen months at the latest, if we were slow. She thinks I'm lazy or negligent, since I'm not pushing my son. My pediatrician says the child has to be ready; but I sure am tired of carrying diapers around."

"I would like my son to be toilet trained by two, but I'm afraid that if I try too soon and he is not ready I will be disappointed. Then he will understand that I am disappointed and will be upset, too. I know that is not a good interaction to set up."

Your attitude is very perceptive and sensitive. That is just what happens when parents try too soon. Our expectations in this area are usually not in keeping with the child's readiness. Very often this can be the start of a battle over training: the parents think it is time for training, and the child resists because she is not ready. The parents are disappointed; the child senses their disapproval but can't comply. The child's inability is regarded as resistance by the parents, who become more insistent and angry. The child becomes angry, and an unhappy interaction is set up between parent and child that may interfere with other aspects of their relationship. The child may view the parents as always angry and displeased with him. He may have angry feelings and also develop a sense of failure and poor self-esteem. These feelings may lead to a very unpleasant angry attitude, which the child may carry on into adult life. We want to help parents avoid this. That is why we advise parents to be careful about the way toilet training is instituted.

Indications of Readiness

"What are some of the indications that a child is ready for toilet training? What can we, as parents, do to help?"

First, the child must have the understanding that everything has its proper place. You have all been teaching your children this concept, both consciously

■   ■

and unconsciously, as you put your groceries away or as you put their clothes and toys away. Once children understand the concept that toys go in the toy box, clothes go in the closet, groceries go in the kitchen cupboard, wastepaper goes in the basket, garbage goes in the garbage can, they will get the idea that bowel movements and urine go in the toilet. That's how they begin to be ready. That's the first step.

"Isn't it also necessary for the parent to notice how long an interval they can stay dry?"

Yes, that is true. When you notice that they have the ability to stay dry for two to three hours, then you know they are beginning to gain control over their sphincter muscles. That is a second indicator that they are getting ready.

"Is it better to try to establish bowel or bladder training first?"

It is easier to train for bowels first, because there are fewer bowel movements a day. Most people train for bowels first when they notice the baby has a regular time for bowel movements. Very few children are ready before two. Some may be ready at two years, some more at two and a half. Some are not ready until they are three years old. Our experience shows that if training is started when children are ready, they learn very quickly without a struggle.

Appropriate Expectations

"What should we be expecting of our children at this age?"

Now the children are all about twenty-one or twenty-two months old. They are just learning where everything belongs. They are just becoming aware of how toilet facilities are used. Some have watched their diapers being emptied into the toilet and enjoy flushing the toilet. Some of them have regular times for their bowel movements and have long intervals with a dry diaper. They are just beginning to gain the necessary control, which depends on the maturity of the central nervous system. This ability varies with each child. There is no one age at which all children can be toilet trained.

"What else needs to happen before they are ready?"

A very complicated set of responses is necessary for successful training. In the first place, the child must become aware of and understand the sensation of having a full rectum or bladder. Then he must have enough language to indicate his need to the parent. He must also have the understanding of the appropriate place for depositing his stool or urine. He must have the muscle control to withhold the evacuation until he has been taken to the proper place, has had his clothing removed, and has been placed in the proper position. Then he has to be able to relax his sphincters in order to release his bowel movement or urine. In addition, there is an emotional aspect to this process. The child must *want* to give up his baby ways and follow this new procedure. He needs to have the satisfaction of being in control of his body functions.

■   ■

Parents often interfere and try to control the child's body, but ultimately they cannot force the child to either eliminate or withhold on command. Such attempts result in a battle of wills between parent and child that may continue into adult life.

"Then should we be introducing the potty chair into the bathroom yet, or is it too soon?"

If the potty is introduced now, some children may become used to sitting on it. They may sit on it as on a chair with their clothes on, which may reduce the fear of sitting on it properly later. Other children use the potty chair as a toy and experiment with their dolls. This is also a preparatory stage. However, others push it around and just play with it, with no association as to its proper use. In that case, it is better to put it away for a few months. Then you can bring it out again and see if its proper use is better understood.

Fears Connected with Toilet Training

"My child watches me empty his diaper into the toilet with a great deal of interest. However, when I flush the toilet he often cries and gets very upset. Why is that?"

Some children are frightened because they feel their stool is part of them; they may be afraid that they will be flushed down the toilet, too. This may also happen in the bathtub if you pull the plug while the child is still in the tub. The child becomes upset because he or she fears going down the drain, too. Children are very sensitive about their bodies, and all are fearful of bodily harm. We need to tune in to their thoughts and feelings about themselves. We need to understand their thinking, which is rather magical at this age. We need to reassure them and wait for them to take the lead rather than imposing our wishes on them before they are able to comply.

"It's reassuring to have this discussion. I was beginning to feel like an incompetent parent because my child wasn't toilet trained."

Your success as a parent should not be measured, by you or anyone else, by how early your child becomes toilet trained. Speech is a much more important indicator of the child's progress; and it is not appropriate to put pressure on the child to control bladder and bowels at the same time that speech is developing. Speech requires that the child be able to "let out" and express himself or herself; toilet training requires "holding in." It is usually too much to expect children of this age to accomplish both at the same time. Toilet training is a complicated physiological, emotional, and neurological process. The maturational level of the child's central nervous system is a critical factor in his or her ability to "get it all together." It is, therefore, important that toilet training be postponed until the child is developmentally ready. You will be pleasantly surprised at how easily it is all accomplished if you have the patience to wait until that time.

■   ■

Manners: What Is Appropriate at This Age?

Are you beginning to think that your children have reached the age when they should begin to learn manners?

"While we were engaged, my husband and I would be with some of our friends who already had children, and one of the things that bothered us most was their lack of manners. It seemed to us their parents were too lax and that the children were being brought up to be brats. We vowed to each other that we would never allow that to happen if we had children. But now I realize it's not so easy, because I can't even get my child to say hello or good-bye. What are we doing wrong?"

Appropriate Expectations

The chances are that there is nothing "wrong"; your expectations from your child are simply not in keeping with her level of development. You are expecting too much social poise from a child who is not yet two. It is true that children of this age can say "Hi" and "Bye." They may say it to family members, but usually they will not greet strangers in this way on request or command.

"I guess my expectations are too high, too. Yesterday a neighbor came to visit. The baby seemed to like her, handed her some of his toys, and then took them back. He also played 'Peekaboo' with her. When she left, we went to the door and I said, 'Good-bye,' and turned to him to say good-bye or wave. But he just leaned close to me and looked at her and wouldn't say anything. I felt so embarrassed and surprised, because he seemed to like her. I felt he was naughty and I guess he felt my disappointment, because he clung to me and wanted to be held when he normally is very active."

It is possible that he was sorry to see her go, since he was enjoying her company. Perhaps he was expressing his feeling of disappointment at her leaving and could not say, "Stay." This is just a supposition. What I am wondering is whether your reaction indicates your concern about what the visitor might think of you as a mother. Perhaps you were more concerned about that than about how your child was feeling. Parents need to try to understand how the child perceives the episode. If they tune in appropriately to their child's level of development, parents will understand whether his or her responses are appropriate. They will feel better about their competence as parents and less dependent on the approval, or lack of approval, of neighbors.

"Well, what is appropriate at this age? When are children ready to say hello and good-bye without a battle?"

The age at which each child will be able to respond with what the adult considers the appropriate social grace varies greatly. At this stage, if they are beginning to greet family members or close friends, that is fine. The parent

■   ■

should make some positive recognition of the child's greeting so the other adult will respond to the child's remark. For example, when Johnny says "Hi," or "Bye," the parent should point out with some pleasure, "Johnny is saying 'Hi' (or 'Bye')," so that the adult also shows approval. This encourages the child and gives him a feeling of recognition and achievement. This is the positive approach.

Parents Model Behavior

"But what if he doesn't do that?"

Then the parent says it for the child so that the child feels included in the interchange. He hears his parent saying, "Good-bye, Mrs. Jones," or, "Hello, Mrs. Jones." If he has the appropriate behavior modeled often enough, he will do it on his own without prodding and embarrassment when he matures sufficiently. Children should not be *badgered* about manners. Badgering only sets up resistance or cowed capitulation. Neither of these attitudes is appropriate for healthy personality development. Nor are they appropriate for the development of good manners.

"Does this hold for thank you and please, too?"

In general the same approach holds true. The parent models the behavior. The child learns more from good models than from verbal direction and exhortation. Often, parents do not say please, thank you, or you're welcome to each other. They consider it understood, or unnecessary, between themselves; but they do expect it of the child. It is very confusing to children when adults behave in one way but expect them to behave in another. Children are very keen observers and very sensitive to nuances of expression and tone of voice.

"When can parents expect children to begin to respond to manners?"

It varies for each child, depending on his or her maturational timetable and the quantity of modeling he or she has experienced. In general, children begin to respond with social manners when they are about three; but the modeling should begin as soon as they are born. Infants recognize the difference between angry and pleasant speech. They can feel the tension of unpleasant feelings when parents speak harshly to each other. Parents who speak gently and lovingly and with consideration for each other are better models. One cannot expect children to behave any better than the example their parents set.

"Should we be teaching them table manners now? My child makes such a mess when he eats. I don't mind so much, but my husband can't stand it."

You cannot expect children of this age to be neat eaters. They are able now to drink from a cup with some dexterity, but there still are some spills. They are managing to feed themselves with a spoon and fork, although their grip may still be with the hand fisted. Some still prefer to eat with their fingers. As they grow older and become more dexterous, parents can demonstrate how to hold the spoon or fork more gracefully. They will notice how the adults eat, and their table manners will change. If parents push table manners too early, before the child is able to respond, mealtime becomes a tense, unhappy time instead of a pleasant one.

"Our child's way of eating doesn't bother us. We draw his high chair up to the table. We understand he doesn't have the ability yet to hold his spoon and fork in the right way. He sometimes drops the fork and picks the food up with his fingers. He always finishes before we do and wants to get down. This bothers us because we feel he should learn to stay until everyone is finished."

You are right in wanting him to learn to wait until everyone is finished, but that is a goal that is not appropriate *now*. At this age, children should be excused from the table because they can't sit still and wait for the rest of the family to finish. Usually, children are not able to do this until they are very much older—about seven or eight years old. Children's manners and behavior are usually better *while at the table* if they are not *forced* to stay too long. It is therefore good to excuse children from the table when they are finished. When they are about four or five, they can learn to say, "May I be excused?" or "May I leave the table?" These children are still a long way from that stage; however, some parents expect it to be happening now.

"How about their leaving the table and then coming back and seeing you eating something they want? Should you feed them what they want or tell them they have finished? Should you say, 'If you had stayed, you would have had a share, but now you can't have any'?"

That concept is really beyond the comprehension of children of this age. It is doubtful whether it is ever appropriate, because it makes mealtime a time of conflict.

"Should you then seat him back in his chair to eat again?"

That depends upon what he wants. If he wants a piece of bread or a cookie that he can hold as he stands by the table with you, it's not necessary. If it's something that he wants to eat, it would seem best to seat him again.

"Well, that approach seems reasonable, but it takes so much patience."

Learning to eat at the table is achieved by parent repetition and modeling, by positive reinforcement rather than scolding. This is not a time to be punitive. Parental modeling of appropriate eating behavior is the best teacher.

Highlights of Development— Twenty-one Months

By around twenty-one months, children's motor coordination has devel-oped to the point that they begin to squat when they play; and they can actually kick a large ball. They can also walk up a few steps alone by holding on to the rail, but may still need the support of a parent's hand in walking down stairs. When playing with blocks, most children can make a tower of five or six small blocks before it topples. They can also assemble two or three blocks horizontally as a "train" and push it in imitation of the parent's demonstration. Most children will have become more skillful with puzzles and will be able to place several pieces. At this age, children also can begin to play with a performance box, a box with openings of different shapes in the top. They should be able to place at least the corner of the square shape in the appropriate hole. If it falls in, with or without the parent's help, the child often opens the box to take out the shape, indicating an understanding of where the shape has gone.

Most children's vocabularies have doubled from the ten words that is the average vocabulary at eighteen months. Many children will have considerably larger vocabularies; and some will be combining two or three words in simple phrases. Gen-erally, the children are communicating more verbally. They can now ask for food and toys and other things they want; but they still pull the parents to indicate what they want or to show something of interest. They often echo two or more words that the parents have said.

While eating, the children can now handle a cup well, if they have been given the opportunity to use one. They are still eating most of their food with their fingers, even if they are beginning to master the use of a spoon.

Tension Situations in the Family's Day

When the children were infants, we discussed what periods of the day and what activities caused tension for you. Are these the same now, or have things changed?

Late Afternoon; Dinnertime

"For me, it is still the late afternoon after we have come indoors and I want to get dinner ready. My son is fussy and wants me to play with him. I feel I've been with him, giving him attention all day. But no, that's not enough— he still wants me to play. That makes me tense and he gets more fussy; then we are in a hassle with each other. I want Daddy to come home and find dinner ready, with us in a good mood; but that isn't the way it usually happens."

"That's the time that I'm under most pressure, but not because the baby wants to play. It's because I want to have dinner ready and the baby bathed and in bed before his father comes home. My husband wants peace and quiet when he gets home. He is in no mood to play with the baby on weeknights. He loves our son, but he can only cope in the morning, when they enjoy breakfast together, and on weekends."

"We find that time of day bad, too. But I guess we're the cause of it. We're both bushed by then from our jobs. We would love a few minutes to unwind before taking on the children. But they're clinging even before our coats are off."

It sounds as though late afternoon, just at dinnertime, remains a difficult time for most families. When the children were infants, the late afternoon was a bad time for them. They had difficulty with digestion and falling asleep. Mothers were tired and anxious to get them off to sleep, and the parents' tension made the situation worse. Now that the children are more active and you can be outside more, you may be planning too many afternoon activities. Many of the children are taking shorter naps, so they may be more *fatigued* at the end of the day. The parent's *timing* of the day's activities may be adding to the tension of the predinner period. In the afternoon, there is no need to stay out so long that the mother feels there is a rush to get dinner. It is better to come home a little earlier and not feel pressured.

The child who has been playing with other children in the park all afternoon or riding in his stroller while his mother does errands does not necessarily feel *he* has been with mother "all day." Mother may feel that way because she has been involved in the child's care. The child may want, *and need,* the mother's attention in one-to-one interaction. So if dinner has to be prepared, the child can be set up with toys or other play materials in the kitchen near mother. She can play with him at intervals, or even involve the child in helping or imitating her cooking.

For those families in which both parents work outside the home, the predinner hour can be very difficult. You have arrived home tired after a day at your jobs. Your inclination may be to put your feet up and talk to no one for twenty minutes. As you have found, this is impossible with a child. The active toddler is at your side or in your lap to *stay*. After a whole day's separation from you, the child really needs your attention and you *must* be prepared to give it. Depending on the hour the parents come home, it is generally a good idea to have the caretaker feed the child earlier. It is often hard for the child to eat in the excitement of the parents' arrival home. Whichever parent gets home first can play with the child. *Then* the other can take over for a while. After some initial attention, the child will be more willing to sit with the parents—perhaps having a snack or dessert—while they eat dinner. After dinner, the child's bedtime routines can be initiated by one parent while the other cleans up. If the parents understand the child's need for their attention, they will be less tense and can enjoy being with the child. The important thing to recognize is the child's need; that is why he or she clings and craves attention. The child is not being naughty; he is behaving appropriately for his age and demonstrating his attachment to the parents. We realize that knowing this may not take away your fatigue, but it may help you to have a more positive attitude. The more cheerfully you respond to the child's need for attention—and the more complete your attention is upon first coming home—the sooner your child will feel reassured and relaxed. As we have said, children sense your tension and become upset; so the more relaxed you can be, the happier the situation will be for all.

"I know you are right. We try to do that. Sometimes I think I just have to get some chores done before attending to my son. It's a disaster; he cries and whines and makes us both miserable! So now I just sit down and play with him. He gets happy and calmed down and will then play in the kitchen while I fix dinner."

"Now I know why we're having trouble: we try to make the baby wait until we are ready to play. It's obvious to me now that he can't wait."

That's right, he can't wait. If you understand this and willingly fill his need for your attention, you will find that a tense situation does not develop.

When Parents Are Busy with Their Own Projects

"What bothers me is not the predinner time, but when I try to do something for myself. Sometimes he won't let me alone when I am doing something such as washing my hair or reading the paper. He just keeps hanging on me and I think, 'Oh, God, when is this going to end?' Sometimes I stop what I am doing and play with him or I put the dryer on low and try to play; but

he really wants to sit on my lap and look in the mirror with me. It really throws me off."

"My worst time is when I try to polish my nails. My little girl always wants something or begins to putter with the polish. I know I should wait until she is asleep, but she seems to be playing all right alone. Then I think I'll manage to get it done, but it doesn't work."

By now, we should all be tuned in to the fact that children of this age have difficulty separating from us and want to be included in almost everything we do, especially something as interesting as using bright nail polish. It's just too tempting. If you polish one of the child's nails and let it dry, that sometimes is sufficient for her to allow you to finish your nails; she will then go off to play with something else. Sometimes the noise of hairdryers frightens children and they need reassurance that it is safe for you to use it. The best solution, if one knows the child will interfere, is to postpone that activity to a time when the child is asleep or being taken care of by the father, another relative, or baby-sitter.

When Company Comes

"In our family most of the tension comes when we have company. I feel I need to entertain them, but the baby seems to need more attention than usual at that time. Then I find I begin to get angry at the baby and that only makes things worse."

The children have to be included now, even more than when they were smaller. Having company is a social experience for the child, and it should be managed so that the child feels included. When the child enjoys the company, the guests will also find the child pleasing. We are all afraid that our child will be considered a "brat" and that our child rearing will be criticized. Parents can have the child help them offer cookies or fruit to the visitors. Naturally, the child should be allowed to have some herself. If entertaining takes place in the dining room, a high chair can be pulled up to the table so the child can participate, too. It is useful to set the example of offering something to the guests. It is a learning situation for the child. If parents regard the event in this way, as an opportunity for the child to learn about socialization, then the aspect of being on trial—as a hostess for the visitors—loses its tension-producing potential.

Shopping

"My worst moments come when I have to go to the supermarket with my son. He used to sit quietly in the cart. But now that he can walk he is not satisfied to sit in the cart; he squirms and wiggles and reaches for items on the shelf. If we pass something he recognizes or wants, he screams. If he knows the name, he shouts it out at the top of his lungs. Whether I want it or not, I have to get it and put it in the cart to quiet him down, because I hate to have everyone looking at me as though I beat him. Sometimes I'm

*told to keep him quiet, that I don't know how to raise a child, or that what
he needs is a good spanking."*

People who are not the least knowledgeable about child rearing are often
the ones who have the most advice to give. Your main concern should be
with your child. It can be a learning experience for him to go marketing
with you. He can be told you don't need a certain food when he pulls it off
the shelf. He can then be encouraged to look for something you *do* need.
Soon he will learn to spot some of the items you want, and you can give
him approval for that. Often it helps to buy something as a snack for the
child when you first enter the store. It is not a good idea, however, to take
a baby along for major weekly shopping. It takes too long. Children can't
be quiet that long, and they get restless. One should shop for fewer items
more often, rather than trying to do all the marketing at one time.

*"My son does fine while I'm shopping. He likes to name the things he knows.
He has learned, after several experiences, which things he cannot have.
But when we get in the checkout line, he gets very impatient. Then I have
to give him a cracker or a piece of orange to keep him quiet."*

You seem to be coping with your son. It might also help to have a toy or
two of his with you that he can play with while you are waiting. It is also a
good idea to shop when the stores are least crowded, so there won't be a
long wait. It takes planning to arrange things so that parents and children
do not get caught in tension-producing situations.

When Parents Are Getting Ready to Go Out

*"The thing that seems to set off problems in our house is planning to go out
at night. I try to be calm and not act impatiently, but somehow or other our
daughter senses there is something different about my attitude. Then she
won't eat her supper as she should or get ready for bed. She senses there is
something up, even before the sitter comes. She knows her and likes her,
but she also knows that the sitter comes only if I am going away."*

Children are sensitive to any tension the parent feels. Unconsciously,
perhaps, you hurry them a little or you've done your hair a little differently.
But parents do have to go out and have time for themselves. If you go out
on a regular basis, then children usually get used to it. It is a good idea to
have the sitter come at times when the mother stays home and does
something she wants to, and does not go away. Then the baby-sitter
doesn't necessarily mean separation, but can be a friend or playmate and
accepted as a good mother substitute when mother is away.

Visits to the Doctor

*"The worst situation for us is the visit to the doctor. My daughter is very
apprehensive when the doctor approaches her, because she's had to have
a few shots. When she has a shot, I get upset myself; I hold her, but I can't
watch."*

Visits to the doctor can be very traumatic. The parent must be as calm as possible and try to reassure the child. Usually doctors try to get the injections done quickly, and parents should be ready to give the child a big hug when it's over. If you bring a favorite toy along, you can then let the child play. Pediatricians' waiting rooms often have interesting toys and books. It's a good idea to stay for a little while so the child can play there and retain some pleasant memories of the visit.

Different children react differently to injections. We all know they hurt, but some children are more sensitive than others. The important thing is to be honest with the child. Never say, "This won't hurt," because when it does the child loses some trust in you. Instead, say, "This will hurt a little, but then we'll play with the doctor's train (or cars or whatever)." Stay as calm as you can. Your attitude will help to make a tense situation less tense.

General Health Measures

Parents are always concerned about their children's health. Earlier, we discussed emergencies. We would now like to talk about your children's general health care.

Infections

"I'm afraid I'm a health nut. Whenever we are invited anywhere with our son, I try to make sure that no one is going to be there who may be ill. My friends make fun of me, I know, but I am just as careful about their children. If my child isn't well, even if it's only a cold he has had for a week, I let them know so they can decide whether to come or not. Is that being too careful and ridiculous?"

If more people had that attitude, perhaps it would cut down on the number of infections children have. It's especially important to do that if you know your child is susceptible to colds, particularly if they are frequently accompanied by ear infections. One certainly doesn't want to expose a child needlessly to another child who is ill. However, one needs to try not to overdo this to the point of keeping a child isolated from fun and social experiences.

"Isn't there a time when children are most contagious? So if you avoid that period, isn't it fairly safe to mingle with the others?"

Unfortunately, during the twenty-four hours before any physical symptoms of illness appear, the child is probably the most contagious. Therefore, such contact is very difficult to prevent. If a child is doing a great deal of sneezing and coughing, however, it's well to stay at home. This is certainly true when you know that some type of respiratory or intestinal flu is going around. There is no need for a child of this age to be exposed needlessly to a bad case of flu.

■   ■

"Speaking of flu, my sister's son just had a terrible bout with intestinal flu. He vomited a lot and had diarrhea as well. Finally, he was so listless that my sister took him to the doctor. He put the child in the hospital for intravenous feeding because he was dehydrated. What should be done to prevent that?"

Dehydration is a serious problem, especially for children. When a child is vomiting a lot, you should consult your doctor about appropriate treatment. In most cases, doctors suggest that you give the child small quantities of fluid frequently rather than large amounts that may reactivate the vomiting.

"When I was little, my mother believed in exposing children to all contagious diseases. When I had the measles, she put the three younger children in the same room with me to be sure they all got it, so she wouldn't have to be bothered worrying about anyone getting measles again. Was that an unwise thing to do?"

Measles can be a serious disease. Many of the childhood diseases can have serious consequences. Not all do, but it can happen; so it is wiser to take precautions. That is why so much money and effort were invested in discovering means of producing immunizations for smallpox, diphtheria, whooping cough, polio, and measles. In fact, immunizations for all these diseases are now a routine part of your child's health care. There has been so much success with smallpox immunization in this country that vaccinations are no longer given in most instances. Although in the old days your mother's attitude was not uncommon, there is some question whether it was entirely wise to force exposure. However, the opposite is not true either: we do not have to "wrap children in cellophane" to keep them away from exposure. We believe that most children develop an increasing immunity to minor infections by the many small natural exposures that occur without anyone realizing it. We know this is an effective way to develop immunity because of the rapid spread of infection in a community that has never been exposed to a specific disease. This is perhaps the proper time to remind every parent to make certain that all immunizations are up-to-date and that you inquire at what age booster shots will be given for each disease. Even though your doctors no doubt keep a record and will remind you, it is important for parents to keep track, too, so no slipups occur.

Appetites; Eating

"I am concerned about my child's eating, in relation to her general health. I know appetites are poor in the second year compared with the first, but my little girl is approaching two and her appetite is still poor. I'm getting resigned to her small appetite, but my husband gets upset with her picky eating. That gives me the feeling that he thinks I'm a negligent mother if I don't get more food into her. Then I try to put a little pressure, but it never works."

"My mother thinks I'm awful because I won't sit for hours trying to get food into my son's mouth. I give him the things I know he likes. If he is hungry, he finger-feeds himself mostly. When he begins to throw his food, I take it away. He takes his milk from a cup and bottle. He gets his vitamins. Isn't that enough? Or should I do what my mother does: sit by the high chair and every time the child opens his mouth shove some food into it?"

Children vary a great deal in their food consumption from day to day and meal to meal. Most children of this age do not eat, or do not need to eat, the portions or the variety of food offered to them. All of us, as adults, eat more than we need, and we try to make our children do the same. When a child is well, hungry, and offered food he likes, he will eat if it is offered in a pleasant atmosphere without tension and pressure. He should have a regular place that he recognizes as the place where he eats and keeps his utensils and be allowed to feed himself as much as he wants. If children like to feed themselves, this achievement should be recognized and enhanced by offering them food of a consistency that they can manage. Other children still want to be fed. Some may request help as a device to keep the parent close. If that is their *need,* it should be met cheerfully, with gradual encouragement to feed themselves.

"Well, I just can't resist coaxing the baby to eat when there is just a mouthful or two left on the plate. Then he turns his head away and closes his mouth. That makes me so mad."

He is telling you he is through. It is much better to remove the food without comment than to put pressure on him. If it bothers you to have food left, serve a little less. Then, when he finishes, you will both be pleased. You can express it by saying, "Good, you finished your dinner." Your comment may stimulate him to finish his dinner the next time in order to evoke that kind of response from you, instead of anger. Everyone will then be happier.

One of the easiest ways to turn a child into a poor eater is to force food on him when he is not hungry.

"Well, isn't it necessary for children to eat in order to be healthy?"

If the child's appetite is so poor that you are worried about his health, then the thing to do is to consult your doctor. Let the doctor decide whether the child is malnourished and what ought to be done about it. Usually, the child is gaining weight, growing, is active and happy, and the doctor will find nothing wrong. If he finds that the child's poor appetite is due to something organic, he will prescribe the appropriate measures.

"Well, suppose there is nothing wrong, but your child is a poor eater and that upsets you?"

Children who are poor eaters are usually more stimulated to eat if their parents pay little or no attention to what they are eating. It is best to eat

■   ■

your own food and express your enjoyment of it. In this way, you give the child a good model to follow. This procedure gives mealtimes an association with pleasure rather than with an unpleasant badgering to eat. The child, if hungry, is more apt to follow that parental example than to use the mealtime as a means of showing resistance to parental pressure. That is a trap to avoid. One very good way to overcome the situation is to place food on the parents' plates but not on the child's. When the parents begin to eat, obviously enjoying the food, a child will usually notice his empty plate and ask for his food.

"When that lucky moment happens, should you then fill his plate and show how pleased you are?"

By no means. The best approach is to give the child a very small amount. If that small amount is finished and he asks for more, pleasantly offer another small amount. Don't overwhelm him with attention and praise; just recognize verbally that he finished. Say, "That's nice," or, "Good," and go on with your own meal. When this procedure is followed, most children begin to eat and enjoy meals with their parents.

"Our child never has dinner with us because his daddy comes home too late. What can I do instead?"

Since he doesn't eat with the family at dinner, it might be possible for you to sit with him at breakfast or lunch and follow the same procedure. During the weekend, when his father is home, you can try to do it. Make sure that his daddy understands the attitude you are trying to convey instead of insisting that the child eats.

"My child won't ever taste anything new. He just sticks to two cereals, chicken and lamp chops, carrots and rice, apples or bananas. He will never touch orange juice or hamburgers or string beans, many things other children like. He drinks his milk; he will take yogurt—but that's it. Is there anything we should do?"

That sounds like a well-balanced diet. Since he enjoys his food, and his doctor thinks he is progressing well, I would be content. It seems that there are some children who are not venturesome; they do very well and do not tire of the same foods. Children don't need as much variety as we think. Some children are found to be allergic to the very foods that parents are trying to persuade them to eat. The child feels innately that they are not right for him. So it is best to respect the child's food tastes; he *may* really know best.

In general, there is too much fussing and competing between parents about how much and how many things their child will eat. For small children, variety may not be the "spice of life" that it will be when they are adults; yet many of these children will grow up to be gourmet eaters, so there's no need to worry now.

■   ■

"Shouldn't children of this age be eating three meals a day?"

When you say three meals a day, you are thinking of simulating adult habits. There is some question whether even for adults three large meals a day is really healthy. More recent thinking is that five or six small meals are more readily digestible and put less strain on the digestive system and heart. There is also some question whether the custom of eating our largest meal at night is a good custom. So the answer to your question is that eating less at the designated mealtimes and having a small snack in between is more suitable for this age and, perhaps, for all of us.

Children's Need for Appropriate Approval and Disapproval

Limits and Approval

Now that the children are getting older and doing more, are you finding that you are spending more time saying "No" and disapproving of their activities rather than giving approval?

"My son is into everything. I am afraid most of our comments are 'No' and 'Stop that'—often for his own or others' safety."

It is very important, of course, to disapprove of the activities that are harmful to the child or another person. The child needs to learn that certain activities are dangerous, and the parents are obligated to teach this. In general, however, parents are often more inclined to dramatize their disapproval than to emphasize their approval. They just accept what the child does that is right, without letting the child know of their approval. The child needs to get a clear message of both what is approved and what is not approved. Unfortunately, many parents are inconsistent about this. One day a parent may feel fine and therefore is not bothered by a particular activity such as the child's loud motor noise when rolling a car along the floor. On another day the mother is under some stress and the sound bothers her, so she scolds the child for making the same sound. The child's activity is actually appropriate, but it just doesn't suit the mother that day.

"Well, isn't it normal for parents to be able to cope one day and not be so in control another day?"

It seems to be all too common, but it gives mixed messages to the child. The inconsistency confuses him. He doesn't understand that he is being restricted because of the parent's *mood*—that it is only all right to make that sound when his parent is in a good mood. We cannot expect a child of this age to make that distinction. If such changes in parental mood are occasional and the parent is usually consistent, then a few instances of inconsistency won't create problems. If the usual situation is one of such inconsistency, then problems are created. The child becomes either inhibited and afraid of the parent's changes of mood or confused and irritable, because he doesn't know what to do. He becomes a "spoiled" child who acts like a "brat" or an ingratiating child who tries always to please. None of these responses is desirable, because it does not lead to healthy personality development and good coping mechanisms in the child.

"Isn't it putting an awful lot of responsibility on the parents to expect them to be consistent all of the time?"

Of course it is. Being a parent is a big responsibility. Consistency is very difficult to accomplish in any field, but it is especially important in the rearing of children. No one is perfect; we cannot expect parents to be consistent all the time. But we should try to be as consistent as possible with our approval and disapproval because of its importance in the child's personality development. It is from the consistent recognition of what the child does right and consistent limitation of disapproved activities that the child learns the cultural norms of her family and the society in which she is growing up. This learning by outside control is the precursor to the conscience, or control from within (self-control).

Appropriate Approval Is Not Spoiling

"But doesn't it spoil children to always show approval?"

When we are very young, we need to learn what is right and what is not right. We can learn this only if our parents and other caretakers label for us what is approved and what is not. This recognition of appropriate behavior and limitation of inappropriate behavior has to be repeated until the child learns which is which. Since human beings seem to thrive on approval (we all prefer that to disapproval), it is better to emphasize approval. Then the child will get a sense of positive recognition and will strive for that. Such recognition also develops a healthy feeling of self-worth and self-confidence.

"It seems to me that children don't really care whether you approve of them or not, as long as they get your attention. Don't children act up just for attention? That's what my mother says."

Children do want recognition. They can't stand to feel excluded. They will demand attention to feel included. If their appropriate behavior gets no response, children may then do something "naughty" to get attention. When a child needs to do something that's disapproved in order to get attention, a very negative cycle of parent-child relations, which we call the "angry alliance," is set up. The responses of parent and child to each other become more and more negative. To get satisfaction and pleasure this way also leads to what has been termed masochism, or getting pleasure from pain. This is not a positive personality pattern. So when people say, "He's only trying to get your attention," indicating that the child should be ignored, they do not understand the real significance of the situation. They do not understand that the child needs *appropriate* attention.

"Won't paying attention to them all the time make it difficult later on? People outside the family won't pay that much attention. I don't want my child to grow up always seeking attention."

Most of us *are* annoyed by attention seekers. We must understand how people get that way in order to avoid it in our children. Children need recognition and attention. If they receive appropriate attention *now*, they begin to develop a sense of self-worth and self-confidence. If they are denied appropriate attention now, when they need it, they continue to seek it, sometimes in very unsubtle and annoying ways, as adults.

Timetable for Learning to Accept Limits

"It seems that we are expecting too much from them. We want them to accept limitations easily. How much time does it take? When should we be expecting some response to our limit setting and approval?"

Learning to accept limitations varies with each child. For some it comes earlier; for others, it may take until they are much older. By three years of age most children understand the common limitations of daily life, but parents want it right away. We remember our parents' demands, and our friends and neighbors keep telling us how the children should behave. That is why we expect so much from our children.

"Just how much is reasonable for us to expect at this age? For instance, my husband has a very complicated and expensive stereo set in the den, where our son plays most of the time. It's a big temptation for him to touch it. That's the one 'No' that he can't seem to grasp. He goes up to it and looks at me, but still fiddles with it. Am I expecting too much from him to leave it alone?"

At this age, he recognizes that the stereo is "forbidden territory." He looks back to see if you will take him away or keep him from touching it. He does not yet have the control to leave it alone himself. To develop that self-control may take him another six months or a year. So you have to assist him by giving him a substitute activity in which he can discharge the need to turn knobs on and off. His own toy record player or a car that winds may be a successful substitute. He may protest, but that's healthy and normal. Finally, he will accept the limitation. When he does, you must show recognition and approval.

"Before, you mentioned the stages that children go through as they learn self-control. Could you just go over it again?"

■   ■

At first, when they are between eight and twelve months old and you say "No," they stop whatever they are doing momentarily. That gives the parent time to go to them, move them away, and give them something else to do. During the next stage, which may last from twelve months to about two and a half years, they know in advance what is a no-no but they look back for help in stopping. Next, they may go up to a forbidden object, say "No" to themselves, but still touch the object unless they have parental help. Around three years of age, many are able to say "No" to themselves and not touch the forbidden object—unless it is exceedingly tempting. Some children achieve this level even later. Each child has a different maturational timetable for this, too.

Discipline Versus Punishment

We were talking earlier about getting a child to respond to limitations, about the importance of appropriate approval as well as disapproval. Are you finding that you are saying "No" less and showing more approval? Do some of you feel that you need to use some physical reinforcement to be more effective?

"I know from my experience with my son that by limiting him consistently he doesn't do the things I minded so much in the park, such as taking toys away from other children. I give back the other child's toy, and he now accepts his own. It is getting much easier. I see other mothers in the same situation hit their children. They think I'm nuts because I don't."

There are many parents, perhaps most, who were brought up that way. That is their image of appropriate discipline to prevent children from becoming "brats." They feel that they must control the child, or the child will control them. They follow the model set by their own parents.

"Well, what harm will it do? They seem like nice people, and they seem to get results."

"I don't think they get results. I have a neighbor who is always slapping her child. Each day she seems to hit harder, but he still does things to upset her. As a matter of fact, I think he is the kind of child you mean when you say a child is a brat."

Slapping

Slapping or spanking may relieve the parent's anger, but it generally does not evoke the kind of response from the child that the parent desires. Most children who are hit do not become sweet and obedient; they become sullen or angry or frightened. When they sulk, hit back, or cry, the parents become even more angry. The next time, the parent uses a little more force—in some instances, the parent may lose control and become abusive. That is one of the dangers of getting this cycle going.

■   ■

"The baby whom I bring to the center is my second child. I know better now how to cope with him. My daughter is four years older, and I have to admit that I more than scolded her. I am sure that my treatment of her made her afraid of me. When I call her name, she seems to cringe, as though she expects to be hurt. Her expression always seemed to be sullen and sad. Nothing seemed to please her. Even in nursery school, the teachers talked to me about it. Now I understand how I should treat her. We are beginning to get better results—sometimes a smile, but there is still a long way to go. I can't emphasize enough what a difference it makes to treat children with patience and understanding, instead of hitting all the time."

Here we have a real-life example of what hitting can do in personality development. You have seen one type of outcome: the sullen and depressed child.

"That was the outcome with one child. Isn't it possible that it would not affect all children in the same way? Maybe that is just the way her daughter was born to be?"

It is true that each child has a different endowment at birth, so not all would respond in the same way to the same treatment. We don't know the endowment of each child, but we do know that children are very responsive to the care they receive. If they are given consistent, patient, loving care, children have a better chance to develop into caring adults and to develop their maximum potential than if they are beaten. It has been well documented that children brought up without this kind of caring relationship cannot form the caring relations with others that lead to healthy personality development. Without caring for others, these children become the delinquent, socially destructive, addicted, conscienceless population that is now victimizing our society—but they themselves were victims of neglect and/or abuse.

"Is that the only outcome we can expect? Are there no other consequences?"

Yes, there are some who, instead of becoming angry, sullen, depressed, or actually destructive, become so inhibited that they lose all ambition and drive to accomplish, even though there is nothing wrong with their intellectual endowment. Their talents are wasted. Because they have always met with negative response and punishment, they give up and don't try. They have never tasted the joy of approval. We have all seen adults like that. They seem to be intelligent and yet they never seem to achieve anything. They never seem to find the thing they want to do. This is not the outcome we want for our children, either.

"This all sounds so scary. It makes being a parent such a responsibility. When I've seen my son about to do something at the other end of the room, I call to him to stop. When he doesn't, then I become angry and holler very loud. That usually stops him, but I feel myself getting very angry when he repeats the same thing another time. My impulse is to grab him and hit

him—not hard, but just so he will know I mean business and remember. That's what my mother tells me to do. She thinks I'm spoiling him unless I hit him."

Certainly, being a parent is a great responsibility, one of the most important responsibilities of life. No one claims that carrying out our responsibilities is easy; but when one is effective in child rearing, there is no greater reward.

One of you spoke about the inclination to hit your child if he didn't remember to respond appropriately the second time. You are following the model of the way your parents brought you up, thinking that it is the right way. Parents often think slapping or spanking will hasten the child's appreciation of what is right and wrong. We forget that the child's immature nervous system does not respond and store messages with the efficiency of the adult's. There is, instead, a long lag before a message to stop gets to the appropriate centers of control in the child's brain and is translated into action. Slapping the child actually jams the overloaded nervous system and often makes it harder for him to respond promptly and appropriately. In addition, it gives the child a negative model of behavior. At some later time, the child will try to slap the parent or another child.

"If a child slaps you, shouldn't you slap him back to teach him a lesson?"

If you do that, you will be teaching the child to *slap* rather than *not to slap,* because you are providing and reinforcing a behavior model. Also, slapping the child back will only aggravate an already tense situation and may seriously damage the parent-child relationship.

Spanking

While we are talking about slapping, we might as well talk about spanking. Spanking a child to "teach him a lesson" does indeed teach a lesson: that when one is *bigger* and *more powerful,* one can hit another person and get away with it. We have seen in our groups here that the children who were spanked tend to hit others to settle their differences. Those who have been restrained verbally in a way appropriate to their age tend to settle their differences verbally.

We are not saying that an occasional slap will create a violent or overly submissive child. None of us is perfect, and there are times when babies and children can be exceedingly trying, usually just at the times when we as adults are tired or upset ourselves. If we realize the bad effect physical punishment can have, however, we can try to control our own actions. All of us have to learn how to handle and dispel our own anger. No one should feel guilty about having angry feelings. They are a natural part of our human makeup, but we all need to help each other learn how to release our angry feelings appropriately. (See pages 157–60 for discussion on how to handle anger.)

■   ■

"That explanation makes a lot of sense. Perhaps, if everyone used this approach, there'd be less violence."

We believe that it could make a big difference. There is another point that needs clarification. One of you said you *called* across the room to get your child to stop doing something. You expect to control your child's activity from a distance. That does not work with children of this age. Often they are so absorbed that they do not hear, or do not understand, your prohibition. The parent must go to the child as quickly as possible and show disapproval of what he is doing, immediately giving him a substitute activity. Then overtly show your approval and pleasure about the new activity. This is how the child learns to use an approved outlet for his impulse. He learns what he *can* do instead of being hit to a standstill, to put it a little harshly.

All parents get tired and out of sorts at times and occasionally use measures they don't approve of themselves. At these times, parents feel pushed too far. An occasional explosion may upset a child temporarily, but the hurt can be mended by talking about it and finding something pleasant to do together. What we are concerned about is using physical punishment as the usual form of discipline, so that it becomes the pattern of life for that child.

"Does a child nearly two years old understand when we continue to be angry long after the event? A friend of mine does that. If her child misbehaves, she will not smile at him or answer except in an angry tone for hours after the episode is over."

A child of this age can't understand the reason for the continued anger after the episode is over. He can't remember the episode and sometimes he doesn't fully understand the reasons for the parent's anger in the first place. That is why it is so important to show disapproval *at the time,* substitute another activity, and show approval for it, repeating the same procedure each time that behavior occurs until the child learns.

Consistency of Limits

"What happens if parents do things in different ways? What bothers me may not bother my husband, so I seem to be the strict one and he comes out looking like the lenient one."

For each child the number of repetitions needed to learn about limits differs. Each parent has to get to know and understand his or her child, and both parents need to apply the same limits for the same behavior. If one is lenient and the other strict, that confuses the child. The results may be a whining, irritable child, the kind that is referred to as a "spoiled child" or a "manipulative child." This child, knowing the parents have differing ways of handling a situation, will try out each one to get something that he wants. But he will not feel secure or happy in that situation, and neither will the parents.

■   ■

"Isn't agreement between parents very hard to achieve?"

It is indeed difficult for parents to agree all the time and to be consistent, but this is one of the learning experiences of parenthood. Parents must be able to communicate with each other and agree on their procedures. They should try not to correct each other in front of the child. This, too, leads to confusion and disparagement of one of the parents, which also upsets the child.

Family Rivalries: Everyone's Need for Attention

Rivalries within the family can cause tension and interfere with the family's functioning in a harmonious and satisfying way. There can be all kinds of rivalries in any one family. We have talked about the rivalry of children with siblings and other children for parental attention and toys. Some of you may have similar feelings regarding the way others in the family relate to the child or to you.

Rivalries with Grandparents

"I suppose it is childish of me, but ever since the baby came it has seemed to me that my parents are more concerned about my baby than about me. It seems as though they've sort of forgotten about me. They always seem to be all eyes for the baby. Of course, I'm pleased that they care so much, but I guess I still want to be their child too—and I'm kind of jealous of my own child."

It is good that you can recognize that feeling. Perhaps it indicates some of your unresolved needs that you could not discuss objectively with your family if you found the suitable moment. If that is not possible, and if you cannot feel that the attention paid to your child is in a way attention to you, perhaps discussing it here will help.

"It's funny you should say that. My parents give me the feeling that I'm still a child and couldn't know how to take care of the baby. When they come, they compete with me in taking care of the baby. My mother, especially, tries to get the baby to enjoy the way she plays with him and acts as though I just don't throw the ball the right way to him or read the stories with the right expression."

"I think my husband's parents do a little of that, too. But what both my husband and I mind most is that when we go to their house, they won't allow us to set limits. They always say, 'Another cookie won't hurt,' or 'Let him stay up a little longer'—things like that. Then when we take him home, he acts as though we are cruel parents and only his grandparents treat him right. Aren't they spoiling him?"

It seems that grandparents do cause feelings of inadequacy or rivalry in different ways. It seems that you are having feelings about these situations

■   ■

that may be interfering in your relations with them and your child. It is good that you can talk about it. Of course, most grandparents show a lot of concern about their grandchildren, sometimes to the exclusion of their own children. They also have a great deal of difficulty in relinquishing their parenting roles and continue to treat you as children. They show you how to raise your children, just as they showed you what to do when you were little. It is well to remember that many grandparents still see their children as children and have a hard time accepting that they are grown up and now competent to be parents themselves. Grandparents often indulge their grandchildren by giving them extra treats. Children thrive on special treatment like that occasionally. It doesn't really hurt them if it is an occasional treat and not a daily undermining of parental discipline. In a day or two, they "recover" from a visit with grandparents. They eventually get to know that there are some extra treats at grandma's and what is expected in their own home, if the pattern is followed consistently. We must recognize that in some families it is just the opposite: the grandparents are more severe disciplinarians and consider the parents too lenient. So one has to cope with each situation and try to establish some consistency for the child.

Rivalries Between Parents

"I have a feeling of need for attention, or recognition, not so much from my parents or in-laws, but from my husband. Ever since the baby came— and he is now almost two—my husband's main concern has been our son. If our son hasn't run to greet him the minute he opens the door at night, he gets sort of tense and wants to know where he is. When he sees the baby, he sweeps him up in his arms and they cuddle. I'm lucky if he turns to me and says hello."

Many parents have these feelings. Often a parent will wish for recognition but suffer in silence until the issue is magnified out of proportion. It is common for a new baby to take up the interest of the father. However, the mother must not shrink back into the kitchen and just let it go on. She must take some initiative and be at the door to greet her husband and try to reinstate his attention and affection on a new level. She can at least say, "Now it's my turn. I'm glad you're home," after the baby has been greeted. That's usually all it takes in a normal situation.

"But it's not the same as before. The minute my husband puts his arm around me, the baby tries to butt in. So we include him, too."

It is normal for the child to want to be included, and that should happen. However, Daddy can say, "First, I'll kiss you, then Mommy, then we'll all have a hug," or something to that effect.

"You know, I've been listening to all this and thinking about our situation. I'd guess that if my husband were here, he would say that in our family it's

just the opposite. I think he feels that I have left him out and that all I seem to be concerned about is the baby. At first, he seemed involved, too; but now he just acts as though the baby is mine, and he has little to do with him unless the baby actively involves him in something. Then my husband seems pleased and gets involved."

You are probably right: your husband is feeling left out and hasn't been able to discuss it with you. It is not an unusual situation. If the wife recognizes this feeling, it can usually be corrected. Some women need to be reminded that their husbands need attention, too. It is best when parents can enjoy the baby together. When one parent feels left out and this feeling is overlooked, the situation can lead to serious consequences, even to the dissolution of a marriage. This result can usually be prevented by dealing with the problem appropriately. In any situation, it is important to be aware of the other's feelings and try to understand how both parents and children are affected and feel about what is happening in their lives.

Rivalries with Caretakers

"One problem that hasn't been mentioned yet is the problem of a working mother who comes home and finds her child so involved with the care-taker—in my case, it's her grandmother—that I feel a little jealous and don't seem to be able to cope with it. If it were a maid, I could change maids and break up this love affair; but it's my mother, and I need her help."

One is very fortunate when one's mother can take care of the child. It is important for the child to establish an involved, close relationship with one substitute caretaker—in this case, the grandmother. However, that doesn't mean the mother needs to be left out. She must establish her own special role with her child. When she comes home, the mother should not try to take over what the grandmother does, but do something different with the child. She should have special games that only she plays with the child.

Even if one is not lucky enough to have a grandparent act as the substitute caretaker, an employed person can establish a warm relation with the child. Such a person is to be cherished, because she is fulfilling a very important role in helping the child to form a stable, trusting relationship with another. This sense of trust will help the child in adult life to form good relationships with his own family. Constantly shifting caretakers is detrimental to the child, because these interrupted relationships interfere with the process of forming binding relations. This insecurity puts an even greater burden on the working parent than the rivalry that might result if the caretaker forms a close bond with the child.

"I think I have a different kind of rivalry problem: it is with my husband and the way he plays with our son. I'm with him all day, giving my all. The minute my son hears his father's key in the door, he drops me like a hot potato and I feel rejected. Is there something wrong with me?"

■   ■

The situation you describe is quite common. The interpretation of many mothers is that the child prefers the father. The child may prefer the father *at that moment* because he is a new face at the end of the day. The child looks forward to the way he plays with him. This attitude is desirable, because most children in our society see their fathers so little. It does not mean the child prefers father over mother. *Parents are partners.* Each has an important place in the child's life. In each family, parents fulfill their roles according to their own personalities and the family's situation and needs. In no two families will these roles be alike, nor should they be.

Spoiling Versus Gratification

The older the children get, the more verbal and definite they become in expressing their desires. Parents are generally pleased with this increase in the children's ability to express themselves. The children are now easier to understand; there is less guesswork. What they need, want, or would like to do are often things that parents can easily satisfy. At times, however, children's requests cannot or should not be gratified. Parents often have a great deal of difficulty about responding to their child's requests. Do you feel that you are "spoiling" if you acquiesce more often than you refuse?

"That's one of the main things my husband and I argue about. He feels that I am too lenient. I say 'Yes' to as many things as I feel are right. My husband thinks that is spoiling. He is strict and has a tendency to say 'No.' If I'm sorting the laundry and my son comes up to me and wants to play ball with me, I'll stop for a minute and play with him. If he goes over to my husband while he is reading the paper or watching a ball game, he'll say, 'No, not now. I'm busy'—and that's that. My husband says I spoil him and am getting him to expect that his every wish will be gratified."

"In our house, it is just the opposite: I'm considered the strict one. I'm the one who says to my son, 'No climbing on the sofa,' because I'm afraid he will fall. My husband comes home from work and says, 'Ah, let him be. I'm here.' My husband just doesn't understand that when he's not there and I'm out of the room, the baby may climb and fall. The baby doesn't understand it's okay to climb only if Daddy is there. But my husband thinks I'm inhibiting him by not letting him climb."

It is evident that there is a great deal of confusion about gratification and spoiling. It seems to cause problems between parents and between generations in many families. Probably the first thing that needs to be taken into account is the child's age and stage of development. Right now, we are discussing children who are not yet two years old. What are their needs? What is their understanding and ability to delay gratification?

At this stage, children should be emerging from the stage when they needed instant gratification of physical needs, such as hunger, to a period in which they are learning to delay gratification for longer periods. Parents should be trying to help the child make this transition. It has to be done in small steps. The mother who understands her child's developing capacity to wait can help the child to delay gratification.

In the case of the child who interrupted his mother to play for a moment, the mother understood the child's need to have some involvement with her. So the mother stopped and responded to his need before going on with her chore. The father, in that case, didn't recognize the legitimate need of a child of this age to feel involved with, and not excluded by, the parent. The mother wasn't spoiling the child; she was being *appropriately* responsive.

In the case of the climber, the mother has a legitimate fear of the child's falling, but she also knows her husband's attitude. These parents should calmly discuss their different opinions. They must come to an agreement either that daddy will uphold the mother's limits or that the child will learn that climbing is something he can do *only* when daddy is there. In fact, it may become an activity that he looks forward to sharing with his father. These children are getting old enough to associate certain activities with each parent. From early infancy, they have been experiencing the differences in the way each parent held them, talked to them, fed them, comforted them, and played with them. At this age, climbing and jumping are motor activities that most children are beginning to practice. The attitudes exhibited by the mother and father, in this case, are both right. These activities should be encouraged and not inhibited; but they must be safely channeled and monitored by the parents.

What Is a "Spoiled" Child?

"I now have a clearer understanding of what is meant by age-appropriate gratification. But what is spoiling?"

A "spoiled child" is one whose needs have not been appropriately met or one whose needs have been inconsistently met. One day the parent will play; the next day, in a similar situation, the parent will refuse. One day, jumping and climbing will be allowed; the next day these activities will be inhibited. Sometimes snacks are allowed before a meal; on another day they are not. This inconsistency confuses the child, because he doesn't know where he stands. He can't learn whether his requests or activities will result in approval or disapproval. This insecurity regarding the parents' responses often causes the child to become cranky and whiny. After much fussing the child may get what he wants. Usually he can't recognize that he has been gratified because such "gratification" often comes from frustrated parents in a grudging way. This child has not had the experience of consistent, appropriate gratification and limitation. When parents learn how to handle these situations consistently, the child will begin to respond better and the whole family atmosphere will be considerably more pleasant and rewarding.

"What I refer to as spoiling is giving a child everything he asks for. That's what happens when he goes to Grandmother's house: she lets him have as many cookies as he wants and he does not have to nap if he doesn't want to. When he comes home, I have to spend several days getting him back into his regular routine."

An occasional break in a child's routine doesn't spoil him. He soon gets back to the routine of the standards set at home. If he visits Grandma's home on a regular basis, he will learn what is appropriate behavior there and what is expected at home. Children can learn that different people expect different things—that prepares them, in fact, for the world outside the family. The way parents help children to cope with these differences is by their own consistent support, by their patient teaching of the limits. This support gives the child the sense of security and self-confidence that will enable him or her to cope with the "hard world" outside the family.

Development of Self-confidence

"I'm glad you mention that. My husband thinks that we must treat our son tough because it's a tough world, especially for a Hispanic child. You are saying that it is important for the family to be supportive, not tough, so that the child develops self-confidence."

That's right. The world is tough in different ways for most children. We want our children to become competent adults so they can cope with the different adversities that they encounter in life. Children learn to cope best when they are helped to develop self-confidence. Parents teach this not by being tough and threatening, but by satisfying their reasonable needs and desires, recognizing their achievements, and setting consistent limits. Treating them harshly to toughen them will not enhance their ability to cope and will set the example for hostile, aggressive relations with others.

Children Need Attention—Not Gifts

"What about the child whose parents give her every toy or game she wants, plus more? She has so much that she doesn't play with any of it. She just flits from one thing to another, acts bored, and doesn't know what to do."

Material overindulgence often occurs in families in which parents have little time for children and try to make up by buying them material satisfaction. What children *really need* is more communication with the parents and fewer toys. The child you speak of needs *attention* from her parents; instead, she gets toys.

Legacies from Parents' Own Upbringing

"That is one extreme. My experience was the opposite. I was brought up in a household where we did not dare ask for anything. We had to wait until it was offered. My parents were exceedingly strict with all four of us. I think that because of that my tendency is to be very lenient. My husband accuses

■   ■

me of spoiling. I think he is too strict. So we often disagree about giving in to our son."

In some instances, we unconsciously follow the example of our parents; in other cases, we consciously avoid repeating their pattern. There's quite a difference between gratifying a child's every wish and responding positively when it is appropriate. We should make a conscious effort to respond appropriately to each child instead of responding as though we are still trying to correct our parents' treatment of *us*.

"I think I've fallen into that trap, but in a somewhat different way. I think I am stricter with my child than I would be if I didn't feel that I had to show my mother, who is a frequent visitor, that I'm in control. I guess I am still reacting to my feelings about my mother. She was very strict; in order to get praise from her, I had to be a perfect child."

It sounds as though you are still trying to get your mother's approval by acting toward your child as you believe she would consider right. This is a very common situation. Sometimes, when we feel we were unable as children to satisfy our parents, we try as adults to satisfy them by treating our children as they treated us—even though it may not be the best way and will only perpetuate feelings of inadequacy.

In general, we do not have to worry about spoiling our children by fulfilling their dependency needs. They are not yet two years old. By our consistent and appropriate satisfying of those needs and our consistent limitations when they are necessary, our children will develop a sense of trust in us and a sense of security in themselves that will help them become competent, likable children, and not "spoiled brats."

Appropriate Games and Toys; TV

Are you beginning to find that your children are getting bored with their toys and are no longer interested in the games that you have been playing together? Are you finding new things to do with them?

"I am so glad that we are going to talk about this. I have completely run out of ideas. My son is happy outside where he can run around, but on a rainy day we both go crazy indoors."

"We were having the same problem. Then a week ago, my mother arrived with some rubber figures of animals and people she bought at Childcraft. My daughter loves them. She plays by herself or with us."

"I was having a problem with my son banging on the furniture with his blocks, so I got one of those benches with pegs you pound with a hammer. He will spend about ten minutes at a time banging on that. He'll probably get bored soon, he uses it so much; but it's just perfect right now."

■   ■

New Activities and Toys

The children are ready now for new activities and toys. Both of the suggestions that have just been made are good ones. The rubber figures will be a source of entertainment and learning for several years because the child will play more and more sophisticated, imaginary games with them—imitating family situations or situations that take place in school. There are also sets of both farm and zoo animals. Playing with them can be enhanced by using plain cardboard blocks that children can build into houses for themselves or for their toys. Children may also like nesting boxes that they can begin to fit inside one another or stack up like towers. They will soon be ready for the beginning set of (large) Lego pieces as well as jumbo beads for threading and stringing and a shoelacing toy. A performance (shape-sorting) box with pieces of different sizes and shapes is an appropriate toy for this age. There are many variations of this toy, including a postbox and a lockbox. Other good toys are puzzles with a limited number of pieces. Puzzles that have little knobs on the pieces are easier for children of this age to manipulate.

"All these toys sound great, but they are all so expensive. Aren't there some things one can make at home?"

There are a number of household items that can double as children's toys and that often amuse children more than expensive toys. Most children enjoy playing with plastic, wood, and metal spoons and pots and pans with lids. An old purse filled with odds and ends such as combs, old compacts, necklaces, and bracelets will often entertain a child for hours. Plastic jars with screw tops are also good for play and for increasing finger coordination. From this age on, children will enjoy cardboard boxes of all sizes. Large boxes can become houses that they play in; smaller ones can become trains and cars that can be set up in a row. Instead of buying pull toys, you can make your own from a shoe box and string.

All children love playing with water. While you are in the kitchen, you can fill the sink, cover your child's clothes with a plastic apron, and let her play with kitchen utensils such as a funnel, measuring cups, muffin tins, empty plastic squeeze bottles, sponges, or plastic containers. The household items that make interesting playthings are endless in number, once you start looking around you; and this manipulation of objects is a great learning experience for your child.

"One rainy day I amused my son with an empty egg carton. He enjoyed putting small objects such as beads and spools of thread into the compartments. When there was something in every one, he closed the lid. Then he opened it and took them all out."

"Another toy that is not expensive and that my daughter loves is a plastic telephone. When I am on the phone, she gets hers. She doesn't talk yet, but she still likes to copy me."

■   ■

Yes, a plastic telephone is a very good toy, not only to keep the child amused while you are on the phone but to encourage verbal communication. You can begin to have conversations with her as she holds her toy phone.

"Another good toy is the Busy Box with gears, bells, and bolts to screw. Our son will accept that as a substitute when we take him away from the stereo."

"What about music? Can't we begin doing musical activities with the children now?"

There are a number of good children's records of nursery rhymes and songs. Children will begin to sing along with the record or with the parent's singing. Children enjoy parents' singing, no matter how off-key. You can get some bells for the child's wrists, so that she can make music herself while she listens. Some children like beating on a drum; drums can be made from a coffee can or oatmeal carton. Children also like to bang two metal pot covers together as they listen to music or dance or march around. Some children may also be interested in playing with a xylophone.

Art Activities

"Can they do some painting?"

It may be a little early for some children to handle paints and a paintbrush, but finger painting is appropriate at this age. It is particularly fun for the child when the parent joins in. A less messy art form is drawing with crayons. Many parents don't let their children draw with crayons because they are fearful for their walls or furniture, but these children should be having the experience of drawing *with parental supervision.* Soon the children will be ready to use "play dough," which can easily be made at home. (The recipe is: 3 parts flour, 1 part salt, and 1 part water. Food coloring can be added to make different colors.) Homemade play dough can be kept about ten days in an airtight bag in the refrigerator. Finished products can be dried in the oven or simply out in the air. The children will enjoy creating varieties of lumps. Don't expect fine art at this age!

Outdoor Activities

"We're okay indoors, but in the park my child is running, jumping, and climbing so much now, it scares me."

Children of this age are much more physically active. They are beginning to climb more, and the playground slide suddenly looks very high when one's small child is heading to the top. Each parent must know her own child's capabilities and be available for appropriate assistance without inhibiting the child's motor development and sense of independence. All toddlers need to be held as they slide down until they have learned to slow themselves down by pushing their feet against the sides of the slides. Some children will fearlessly climb up; their parents need to be close by to avert accidents. Children's accomplishments should be acknowledged by the parents; the sense of physical mastery is important to the child's self-confidence and self-esteem.

"Are there other physical activities that we could be encouraging now?"

Some of the children may be ready for a riding toy that they can propel with their feet on the ground. Children can be encouraged to gain motor control by walking backward and standing on one foot. They enjoy copying how animals walk or hop or jump. This can be made into a game that other mothers and children can join in.

Television

"What about TV? The child of one of our friends loves watching 'Sesame Street,' and I am tempted to get that hour of peace and quiet; but I am afraid TV will become a habit. Is that true?"

There have been many studies and surveys on how much television children watch. We have learned that many children spend more time watching television than going to school and that most watch three to four hours a day. So the answer to your question is, "Yes, TV can become a habit." Television provides easy entertainment; the child (or adult) can sit passively without making the effort that goes into reading a book. At this age, children should spend time being read to and exposed to appropriate books. Many educators think that the decline in national reading scores is the result of too much television and too little reading. It is therefore recommended that the introduction of television be delayed for as long as possible. There are really very few programs that are appropriate for two-year-olds. "Sesame Street," for example, was designed for four-year-olds as a substitute for nursery or preschool experience. Following the production techniques of advertising, many children's shows use fast-paced, jam-packed formats. Children are therefore bombarded with attention-getting scenes and visual effects. It is true that children can recite letters and numbers earlier after viewing "Sesame Street," but whether this helps them to learn concepts is still in question. Using television as an educational tool is an important idea. There have been many articles written on the merits and disadvantages of "Sesame Street," and we encourage parents to read them. We are inclined to think that it is too stimulating, fast-paced, and skills-oriented for children of this age.

In general, we strongly recommend *very limited* viewing for *all* children, both in time spent and programs watched. Television should not be used to keep the child quiet while the parent does chores. Often the quieter the child, the better the parent likes it. But the electronic companion is not a substitute for human contact and stimulation. If the child is exposed to TV for too long, he or she is deprived of the parent's stimulation of speech, touch, and involvement. If the parent leaves the child alone by the TV, she may be away too long. When she returns, she finds that the pleasant, harmless program has ended and the child is watching something frightening, unpleasant, or violent. As yet, there have been no conclusive studies of the effects of violent programs on children, but violent programs clearly are bad models for life and seem to foster aggressive behavior in *some* children. In addition to limiting the time, therefore, we advise you to monitor carefully the kind of shows being watched by your children. To do this effectively, you should watch with your child and make sure that both the overt and the hidden messages of the program are acceptable to you. In addition to violence, there are many stereotypical portrayals of minorities, women, and the elderly that can contribute to children's prejudices. The commercials on children's programs can foster desires for products such as sugar-coated cereals, which are unhealthy, or for expensive, short-lived toys. If parents watch television with their children and discuss the programs with them, it can be a valuable learning experience.

Cognitive Development: Parents as Teachers

Now that the children are getting to be more verbal, how do you view your role as a parent?

"We are finally comfortable with the mechanics of child care and we are able to concentrate on the fun of playing with our daughter. Now that she is talking, I am wondering when we should teach her the alphabet. I have friends who are doing that."

Teaching the alphabet may be possible, but teaching a song or a rhyme is more appropriate now.

"My surprise at the beginning was how little the baby could do and how much care she needed. She was totally helpless. Now I'm constantly amazed at how much she can do on her own."

"My husband and I experienced some of these same feelings. It wasn't till we came here that we began to recognize that playing with the baby in the right way could help her development. That's when we began to feel a new kind of importance in her life and a new kind of involvement with her."

Development of Trust and Attachment

You all seem to be well aware of your roles as caretakers. Certainly, that is a primary element in parenting. However, while you were responding to the baby's needs, you were also teaching the baby that you were reliable and that you could be trusted. In addition to being caretakers, therefore, you are the *first* teachers. As the children developed basic trust in you and the world, they became attached to you. That primary feeling of attachment and affection is one of the most important "lessons" to be learned in life. Learning to relate to the parent is the forerunner of being able to be involved with and relate to others: teachers, friends, and, later in life, associates, spouses, and their own children. This ability is also the groundwork that is needed for cognitive development and a drive for learning. It is becoming increasingly recognized that the lack of this early affectional relationship may account for the difficulty many children have in school and for the ineffectiveness of much of the remedial efforts to help them.

"That was a good period for us when we understood about establishing trust and affection. After he learned to walk and get about, it was difficult— he got into everything. It seemed we were always running after him, trying to show him the right way to use things."

Understanding of Environment

That is a large part of the parent's role in the child's early years. The child needs to learn how to manipulate toys and objects around the house: how to open and close doors without getting fingers caught in them, how to open and close boxes and jars, how to eat, how to dress. Parents are teaching all the time, consciously or unconsciously. Each new experience adds to the child's understanding of the world and to his cognitive development.

"I know that I should be looking at myself as a teacher. But when I'm in a hurry and I have to stop him repeatedly for doing something he is not supposed to, I get angry."

Of course, there are moments of anger when something is boiling over on the stove or the telephone is ringing. As the mother tries to attend to these, she notices the child doing something he or she should not be doing. She gets irritated at the child—that will certainly happen occasionally. In general, when one becomes a parent, new priorities should be set. Adaptations have to be made so that the first priority is attention to the child's needs; the household chores then come second. Children absorb most of the information about their lives by being around the parents, watching them, and participating in simple things such as setting a table or putting all the teaspoons into their slot in a drawer. Learning where everything belongs and what objects are for is part of cognitive development. Parents often take this aspect of learning for granted. Parents need to discuss what they are doing and allow the child to make comments as well. There is nothing so satisfying to parents as a verbal child. Learning how a child interprets events is a fascinating and enlightening aspect of child rearing.

"Well, does that mean you have to speak almost every minute with the child? I've been looking forward to his playing by himself so I'd have more time for myself."

■   ■

One does not have to spend every minute playing or talking with a child. But one has to be available to help fix a broken toy, or point out an alternate way if a toy is too wide to go through a door, or make suggestions about how to do something *after* the child has exhausted his resources. The child has to have a chance to arrive at his or her own solutions. Parents have to stand back and give children this opportunity—up to the point of frustration. Then they should step in and offer help.

Children also need to learn about time and when it is time for various activities, such as playing, taking a bath, or eating dinner (as well as when it is time for mommy to cook dinner or do her nails or go shopping). These are concepts about everyday life that two-year-olds begin to comprehend when they are discussed and incorporated regularly into their lives.

"All the things that you are mentioning happen naturally in the course of a day. I don't regard them as enhancing cognitive development. My feeling is that I should be teaching my son the letters of the alphabet, colors, how to count, and maybe even how to read his name and other words. I've even read that someone devised a system of labeling different items in the house, so that when the baby saw the label and named the object he learned to read as well as talk."

There are all sorts of systems that are advocated for enhancing children's education. There is as yet no proof that learning to read at two is important for intellectual development. A two-year-old has far to go in concept formation, which he learns best from contact with his parent and from everyday situations in his home and its environs. We sing songs about the alphabet that children enjoy, but at this point such learning is mostly rote memory. The association of the sound with the written symbol is perhaps beginning for a few exceptional children; they may respond to learning letters if the parent's approach is casual and unpressured. The danger is that most children are really not ready and parents apply too much pressure. Their impatience at the child's lack of response gives the child a sense of failure and can actually turn the child off reading later on. In general, kindergarten is soon enough for most children to learn the alphabet. Now they should be learning other things that will not be as appropriate later.

Learning to Talk

"What special things should we be teaching them now? What is appropriate that we might be missing?"

A major accomplishment of the two-year-old is language: an increasing vocabulary and the ability to speak in three-word sentences. Some children may use even longer sentences. As we have said before, parents play a very important role in the child's acquisition of language. A child will make sounds but never speak a language unless he or she is spoken to. Language development requires stimulation and modeling by the parents.

■   ▧

They label objects and encourage the child to repeat words. They point out objects and situations in books and describe what they do around the house as they cook, clean, put things in order, and play games. Parents also name and describe more abstract things such as work, play, pleasure, happiness, and sadness. This parental teaching takes place in natural situations and contributes to the child's cognitive development, even though it is not usually labeled in that way.

At this age, the child is also learning how to manipulate toys such as toy cars and trucks, arranging them in various ways. Playing with dolls and stuffed animals also helps the child to work out difficult life situations and to express emotion, both affection and anger. Children mimic what they see, following and internalizing the parental models.

Games

"What about games? I understand 'Peekaboo' is an important teaching game."

That's right. "Peekaboo" is a game that gives both parent and child fun and pleasure. At the same time, it teaches the child that some person or thing that he or she cannot see for a moment continues to exist—that someone or something that goes away can come back. There are also nursery rhyme games like "London Bridge" and "Ring-Around-a-Rosy" that help teach the child words and understanding of language in an entertaining way.

Another skill that parents can appropriately encourage at this age is drawing. Children should be encouraged to draw with crayons: free scribbling and imitations of simple forms such as lines or circles. Parents often prohibit this activity out of fear that the children will scribble on the walls. The answer is that parents must *monitor* this activity, not inhibit it.

Learning Concepts

Finally, this is the age at which it is appropriate for children to be learning the concepts that will make reading and more formal reasoning meaningful later on. A child has trouble giving meaning to abstract symbols (reading) if he or she doesn't understand what the words mean, even if they have been properly sounded out. Children obviously need to know the names of all the common objects before *reading* them will give much pleasure. Additionally, children need to learn the concepts of up and down, in and out, on top of and under, and in front of and behind. It is really very difficult for a first-grader to progress if he or she, in learning to read, sounds out "behind," for example, but doesn't know what it means. The teaching of these concepts, therefore, is a most appropriate activity for parents of children around two years of age. Children can also begin to learn about shapes, and which shapes belong together, from doing puzzles with three or four simple and complete geometric shapes such as circles,

■   ■

squares, triangles, and rectangles, or puzzles with complete animal shapes of three or four different pieces.

After this discussion, you will understand why children can learn more from their parents during these first formative years at home than they may learn from many academic situations. Additionally, you will realize that it is considerably easier for children to take advantage of school when they have had this kind of appropriate preparation at home. Children who have had recognition for their achievements at home generally continue positive involvement in formal education.

"This discussion gives me more of an idea about natural teaching and makes me feel more comfortable with what we are doing already. Though I didn't want to, I felt I had to drill the baby to repeat words, and he just turned away. I was afraid there was something wrong with my child's intelligence. I guess I was so anxious that he should progress later in school that I got way ahead of him."

That is a very common error. Parents' expectations are often beyond their child's capacity. This often happens when they compare their child with friends' children who are older, or even to older siblings. All of us have a way of forgetting at what age we ourselves or an older child actually accomplished a certain activity. Then we expect too much of the younger child, disappointing ourselves and giving the child a feeling of failure. We are trying to help parents avoid this by developing expectations that coincide with the level of the child's development. Appropriate parental expectations combined with appropriate parental guidance and teaching generally lead to accomplishments by the child that are satisfying for both parent and child. The patient helping of children to understand concepts and the fostering of feelings of accomplishment and self-confidence are the best ways parents can give their children a head start for school.

Sleep Changes: Nap Patterns; The Move from Crib to Bed

How are the children sleeping now? Do you have any questions about sleep patterns or naps?

When Do Children Give Up Naps?

"We are just beginning to have a problem. Our little girl, who used to take naps very easily—a short one in the morning and a really long one in the afternoon—is beginning to resist her afternoon nap. If she doesn't have it, she gets very cranky late in the afternoon; in fact, she is impossible. She is cranky for her bath and hardly eats her supper, but she does sleep at night. It may be a good idea to eliminate the afternoon nap, since she sleeps so well at night. Her morning waking is about 6:00 A.M., which is very early; but my husband gets up early, so it is not such a problem."

■   ■

"My child is trying to eliminate her afternoon nap, too; but she falls asleep at 5:00 or 5:30 from sheer exhaustion and sleeps till 6:00 or so. Then she gets her second wind. We can't get her to bed until 9:00—sometimes 10:00 P.M.—and that cuts into our evening together."

It is apparent that some of the children are going through a transition period. There is no set time when children should give up their naps. It depends entirely on the child and his need for sleep. Some children nap until they are four or five years of age; others stop around two. The child who has been taking two naps usually consolidates them into one at this age. Parents can tell by experimenting whether a morning nap or an afternoon nap is better for the child.

A child who wakes very early in the morning may need a late-morning nap, or his lunch can be given earlier, followed by an early-afternoon nap. The child who takes only an afternoon nap and tries to eliminate it clearly is not quite ready if she falls asleep just before supper. It may be necessary to shorten her day and give her an early bath and supper and an earlier bedtime. Even if children won't nap, a quiet period should be instituted when they can rest in their cribs or beds and play quietly alone. A quiet time can also consist of sitting quietly with mother and looking at books or listening to records.

Gradually all these changes in sleep patterns emerge into a new pattern; but during the transition one has to experiment and see which solution works best for each child and family.

Climbing Out of Cribs

"We are lucky our little girl still naps and sleeps all night. But now when she wakes, she no longer waits for me to come to get her; she climbs right out of her crib. When I come into her room, she is playing on the floor. She hasn't fallen out, but I am afraid she will. Is there something to do about that?"

It seems that some of the children are not sleeping as long as their parents thought and they may be left waiting in their cribs too long. When they were younger and less mobile, they stayed in their cribs. Now many won't stay, and parents have to be alert and take them out sooner, so they won't fall.

Another problem when children get out of their cribs without the parents' knowledge is that they may get involved in some activity that is harmful. As you well know, children of this age should not be wandering around unsupervised, especially in the kitchen or bathroom or near stairs. You can all imagine the possibilities for trouble without our listing them. Some parents may find that placing a gate in the doorway to the child's room is helpful. Many children will not be content to stay in their rooms, but they will call out. This will alert the parents that they are up. For the child's safety, it is best for a parent to get up when the child is up. If you wake up when she does and then take her out of the crib, she may never have the need to climb out.

"My child wakes up, climbs out of his crib, comes onto our bed, and wants to play. It may be four in the morning, and we are not ready for that. But we don't want to upset him or scold him. What should we do?"

It is important for him to know that it is still "sleep time," not "getting up time." Take him back to bed, tuck him in, and assure him everyone is going back to sleep. Tell him you will come and get him in the morning when it is "getting up time."

Readiness for Big Beds

"We are having a different situation now. Our little girl takes her naps in her crib. At night, however, she will not fall asleep unless she is put to sleep in 'the big bed,' our bed. Then we move her to her crib."

"We were having the same situation with our little boy. Last week, we spent the weekend with friends. They had no crib for him, just a studio couch in the den. We were a little bit worried because of the new place and the big bed with no rail, we put chairs around it. He liked it and slept all night. So we wondered if that was a signal that he is ready for a youth bed."

Children's enjoyment of sleeping in regular beds is certainly one of the signals that they are ready. In most cases, when the children are a little older, they enjoy selecting a real bed and seeing it installed in their rooms. They feel very grown up then. In many cases, having their own beds eliminates the problem of their getting up and coming into parents' beds. Some children are ready for a bed around two years of age, but most are really not ready until two and a half or three, some even later. If the child is not ready, the change should not be made. Some children are attached to their cribs. They are their havens and castles.

"We are expecting a new baby in about six months. Our son will be about two and a half then. We were planning to give his crib to the baby and give him a bed, but he seems very attached to his crib. So we are wondering if that's a good idea."

In general, it is not advisable to give the crib to the baby when the older child is still using it and is attached to it. His sleep pattern may be disturbed. In addition, the older child's loss of his crib may heighten his feelings of loss of his mother's attention when the new baby comes. Because the baby has mother *and* his crib, the older child may feel doubly displaced. This feeling can initiate or intensify sibling rivalry that parents find difficult to cope with. Most of us would like to minimize or avoid this kind of stress if at all possible. Although it may seem like an unnecessary expense to have two cribs, it may turn out to be a valuable investment for the emotional well-being of the family. Some families may be able to borrow a crib for the baby until the older child is ready for a bed.

■   ■

"We are expecting a new baby, too. Our son is climbing out of his crib and prefers to sleep on the daybed we already have in his room. We have told him that as soon as the baby comes he can have that bed for himself because he is going to be a big boy by that time. He is looking forward to that."

Your son sounds ready to make the change. In addition, you have made it a privilege and reward for being the older child, so that any feelings he has of being displaced from his crib will be minimized. In all cases, when a new baby is expected, it is a good idea to emphasize the advantages of being the older child. In the next six months, the child who is attached to his crib may have matured sufficiently to want a big bed and may relinquish the crib easily to the new baby. On the other hand, the child who seems ready may suddenly decide he wants to keep his crib when he actually sees the baby using it. It is therefore important for parents to be sensitive to the child's feelings about his crib and not force him to give it up prematurely.

"We are not expecting a new baby, but we have a big bed for our child in his room. Luckily, we left the crib up, mainly because we haven't decided where to store it, and we find that sometimes he prefers to sleep in the crib again. Now we will leave it up until he is really ready and doesn't ask to be put into it anymore."

The move from the crib to a bed is a big event in a child's life. Most of us regard it as just a matter of refurnishing the child's room. To the child it is much more than that—it is a move from infancy to childhood. The move is often accompanied by a mixture of excitement and joy and a little fear and regression, for which parents must be prepared. It is another change in the child's life that is better dealt with on the child's maturational timetable, and not at the parents' convenience.

The Second Child: How to Cope

We want to discuss what happens in the family when a second child is born, especially when the older child is under three. Some of you already have a second child, and some will have one soon. Others may be thinking about it. What are your feelings and experiences?

"Because of my profession and for medical reasons, I could not wait. There are only twenty months between my boys. I knew from our earlier discussions what some of the difficulties might be. Although I knew there would be great demands on my time, I did not know how difficult it would be to give both children at least some of what they needed. Fortunately, the second is less demanding than the first. To fulfill the needs of my first child, in fact, I may be taking too much advantage of the second baby's placid disposition. Sometimes I feel I actually neglect him."

■   ■

When the second child is placid, parents frequently tend to exploit his or her good nature. It is important to recognize that this is happening and try to give the baby the attention he needs. Sometimes arrangements have to be made to have some help for a few hours a day. Someone can entertain the older child while mother attends to and stimulates the baby. When father comes home, he can play with the older child, or the parents can take turns, so that both children have special times with each parent. Sometimes, if one is lucky, a grandparent or other relative is available to help.

Helping Toddler Relate to New Baby

It is also possible to enlist the older child in helping to stimulate the baby. While an older sibling of three or four is very good in this role, it takes thought and ingenuity to help a two-year-old do this. The parent can encourage the toddler to wave a rattle for the baby, or to place a small stuffed toy in his range of vision, or to place something in his hand. (The parent should closely supervise this activity, because the two-year-old is not mature enough to understand which of his activities might be harmful to the baby.) Helping with the baby in this way enhances the older child's feeling of importance while giving the baby appropriate stimulation. At the same time, the older child can be helped in his language development by talking to his sibling and imitating the parent's way of communicating with the baby.

"We have the opposite situation. We have to give our second child a great deal of attention. She required an operation, and I had to stay with her in the hospital. It was too much for our two-year-old—first to have so much attention centered on the baby, then to have me away. He had to stay with his grandparents. Although he knows their house and likes to be with them, he had never been there alone overnight. He has an adequate vocabulary for his age, but not sufficient for us to explain that I would be back, that we still loved him as much as ever, and that soon he would be home again. From a happy, active boy who could amuse himself, he has become a whining, clinging 'baby.' I know why; but it is so hard to give both of the children the attention they need. How can I get him back to his former state?"

That was a very difficult situation. You did all you could to make it easier for your son, but it was beyond his experience and level of comprehension. It is good that you understand the cause of his clinging and regression. Now he needs time with you in order to be assured that you are not leaving him. It would be helpful if someone else could care for the baby for a little while each day, so you could have a separate time for him alone. He needs some undivided attention from you to get over his feeling of abandonment and to help him reestablish his former sense of security. If the baby has recovered, he can also be involved in playing with the baby. Then he can experience a sense of pleasure in relation to the baby and have less of a feeling that the baby only keeps you from him. It will take time to accomplish this; but if you are sensitive to his needs, the situation will improve.

"Since I brought my baby home, my little girl, who is twenty-two months old, has behaved as if she were bereft. When I went to the hospital to have the baby, my mother, whom she adores, came to stay with us. We give our daughter lots of attention, and our friends are very careful to include her, but she still clings and whines. She wakes at night, which she didn't do before, and she doesn't eat as well as she did. Both my husband and I have tried to spend a little extra time with her and keep her away from the baby, but it doesn't seem to help. We want her to love the baby."

As adults, we often make the mistake of expecting children to "love" the new baby brother or sister right away. We must recognize that the first child feels displaced—and to a certain extent this is an accurate perception. The parents, particularly the mother, who is probably nursing the baby, are no longer able to give the older child *their* undivided attention. Parents can help the older child to begin to verbalize his or her feelings of anger or disappointment (often young children expect a new baby to play with them immediately). The main thing is not to expect too much in the way of affection and not to criticize the child for lack of enthusiasm. In most cases, acceptance of the baby develops gradually if the parents help the older child to feel loved and secure.

"Of course, I expected some of these reactions and I think we are coping. But we haven't talked yet about the mother! What about her needs when there is a second child? I hardly have had time to put on lipstick since the new baby came!"

The Needs of Each Child

Having enough time to give a new baby and a toddler the attention they need is one of the hardest problems to solve at first. The first child is still quite immature and dependent, but very active; the new baby is totally dependent and relatively inactive. Their individual needs at a given moment may be quite conflicting, and the parent, most often the mother, feels torn between them. Some mothers are very easygoing and casual. They have an easier time coping than more tense and exacting parents. A great deal depends on the mother's personality and physical endurance. Much also depends on the assistance she receives from her husband, relatives, friends, or hired helper. Caring for a toddler and a new baby requires a great deal of organization and stamina, perhaps even more than is required in another profession or business. Parents' needs for support are not widely recognized by our society, nor is the value of good parenting. Without support, child rearing can be a lonely and frustrating experience.

One of the ways for a mother to preserve her health and pleasure in her children is to try to have a rest when the children nap. If the children do not nap at the same time, and no relative, friend, or hired helper is available to take care of the children for a short period each day, then the father must give her a breathing time when he comes home.

"Well, that is usually not the way it works when my husband comes home. He wants dinner, and the children are cranky and hungry. Everyone wants something, and I only have two hands!"

One cannot expect the children to understand your need for a little rest and relief, but your husband needs to be aware of his responsibility to help. He has the more mature central nervous system and he can wait for his dinner. Or he can help make it, or go out to the deli and get something for your dinner. This period when everyone seems disorganized will not last forever. In a while, a better routine will be established. The baby's schedule will become more predictable and gradually it will be more like the older child's. Dinnertime, as we discussed before, is a particularly difficult period of the day. Parents need to discuss ways of making it easier for themselves and the children.

"I can cope with the daily juggling of each child's needs, but once in a while I need to get away. Is that unfair to the children?"

It is absolutely essential that every parent get some time off. As we have said, no one can do a job twenty-four hours a day every day without relief. A mother's job is no different. Some arrangements must be made so she can have some time for herself. It is important for her emotional and physical health. She can then do her job better and enjoy it more.

"I went back to work after my second child was born, because I just couldn't take it at home. Then when I came home, I was so glad to see the children that I think I was nicer to them and not so irritated. But I noticed that my younger child, who is nearly two, is not speaking as early as my first. Do you think that may be because my housekeeper is not talking to her enough?"

Your housekeeper is just as busy looking after two children as you were. In addition, she is probably more concerned about the housekeeping. Some housekeepers feel that the employer is more concerned about the state of the house than the children, because that is what the parents notice most when they come home. It is important to emphasize that you are more concerned with the children than with the housework. Some housekeepers may have trouble changing their priorities. If you have noticed a speech lag in your younger child, you can spend time stimulating the baby's speech when you and your husband are home on weekends.

Problems Regarding Sharing

"Our problem has been the sharing of toys. Although my older child has an abundance of age-appropriate toys, he seems to want only what the baby

is playing with, such as his rattle or squeeze toy—toys he had given up before the baby came. I don't like to push him away from the baby and take the toys from him, but it upsets the baby. I find I am getting angry at my son more often than I should. I feel he is selfish."

It is very common for the older child to want the baby's toys, especially if they were once his. Sometimes, it is best to give the baby new toys and let the older child play with his own again so that he won't feel displaced by the baby. His old toys revive memories of a pleasant time when all attention was paid to him; he also notices the attention you pay to the baby, helping her manipulate the toys. His behavior isn't "selfishness"; it's immaturity. He still needs to be included. So you can try to include him in the baby's play. Have him dangle the toy for the baby and pick it up when the baby drops it; recognize how well he does it. At such times you can also get one of his new toys and by playing with it show him how much more interesting it is than the rattle he played with when he was a baby. You can also show him how he can roll a car along the floor now because he is a "big boy." Try to make being the older child an asset rather than a privation.

"In our home we have the opposite problem: the baby wants everything the older one has. He is now able to crawl and get into all of my older child's toys. She resents it. I tell her the baby is too young to know not to touch them, but it doesn't seem to help. I feel an uncomfortable relation is developing between them. Is there any way to deal with that?"

It is natural for the younger one to want to explore, but the older child has a right to her toys and privacy. You must help her by giving the younger child the toys he can have and by protecting the older child's toys. Some toys they can share and play with together, such as rolling a ball to each other; but special toys belonging to the older child must be guarded from the baby's grasp. When the older child recognizes your protection, she will have a better feeling toward her younger sibling and may be able in time to share some toys with him.

"All of these issues are important, but the hardest thing for my husband and me is to find time to be together. We always seem to be doing something for the children. Perhaps it is because I have a job outside. When we come home we feel the children need all of our attention. We haven't seen our friends or been out to dinner or a movie in months."

When both parents work outside the home, they may feel guilty about leaving the children for their own time alone together. This is a situation in which many families find themselves. The family's pattern of living must include time for the parents alone. No matter how much one enjoys one's children, or how seriously one feels the responsibility to gratify the children's legitimate needs, time must be arranged for parents to do things for themselves on a regular basis. It is important for them as individuals

■   ■

and as a couple to have time off from child care. Otherwise, parents may become overtired and resentful of their children. This is a situation that everyone wants to avoid.

Weaning: What to Do About Bottles

Now that the children are approaching two, have you begun to consider them old enough to give up their bottles? Have you been getting pressure from friends or relatives to wean your children?

"Well, I remember that we discussed weaning earlier. At the time, I was worried because my mother was urging me to take away all the baby's bottles. It was pointed out that doing it abruptly was upsetting to the child because it was like a separation from mother. That made me slow down and think about it. So instead, I have been giving him as much milk as he will drink from a cup after each meal. Some of the time he drinks well without spilling. Now he takes a bottle only early in the morning and at bedtime."

"My little girl will take a little milk from a cup at each meal, but she spills most of it. So I'd just as soon have her take bottles. It is so much easier for me that I usually don't bother with a cup."

Drinking from a Cup

All parents have to satisfy their children's and their own needs, but at some point all children need to learn to drink from a cup. Sometimes parents push children to give up their bottles too soon, and sometimes they don't encourage children to learn to drink from a cup soon enough because they want to avoid a mess. There is, of course, a "happy medium." It is a good idea to start with a cup at one meal a day, perhaps the noon meal. When that is successful, the cup can be introduced at another meal or afternoon snack, whichever is most suitable to the daily routine.

"When should parents really expect children to give up their bottles entirely? You hear so many varied opinions stated with such authority that it's really confusing and more than a little upsetting. My child enjoys his bottle, even though he is two."

Most specialists in the field of child development now feel that most children can relinquish their bottles with little trauma by around three years. The age varies with each child—some are ready earlier, some a little later. Each child has his or her own timetable and needs; and parents should be concerned about their own child's needs rather than unsolicited advice, no matter how well-meaning.

"Well, I don't see what all the fuss is about. My baby takes his milk so much faster from a bottle. He can hold it himself, and I am free to do whatever I want. If I give it to him from a cup, I have to sit with him so he won't throw it or spill it. It takes so much time; I just don't have the patience for it."

■   ■

Taking care of a child does take time. Children cannot be hurried, especially in eating or drinking. By the age of two, a child should be learning to use a cup so that he can gradually give up his bottles. A little patience *now* pays off well *later*. Sitting with a child to assist him in drinking from a cup once or twice a day helps him advance to a more mature level of drinking. It also continues intimacy with the parent at mealtime, which is important.

Parents seem to like to have their children do things early or fast. Having the child give up his or her bottle *early* makes parents feel successful as parents. What *really* is important is that the child be allowed to relinquish the bottle when the *child* is ready. Pushing the child may be counterproductive and cause resistance instead of cooperation.

"Along with weaning, another thing that concerns me is when to begin toilet training. I'm being criticized by my family because my child isn't weaned or toilet trained yet."

It is not advisable to begin toilet training when the child is concentrating on other areas, especially weaning. Most children are hampered in their progress if too many tasks are introduced at once. It is best to tune in to the child's readiness for new development and respond to her cues.

Toilet Training and Weaning

"We have a different problem. Our son was giving up his bottles and just beginning to use the potty. Then our daughter was born, and he refuses to use the potty and insists on having his bottles."

Your son is exhibiting a very natural regression. He sees the attention that his baby sister gets having her diapers changed and being fed. He thinks that these baby ways are good ways for him to get attention, too. Since he is still quite young and needs to get adjusted to the baby, it would probably be best to slow down on the weaning and toilet training.

"We have the same problem and stopped talking about it altogether. We did continue giving our daughter milk from her cup (except at night), however, telling her that the baby was much too young and small to do that. She seemed to feel proud about that."

That's good. You have given her an idea that there is some advantage in being older. Often all the child can see is the attention the baby gets; being older seems like a disadvantage. Parents have to be careful not to say constantly, "The baby is so small and helpless, he needs my attention. You are a big girl so you have to wait for Mommy." Parents sometimes unconsciously convey the disadvantages of being bigger instead of pointing out any advantages. That is a trap we all fall into. We forget that the two-year-old is still a baby in many ways. Besides, when children are close together in age, the demands on a parent are very great. The parents want the child to act older so she can help, or at least wait her turn. If the older child is very compliant, we can rob her of her babyhood before it is time. If the child is assertive, the parent often labels the child "spoiled" or "bratty" or "naughty." Because the child wants attention like the baby gets, she regresses. If the child is verbal enough, the parents can help her begin to understand her feelings by saying, "I guess you feel like being a baby again. That is all right. In a little while, maybe you will be my big girl again."

The important point is that two years old is really on the young side for most children to give up their bottles or begin toilet training.

The Child's Understanding of Family Events: Illness, Death, Separation, Divorce

There are many situations that occur in a family that disrupt the usual routine. Some are happy events such as visiting relatives or friends, celebrating a birthday or anniversary, moving, or going on vacation. There are also unhappy or unpleasant situations such as illness or death in the family as well as separation and divorce. Even though the children are older and are becoming more verbal, they still have difficulty understanding and relating to all the different events that can occur in a family. Parents themselves have difficulty dealing with such situations and often do not know how to help their children handle them. Because such occurrences usually arise unexpectedly, we would like to discuss different ways of handling them so that you may be better prepared.

Illness

"Just this week my mother took sick and I had to rush over to her house. I had to take my little girl because I didn't have time to get a baby-sitter. Mother had a heart attack; I had to send for an ambulance. I called my husband, who came from his office; but all the time I was rushing around to help Mother, my little girl was very upset. She is very fond of her grandmother and cried. She couldn't understand why Grandmother was not paying attention to her. I knew that, so I held her in one arm and did things with the other—but was very upset myself. By the time the ambulance came, her father was there. He took her home while I went to the hospital. Mother is still there, and I have to visit her every day and leave the baby with a sitter. She continually asks for her grandmother. Her appetite has fallen off, and she has begun waking during the night. I'm not sure I'm handling things right, because I am so upset about my mother, even though she is improving."

Situations that are so serious and sudden are very difficult to cope with, even for adults, as you have so clearly stated. It seems as though you were very sensitive to your little girl's needs by holding her close as much as you could. At this age, children can understand if you tell them that

Grandmother is sick and that you have to take care of her. It is important to emphasize that you will be back soon. You can also talk about what you will do together when you get back. Then go as quickly as possible and return as soon as you can manage.

"What about her not eating and sleeping?"

Whenever there is a change that causes anxiety, children may respond by not eating or not sleeping—or both. These disruptions are to be expected. All that a parent can do is to be patient and comforting and not get upset. When life gets back to normal, the child's appetite and usual sleeping pattern will return.

Death

"We had a similar but less fortunate situation in our family. My husband's father, who was a constant visitor and a great pal to my little son, was hit by a car. He did not recover after being taken to the hospital. Our little boy keeps asking for him, and we keep saying he is away. But we know we can't say that forever. One day, we are going to have to tell him. What should we say? We try not to talk about his grandfather in the hope that he will forget about him."

If you don't mention his grandfather and your son stops asking, that does not mean that he has forgotten. Furthermore, we won't know what sort of fantasy the child may have about his grandfather's sudden disappearance. He may begin to worry that his parents will vanish that way, too. He may even think *he* has done something wrong. So, difficult as it is, it is best to tell the truth. The truth about his grandfather will be difficult for him to understand but less bewildering than silence or the idea that in some way he is at fault.

"We would like to, but we just don't seem to be able to begin."

When your son asks again, say that Grandfather had an accident and was hurt very badly and that's why he can't come over. The next time he asks, or a few days later, it may be easier to say that the doctors and nurses tried their best to help Grandfather, but he just couldn't get well. By this age, children have heard the word *die* in reference to flowers, animals, and insects. So, if you say Grandfather died, he may have some awareness of what you mean. He may ask more questions about where Grandfather is and wonder if he will return. Some children have difficulty understanding and accepting the finality of death, even at seven or eight years, so do not be upset or surprised if you are asked these same questions over and over again. The important thing is not to give the child the feeling that this is a topic that must not be discussed. It is a good idea to talk about his grandfather.

"What if the child cries?"

■   ■

You can say how sad you feel and how much you miss Grandfather, too. Tears of grief do not hurt anyone. They are an appropriate expression and release of emotion.

"Can't one tell the child that Grandfather has gone to heaven and that he is resting in a nice place?"

If that is part of the family's belief and a comforting idea, one can explain it to one's child that way, even if the child doesn't yet understand completely. One must do and say what is appropriate to the family's beliefs, whether cultural or religious.

Mourning

"Do children mourn? How can one tell?"

Children do mourn. Some children do so by avoiding the subject—never looking at the dead person's picture. Others want to look at the relative's pictures and talk about him or her all the time. Some lose their appetite or experience a change in their sleep patterns. Some become very irritable or tearful for no apparent reason. Others show a great deal of anxiety about their own health and body parts. Others become very clinging to parents and worried about the parents' health, always wanting to know where they are going and when they will return. Others have difficulty playing with peers. If a parent is sensitive to the child's behavior, subtle changes may be detected. That is why it is best to be open with the child and try to answer his or her questions as simply and directly as possible. It is also important to remember to reassure children that your own health is good and so is theirs.

"After talking about the death of a grandparent, I hate to bring up the death of a pet—but our son's kitten is very sick. I'm afraid she's going to die. I've been thinking we should find another cat for him so he won't be upset."

If your son is very fond of his kitten, he *will* be upset by her death. That's only natural. It is better not to try to gloss over his loss and to let him know that you are sad, too. Children have a right to mourn the loss of a pet. It is really better not to get a new pet until the child asks for one. No one pet should be any more replaceable by another than one person is replaceable by another.

Family Arguments

"What about angry feelings? Sometimes my husband and I get into a discussion that is very heated; there may even be a quarrel in front of our son. What do we do about that? He often acts frightened."

It is best not to have a heated argument in front of a child, particularly if it involves some difference of opinion about the handling of discipline. It confuses the child and may make him feel guilty. He may even fear that his parents will come to blows or hurt him.

"Well, what if you just can't help it? What if it's something that doesn't really involve your child? Do parents always have to wait until the child is out of earshot? That's just not normal to be so controlled!"

That's true. It may not be the usual way two adults have related to each other. However, one has to bear in mind the child's presence, feelings, and possible misinterpretations. So if you are arguing in front of the child, tone it down if you can't postpone it. Explain to the child that Mommy and Daddy have different ideas about something and that you are not angry at the child.

"When we argue, my little girl covers her ears and cries. She runs either to me or my husband, depending on who is yelling the loudest, and pulls on my (or his) arm. That always brings us to our senses. We are learning not to discuss things that are apt to start trouble in front of her."

"Doesn't it give the child an unreal view of the world if he never experiences any dissension in a family?"

We are not advocating that families give their children an unreal picture of life, as though there are no difficulties. We are suggesting that you bear in mind how children may interpret and respond to arguments and that you be sensitive to their needs. We also have to remember that parents are models for their children. If children see parents quarreling all the time (sometimes violently), this becomes their model of how adults relate to each other. It is likely to influence their behavior when they grow up. None of us wants to set this kind of example for our children. You may argue like this because that was the model set for you. Now, as you bring up your own children, is a good time to try to find a more constructive, more respectful way of relating.

Separation and Divorce

"There is another subject that is bothering me: separation and divorce. I've wanted to discuss it for a long time, because my husband and I contemplated divorce before the baby was born. Then the baby came, and we thought maybe that would make us closer again. Things are a little better, but we still have problems. What would we say to our son, and just how would divorce affect him?"

One would hope that parents would be able, with appropriate help, to avoid divorce. But if that is not possible, the child should be told that the parents love him and that they will always remain his mommy and daddy but that one of them will not be living with him anymore. (We say "one of them" because some mothers leave their children with the fathers. We can no longer take for granted that children will remain with the mother, although in most cases, especially with young children, that is still so.)

■   ■

Explain that the other parent will live in his (or her) own house and will come to visit and play with the child, that they will still have good times together. The exact details of the arrangements should be explained to the child in terms that the child can understand. For example, "Daddy will come and take you to the park every weekend." If at all possible, it is best for the child to remain in his own home, at least until he has adjusted somewhat to the separation.

"If the separation does go on to divorce, should you tell the child?"

Usually children try very hard to effect reconciliation between parents. By the time the divorce is final, the children may be old enough to understand that the separation has been made permanent by divorce. However, even with children three or four years old, one needs to take care to explain how they will be affected. The parents need to try to understand how the child interprets and feels about it. Some children think that divorce means some surgical process like cutting someone in two, and they are not sure whether the parents are cut apart in some way. Parents have to allow their children to express their ideas and fantasies in order to be sure the children have no misconceptions that cause them undue anxiety. Most important, the child must be reassured that *both* parents still love her or him.

Single Parents: Special Problems

We have been discussing how families cope with a variety of child-rearing issues. Usually we discuss the role of the members of the traditional two-parent family, but it is important to recognize that an increasing number of families consist of only one parent and that these families have many special problems. We were wondering whether there were some special issues that those of you who are single parents would like to discuss.

"Where Is Daddy?"

"It's no secret to all of you how I've had to struggle to arrange appropriate care for my little girl, since I am not married and have to work. You've all helped in discussing different child-care arrangements and how to cope with all my other chores. I'm managing, but now I have different worries. As my daughter gets more verbal, I imagine she is going to ask me where her father is or why she doesn't have one. What is the best thing to say?"

There are many questions children ask that are difficult to answer. It's best to try to understand the level of the child's thinking when the question is asked. To help in understanding what the child is thinking the parent can ask, "What were you thinking?" or "I wonder why you're asking?" Then, when you have received a reply, you will be in a better position to answer the question. Any answer you give the child should be as simple, direct, and honest as possible. Often adults make the mistake of giving involved explanations, which the child is not able to comprehend.

"Well, in my case, I didn't want to be married or to live with the man. I just wanted a child before I was too old. I wanted to be a mother and I thought I could be a good one. It's harder than I thought it would be. But I enjoy my child. How can I tell her about that? Her father moved away and I never even told him of her existence. And that's the way I want to keep it."

For the present, if your daughter asks where her daddy is, you can answer truthfully that he has gone away to work.

"Suppose she wants to know whether he knows about her?"

That is a question *you* are worrying about her asking, but it is probably beyond her level of conceptual thinking to ask that now. At this age, she assumes *everyone* knows about her. She is more likely to ask when he will be back. If she does, you can say that you do not know when he will come back but that you do not think he will come back for a long, long time. After all, it is possible that he might at some future time be in contact with you again. At some future time, she may want to know him and you may make a different decision. For now, you can make it clear that she can rely on your care and love.

When she is older, she may ask why her father does not write her or want to visit her. Then you must tell her that he does not know about her, so that she will not feel rejected or deserted by her father. You will have to explain that he moved away before she was born and that is why he does not know.

"Well, suppose she asks why I didn't tell him?"

If you don't know where he is, you can say that. You can also say that you wanted her very much and felt you could bring her up alone and make her very happy by yourself. You may also need to explain that you love her but you did not want to live with her father. It is good to be prepared to answer, so that you will not be taken by surprise.

"My situation is different, but I've been wrestling with similar questions. After three years of a calm and pleasant marriage, my husband found out that we were going to have a baby. He became very upset. He just couldn't cope with the responsibility of being a father and wanted the pregnancy terminated. I couldn't do that; I wanted the baby. We separated and are now divorced. My husband still lives in the neighborhood. We pass each other occasionally in the street as though we were strangers. He doesn't look at our son if he happens to be with me. He has never inquired how we are or made the slightest gesture of concern. I have resumed my maiden name, which is my son's last name, too. There is no financial problem; I have just continued with my job. My son is a happy, easygoing child. Can I tell him that his father didn't want him? That is the truth. What will it do to his self-image to find out his father didn't want him?"

■   ■

In the first situation, the mother didn't want the father as a husband. In this case, the father rejected his role. The problem is how to tell the child the truth when he asks about his father without giving him a sense of personal rejection. You could say that his father didn't understand what to do as a father. He just wasn't ready to be a father. But you were ready to be a mother because you knew how and wanted to be a mother. Therefore, you decided to take care of him yourself without the father. This may satisfy him at first. As he matures and asks more sophisticated questions, more explicit answers will have to be given. It so happens that this is not such a unique situation. As he grows older and goes to school, he will meet other children of one-parent families. Then he will not feel so alone and different as you now worry he will feel.

Male Role Models

"There is another problem that bothers me, which I suppose is more serious for a male child, and that is: what does one do when there is no male role model? Isn't it true that boys have to have a man around to establish their masculine identity?"

Both parents are important models for children of *both* sexes. The girl, perhaps, has an easier time because she identifies with her mother, but she needs to be aware of what to expect of a male. In two-parent families, the father is the model for her future heterosexual relationships. While the boy in his earlier years may be close to his mother, and even his father's rival, he eventually needs to identify with a male, which is usually his father. Although they can hardly escape some influence from the parental models, some children identify with other family members. In the case of an absent father, a child may identify with a grandfather, uncle, teacher, or minister. It is good for *both* girls and boys to have some contact with an interested adult male.

"In my case, I have an aunt and uncle who live near enough so we can visit them often. They have been baby-sitters in many an emergency. My son loves them dearly and plays ball with my uncle. Their children are grown up and live far away, so they are very glad to be surrogate parents. I am very lucky, I know."

"I live with my parents. My son has my father as his model. He also has the advantage of having my mother, who takes care of him when I go to school three days a week. I was afraid that he would mistake them for his parents. I've been insisting that he call my mother Grandma and me Mother to avoid that."

"You are lucky. I have no family nearby. Though I date occasionally, I do not like to keep introducing my child to different men. I've tried some of those groups for single parents, but they are made up mostly of women and the few men are not particularly compatible. I just don't know how to

*bring my daughter into contact with appropriate males. She is obviously
confused because she calls all men Daddy—and that embarrasses me!"*

Child's Adjustment to Parent's New Friends/Partners

You are raising a very important issue. It is not good for a child to have to
keep adjusting to different friends of the parent. The same thing applies
when the child visits with the father and his girlfriends. Sometimes these
friends of the mother's or the father's are not interested in the child—or
worse, they are jealous of the child who resembles the former spouse.
There is obviously a need for groups in which single men and women and
their children can come together in a family-like atmosphere. Some groups
like this have been established by Ys, community centers, and religious
institutions. There will need to be many more of these to satisfy the
numbers of single-parent families. Also, you can try to get male baby-
sitters; your children can benefit from contact with them.

*"My husband died before our little boy was born. Now I have a friend
whom I like very much, but he seems too strict with my baby. My son seems
a little afraid of him and clings to me. I'm afraid that if we marry—and I
do want to marry again—we'll have problems over discipline and the
marriage will be an unhappy one. That I don't want. I haven't said anything
to my friend about it because I don't want to offend him. Is there some way
to deal with that?"*

Before any marriage, the partners should get to know each other's ideas
about how they want to live. Their ideas about rearing children are an
important aspect of this. So if you both are interested in marriage, it would
be appropriate to discuss your feelings about children and their need for
approval as well as discipline. Perhaps you can come to some agreement
before you run into trouble.

Living with Grandparents

*"My problem is a little different from the others because I have to live with
my parents. My mother is very good to me and lets me go out and take
courses. But I have a feeling that she thinks she knows more about raising
the baby than I do—and maybe she does. But I decided to have my baby
so I could raise her, and my mother makes me feel left out. The only time I
feel like a real mother is when I'm here. Then I can see how well my baby
is doing and how good I am as a mother. It's been on my mind to mention
this before, but somehow I felt I would seem ungrateful to my mother."*

It is hard for you to be in the same house with your mother and try to be
your child's mother when your own mother is still mothering you. She is
having a hard time recognizing that you are grown now and a mother in
your own right. This often happens between mother and daughter, even
when they don't live together. It is very hard for a mother to recognize
that her own daughter is grown up and may be very competent to bring up

her own child. It is not ingratitude on your part, just your desire to be recognized and respected in your new role.

Financial Concerns

"My major worry since my divorce has been financial. The child-support payments aren't adequate with the increase in the cost of living. I work part-time but hardly have anything left after paying the baby-sitter. I've decided to try to find another woman in the same predicament. We could pool our resources and live together. I'm lucky to have an apartment that is large enough to share."

These ideas for developing your own "extended family" units are good ones. It is interesting that other people—single people without children and elderly people—are also beginning to think of sharing living arrangements. Though compromises may have to be made as one adjusts to these new groupings, they can be a mutually beneficial way to solve some of the problems we have been discussing.

It is quite clear that being a single parent, whether mother or father, poses many problems that complicate parenting. No two single parents have exactly the same problems to solve. Each parent has to use his or her own available resources and ingenuity.

Nursery Schools and Day-Care Programs: At What Age Are They Appropriate?

Some of you have been asking us about the appropriate time to send children to nursery school or to a day-care center. What are your ideas about this?

"In my neighborhood, all the parents of children my child's age are madly investigating nursery schools. I'm not doing that because it seems ludicrous to me to take my child to an interview for a prenursery program when he isn't even two. Am I naive? Am I making a mistake? Will his education be impaired if he doesn't enter a group when he is two?"

In large cities or the suburbs, where appropriately aged playmates may not live nearby, parents are tempted to provide play experiences for their child by enrolling them in a prenursery program. However, there is really no necessity for such a formal experience at this age. You are not depriving your child or hampering his development because he is not attending a formal preschool program. Registering a child in a preschool is often looked upon as a solution when families do not live near other children. Some of you live near parks or playgrounds where playmates are available. All you need to do, then, is to go outdoors to these areas and there will be plenty of opportunity for your child to play with other children. There will also be other mothers available to watch them and to socialize with each

■   ■

other. There you will make friends whom you can visit on rainy days. For those of you who worry that the children are not learning enough, it is important to remember that your children are learning a lot at this age from their contact with you and by going with you on errands around your neighborhood.

Informal Playgroups

"But what if you don't live near a playground and you can't afford a preschool? Then what alternative is there?"

We feel the best arrangement for this age, even if you could arrange for a prenursery school experience, is the *informal* play group of about four children and their mothers. This group could meet in each other's homes or at the park two or three times a week for an hour or two. If the same group meets fairly regularly, the children get to know each other. They begin to socialize and form friendships. They will need to have their own mothers present at first, but after a while they will feel secure enough so that the mothers may be able to take turns leaving for a short time. This kind of group is very good preparation for nursery school and should precede a formal school program, if it can be arranged.

"That sounds like a good idea for mothers who know how to organize play for children. I don't think I could do that. But I realize my child isn't ready yet to go to a school away from me. What can I do so that he is not deprived of interesting activity and stimulation?"

Special Activity Groups

In many communities, the local Y or religious institution has arranged some activities for young children and their parents. Some groups are organized specifically for large motor activity: climbing, jumping, running, and active games. There are even a few for swimming. Some parents like participating in these programs with their children.

There are also programs for children who would be happier with something quieter, such as pasting, crayoning, and finger painting. Parents often appreciate that kind of group because these activities make a mess at home, or because they do not have the proper equipment or space.

There are also music schools that have groups for young children that meet once or twice a week. The children participate in activities such as rhythm exercises, marching, dancing, or playing simple instruments. Some programs also teach songs that appeal to children, and they learn to enjoy listening to music.

There are many things to do with young children that enhance their experience. You will need to research your own community to find these resources. Then you can spend quality creative time with your child before he or she is really ready for a formal school program. Most parents enjoy these experiences as well, as they enhance their ability to spend quality time at home.

"I have always thought that a child would get more benefit from trained teachers in a setting designed with age-appropriate play areas and materials and a larger choice of playmates than being with three or four other inexperienced mothers and their children."

This is a very common attitude for parents to take. Children can certainly benefit from teachers who are well trained and empathic, working in a good physical setting with the appropriate equipment. However, there is still one question that is very important and that we have not yet considered. We must consider whether the child is *ready* for this experience. The parents may overlook the child's lack of readiness in their great desire to enrich the child's experience.

Signs of Child's Readiness for School

"What are the developments we should be looking for when we make a decision to send our child to a nursery group?"

One of the first considerations should be how well the child is able to separate from the mother or other caretaker. Most children of this age are not yet ready to separate from their mothers away from home and need to have the experience of being with other children while their mothers are present. The children are starting to play together here in this group but are just beginning to spend time in the children's area with the play teacher. Most of them still come back and touch base with mother a few times during the session, if only for a moment. Not many of them feel comfortable yet leaving the room for a walk down the hall or for play in the playroom across the hall. Most of them run back quickly to see their mothers or to show them something. It is very important for children that their mothers be available so they can do this. Children who do not need to do this are further along in their ability to separate. Each child has his own maturational timetable for separation, as for every other facet of development. It is very important that each child's need be understood so that a separation problem does not develop. This can be difficult to resolve and can recur at separation situations in adult life.

"Well, that is a good warning for me. I was thinking of taking a job so that I could afford a nursery school. I noticed that my little girl has great difficulty staying even at her grandmother's without me. She does a bit better without me if Grandma comes to our house. I thought what she needed was to separate from me, that nursery school was just the thing for her. All my friends have told me that I am too close to her."

It sounds as though the contrary is the case: that she is not ready to separate from you yet. Instituting separation too early would probably be too costly for her emotionally and would actually make her more dependent.

"I have noticed this about my son, too. My family has given me the same line. My husband has intimated that I'm making a sissy of him."

That is a very common fear. As we have said, forcing separation prematurely would intensify the clinging that a father interprets as being sissy. Actually, this kind of behavior indicates that the child still needs to be close to the mother and is not ready to separate.

"Well, I used to think that my son didn't care about my leaving because he is so fond of our sitter. I have noticed lately that he won't let me out of his sight when I come home. He wants me to hold him the minute I come in. That bothered me. Now I understand it. I remember that we had discussed this, but somehow until it happens in your own experience you don't really understand it. I guess he isn't as ready to go off to nursery school as I thought."

Another important sign of readiness is the ability of the child to communicate verbally. These children are quite advanced in this area; most of them are saying words and phrases, and some are trying three-word sentences. Their pronunciation is not always clear, however, and perhaps only a parent can understand them, so it might be difficult to be in a nursery school, where the teacher may not understand them or where they may not understand her. The level of a child's language development is important—both how much he understands and how well he can express himself.

"I can understand how that can be a problem. But I know a situation in which the child was late in talking, and nursery school was advised to encourage her speech."

That may have been good advice for that child. I would suspect, however, that the child was older than these and that there was some deficiency in speech stimulation at home.

"I'm a working mother or, as you prefer to say, a mother working outside the home. I prefer to leave my child at home with his old nurse, whom he adores. I don't think he is ready for nursery school. But he doesn't talk as much as some of the other children here. Do you think he would be better off in nursery school part of the day?"

In general, we think that two years old is still young for nursery school. If the child is not ready for nursery school, it is much better to leave him with a devoted caretaker, even if she doesn't stimulate speech sufficiently. The parents can make up for this lack by their own attention to speech when they come home in the evening and on weekends. They can also encourage the housekeeper to spend more time talking and playing with the child and not so much time on housework. Sometimes, parents need to model for the housekeeper what she is to do. If she is non–English-speaking, reading books with simple pictures and words will help her learn the language. She may even be pleased at the attention paid her by the parents. If parents understand the situation, remedial steps can be taken in time to prevent later problems. A speech deficit can be detected early and overcome. The anxiety produced by sending a child to school too soon is harder to overcome.

"So far, everyone has been approaching this question with the options of doing it or not. I simply do not have any option. I can't afford a baby-sitter. I must find a day-care center. Now that I am separated, I must return to work."

Each of you must weigh your child's need and the family's needs and then look for the best solution considering your own circumstances. As we have said, there are a growing number of programs for two-year-olds, and, if given sufficient time to feel comfortable in this situation, your child can learn to cope.

"I have taken my little girl to a music group a few times, just to see how she would respond to other children. She seems to like it, but she only wants to watch the activities from my lap. I haven't urged her to join the group, but I feel that the teacher is making overtures and is trying to entice her into the group. This only makes her cling to me. Do you think she is too young for this experience?"

It seems to me that she is indicating that she is. This brings up another guideline for judging whether a child is ready for a group experience. If the child has had enough social experiences with small informal groups, as we have mentioned before, she may be ready to participate in a larger group—at first with mother and then alone. There are some children whose personalities are such that they have to observe the activities of the group for a while before they can participate. There are others who bound right into a group and take over. The social behavior of these children indicates an earlier readiness. Even some of these children, after the first rush of enthusiasm, may want to return to mother's side. So the level of social development is important. Each parent has to know her child and try to assess this readiness.

"Whenever we are in the park and there are more than two or three children, my little boy moves away from them and finds a corner to play in by himself. This upsets me. I thought of sending him to nursery school to get over that."

Parents often come to that conclusion, but the children will do the same thing at nursery school. They are either not ready for that experience or the encounters they have had with other children have not been pleasant ones. Perhaps their play hasn't been appropriately monitored by the parents, so they respond by isolating themselves. It takes patience and understanding to help overcome this. The child needs time to reach the necessary maturational level *on his own timetable.*

"Most nursery schools require that a child be toilet trained before they will accept the child. Isn't that another guideline?"

In many nursery schools that is a requirement. Parents often hurry toilet training in order to meet this requirement and cause themselves a great deal of unnecessary disappointment and conflict with their children. They try to teach bowel and bladder control before the children have the neurological control and psychological readiness for this achievement. So this, too, is a consideration in deciding whether your child is ready for nursery school. In this case, as in many others, parents are ready before the child. Each child, as we have said before, has his own maturational timetable. The best results for all concerned are obtained when this is understood and accepted.

How to Choose a Nursery School or Day-Care Center

Many of you have expressed concern about how to tell whether a preschool program or day-care center is a good one and will be appropriate for your child.

Importance of First School Experience

"Yes, I didn't know anything about young children until my daughter was born. Now I have no idea what to look for in choosing a school, but I want to make sure it's the right one. I don't want her 'turned off' by her first school experience."

It is appropriate that you should be concerned about that. Children's problems with school often stem from their very first experiences, and we should make every effort to get them off to a good start. We talked about the importance of the child's readiness for the group experience of a preschool and his or her ability to separate from parents and home environment. How the parents and the school handle the separation process will have a major effect on the child's adjustment to school. We have talked earlier in the year about the importance of making the introduction of new caretakers or baby-sitters a gradual process, so that the child may become familiar with the new person within the secure setting of the home. This gradual process is even more important when the child encounters new adults and new children within a *new setting,* the school. Parents should therefore expect to stay at the school with their children for several days to a week, or even longer. Young children, especially those under three years of age, need help in making the transition to school. Trying to hurry their adjustment just makes them less secure and more uncomfortable.

"A friend of mine was told that she should stay for the first two days, and that was all. Her son screamed for the whole morning on the third day, after she left. Then he cried so much the next day that she took him home. Now she has decided to give up that school."

Adjustment to Separation

How the school deals with the separation needs of the child and what provisions are made are important questions to ask. One can learn a lot about the general philosophy of the school and about the administrator's understanding of child development from the answer to these questions. No preschool or day-care program for children under three should expect a child to begin the experience *without* separation anxiety. The parent should be allowed and encouraged to stay until the child, the teacher, and the parent herself feel that the child is ready to stay alone. If the school you are interested in has no particular plans for dealing with separation or says there is a policy allowing parents to stay for only a set number of days, it would be wise to look for a different school.

Many preschool programs facilitate the adjustment of children by having the teachers visit the home first. That way, the child is able to become familiar with the new adult. Conversely, the teacher is able to see how the child behaves in the security of the home environment.

Children's adjustments are also facilitated when the program begins gradually, starting with forty minutes to an hour the first day and working up to the full three-hour program over a period of a week or two. Some arrange to have the children begin coming in groups of three or four instead of meeting with the whole class of ten or twelve at once. We must recognize that having to adjust to two or three new adults, ten or twelve children, and a new environment is quite a large assignment for a two-year-old. Most are simply not ready to do it without a lot of support from the parent. For this reason, we are not recommending school for most children at two. However, some parents find they need to send a child to prenursery school or day care because of their work schedules. They should still take into account the child's needs and capabilities so that the best arrangement is made for both parent(s) and child.

Signs of Readiness for Separation at School

"Say you like the school's attitude. How can you tell when the child is ready to make it on his own?"

The first sign of readiness is the amount of time the child spends away from the mother engaged in the activities available in the classroom. If the child spends most of his time away from you, only checking back occasionally, he may be ready. You can test this by saying that you need to go on an errand and will come back in ten minutes. Some schools have rooms where parents can go for coffee to be somewhat removed from the children but available if needed. If parents leave for a brief period, they should stick to their promise. A ten-minute errand should take ten minutes, not an hour. If this brief separation goes well, then you could try leaving for half an hour or so the next day, until you are staying away for most of the session.

"What if your child says 'No' and clings?"

Then you know that she is not ready and you stay. After a few more days, you can try going to the parents' room for coffee or out to make a quick phone call. If, after several weeks, your child still makes a fuss when you try to leave, or still sits by your side and doesn't engage in activities with other children, it may be best to withdraw from the school. A good school director should be cooperative and consult with the parents about this decision.

"I can see that the school's policy on this issue indicates an understanding of the child, but also an attitude toward parents: whether they are to be gotten out of the way as soon as possible or treated as partners."

"I've heard that schools require that children be toilet trained before they will admit them. Is this possible for two-year-olds?"

As we have discussed, toilet training should take place when the child is ready—and most children are not ready at two. Good schools should know this and not require that children be trained as a prerequisite to admission. The teachers in prenursery programs should also be willing to accept the child's own maturational timetable regarding this issue. So the school's policy on toilet training is another important matter for parents to ask about.

What to Look for in Toddler Programs

"I'd like some guidelines on what to look for when I visit a classroom. Obviously, I will look to see how the children seem: whether they are happy and busy, or crying or withdrawn. I will look at the toys to see if there is a good variety. Are there other things I should look for?"

One should pay considerable attention to the teacher. Notice whether she looks interested in the children. Is she patient, relaxed, and calm? Does she bend down to talk with them and sit on the floor or on small chairs with them? Listen to the way she speaks to the children. Is she soft-spoken, or does she shout commands? Observe how she handles arguments and aggressive behavior. Two-year-olds, as you know, have not yet learned how to share. Observe whether the teacher protects *each* child's rights. Is she sensitive to the needs of both the aggressor and the victim without being harsh or punitive? Is she warm and comforting to the child in tears? Try to observe how well the teacher(s) and assistant(s) work together on the activities and with the children.

"You're really saying that the teacher is key to what happens in the classroom."

Yes, that's right. She and her assistant(s) set the tone for everything that goes on in the classroom; so if you see a school where you think the teacher is great, it is good to make sure that she will be there the following year. If she is replaced by a new, inexperienced teacher, the classroom experience could be quite different, although a good director will certainly try to make sure that all the teachers in the school follow the school's particular philosophy.

Other things you can observe or ask about relate to the curriculum and program. Observe (or ask about) the day's activities. There should be a schedule that alternates active and quiet activities, with a sequence of certain activities to start and end the day. This sequence gives the children a sense of knowing the beginning and end of the day. A certain amount of routine at school gives the children the same sense of security that we have encouraged you to provide at home. The classroom should have equipment for a great variety of activities, which the children can explore on their own or with guidance from the teachers. Try to decide whether the activities seem appropriate for two-year-olds. There should not be too many *group* activities, since they are just beginning to play together. There should not be too much emphasis on sharing or taking turns, especially at the beginning of the year. The children should not be expected to do things neatly or sit quietly for very long, and there certainly should not be any emphasis on letters or numbers. You should be looking for a happy, relaxed atmosphere with some structure—not an environment that is pressured or restrictive or academic. Finally, children generally do best when the atmosphere of the school is not too dissimilar from that of the home.

All-Day Programs

"My mother has been taking care of my son while I work, but now he is getting to be too active for her. I feel that I must find a day-care center where I can leave him for most of the day. I guess I should be looking for much the same things. Are there any additional features to all-day programs?"

Certainly, the schedule is very important in an all-day program. You would want to know what provisions are made for mealtimes and for naptimes. Children of this age should have one or two definite rest periods during the day. You would also want to ask about the consistency of care that the center will provide. For example, will the same teachers and assistants be there for the whole time the child is there, or will there by many changes in personnel? Changing caretakers is difficult for two-year-olds, so programs for this age should have a minimum of staff rotation.

It would probably be a good idea to visit a day-care program a couple of times, once in the morning and again in the afternoon. Observe how the children seem to be faring at each time of day. See whether they appear happy and calm or whether they sit off by themselves, looking sad or bored. Day-care programs for children under three are expensive because of the required ratio of adults to children. A good one may therefore be hard to find and too expensive. Sometimes family day care, in which a woman takes several children into her home, would be another possibility for you. Or you might find a program that runs from nine to three that would relieve your mother for most of the day.

Adequate and appropriate day-care facilities for working parents are greatly needed in our society, but parents should try if at all possible to be selective in choosing a center for their children. A child is not *automatically* better off either at home with a relative or at a day-care center with other children. It depends on the relative (or other caretaker), on the type of center, and on the particular child.

"I have been looking at two programs. One is three blocks from our apartment and is very nice and simple. The other is a twenty-minute bus ride. It is much better equipped, but I'm concerned about the ride."

In general, it is better if the school is closer. There are other considerations, of course. We would not advise a nearby school that did not meet your other expectations, but a nice, simple school may be just fine for two-year-olds. Remember, the school that you choose now does not have to be the child's school forever. The kind of school that is appropriate for a two-year-old will not necessarily be appropriate for a five-year-old. The important thing is to try to select the appropriate one now, one in which the child will feel comfortable and secure. In several years, you may decide to select a different school in any case. In fact, you may have to, because there are few schools that combine prenursery and elementary school grades.

Ratio of Adults to Children

"What ratio of adults to children is best?"

For two-year-olds, we think that one adult to three or four children is the best. In New York City, the Health Code requires one adult to five children for two- and three-year-olds. Other cities may have different requirements. Licensed programs are visited regularly to make sure that these requirements as well as those relating to toilet facilities, outdoor play space, and safety measures are all being followed.

Once your child is enrolled in school, it is important to keep in contact with the director and the teacher to be sure that you have made a satisfactory choice. Visit every once in a while and talk with the teacher occasionally to ask how things are going. Encourage the teacher to call you if she sees anything different or puzzling in your child's behavior. It is important for teachers and parents to be supportive of each other in their roles. As one of you mentioned earlier, teachers and parents should be partners.

Involvement of Working Mothers

"I work full time. How am I going to be able to be that involved in my child's school?"

It is important for working mothers to talk with the director about the availability of teachers for conferences in the early morning before school and work or in the evening. Many schools have been slow to accommodate the needs of working parents, but some are doing it now. Occasionally, working parents should take a couple of hours off from work to visit the school. This is particularly important on the days when other parents will be visiting. Children feel very neglected when other parents come and theirs do not. Some schools require that parents help out occasionally, and that is something that parents should ask about before enrolling the child. Often, working parents can be involved in this way; but if it is impossible, another school should be selected.

All in all, the selection of schools for one's children requires common sense and recognition of the validity of one's intuitive feelings about the general atmosphere and the people involved.

Highlights of Development— Twenty-four Months

The child's second birthday is another one with special significance for parents. There has been tremendous development over the past year. At the beginning of the year, some of the children were walking with one hand held; a few were toddling on their own. Now, most of them run with little or no falling. They can also negotiate stairs alone, both up and down, some even without holding on to the railing. They can kick a large ball upon request without demonstration. When interested in looking at a book, they can turn the pages singly.

At one year, the children could sometimes make a tower of two blocks after demonstration by the parents. Now the children can build a tower of six or seven blocks without demonstration. They can also align two or more blocks into a "train."

The two-year-old no longer scribbles when clutching a crayon in his hand; he may be able to imitate a V and circular stroke. Now when a puzzle with simple geometric shapes is presented, the child may put all the pieces in place after several attempts, indicating that he has learned to associate shapes. He can also successfully insert the square block into the performance box (instead of just inserting the corner as three months ago).

Most children have progressed from the three or four single words they knew at one year to many phrases and two- and three-word sentences. They may even have discarded jargon, the imitative sounds made before words and meaning become associated. They may even use the pronouns *I, me, you*. In communication, the children may be able to refer to themselves by name and verbalize an immediate experience, as well as ask for "more" or "another."

The children have also made great progress in their social development. They are now able to eat with a spoon without turning it over, although finger feeding may still be preferred and eating may still be quite messy.

While dressing, they may be able to pull on simple garments such as underpants, pants, or an open sweater, often with the arms in backward.

Review of the Accomplishments of the Second Year

We have reached the end of the second year, and this is quite a milestone. Can you remember a year ago and compare your children's abilities then with their present achievements?

Motor Development

"Well, yes, I can remember very well that our boy was just taking his first steps alone, and my wife and I were so proud to report it to the group. Now he seems to run more than walk, so he's a handful to watch; he gets away so fast. I like to see him so energetic, but I can see that a full day of watching him may be trying to his mother sometimes."

"I remember at a year our little girl was not walking yet, and we were getting anxious because other children were beginning to totter around. You encouraged us by saying that each child was different and not to worry because she was saying more words than some of the others and that was where her energy was going. Now she, too, runs around instead of walking."

It's obvious that the children's increase in motor activity has been very marked and that, in general, it has been a joy and a relief to know that their motor ability is not impaired in any way. But this development has also brought a need for more careful watching, which parents may find difficult at times.

"Our situation seems to be different from most. My husband thinks I have inhibited our son because he is so cautious. He doesn't run helter-skelter

everywhere. He sort of sizes up the situation before he climbs up or down anything. He never runs very far away or too fast for us to keep up. My husband thinks there is something wrong with him because he prefers to sit and put his blocks in various arrangements and run his little car up or down a chair."

Not all children develop at the same rate and not all children's energies go into large motor activities with the same intensity. There are variations in the amounts of energy devoted to different aspects of development. That's what makes for the uniqueness of each child and the differences in personality. There is nothing wrong with a child whose interests lie in fine motor skills. Problems often arise when a parent has a set image of what a child should be like and feels that any variation from that image indicates a deficiency in the child. The child is actually perfectly normal, just different from the parent's expectations.

"Well, for a long time I've been noticing our child's increased interest in how a toy is put together. He inspects it from all sides, turns and twists each part, takes it apart and tries to reassemble it, and sometimes manages to do it without help. That pleases me a great deal. His favorite toy is his Busy Box, which has all kinds of fasteners and knobs to turn."

You all recognize how much more your children are doing now than they did a year ago. At that time, they barely could put one block on another, or make a scribble on the paper, or put the round piece in its place on the form board. They have come a long way in fine motor skills. What have you noticed in their speech?

Language Development

"Oh! I think that has been the most exciting for us. I remember last year how disappointed we were when our little girl could only say about four words. We wanted so much to have her say more, even though we knew that what she was saying was normal for her age. Her vocabulary has grown so, we have lost count; and she even puts three words together in a sentence, such as 'Daddy go work.' We are thrilled."

"Yes, I think talking is the most thrilling for us, too. We seem to have gotten past the stage of his saying things in a tone imitating us, but with no discernible words, to saying words clearly so we can understand them. He can name pictures of animals and other things in a book, too. He loves to sit with us and do it for a long time. I enjoy the half hour we spend doing that while my wife gets dinner ready."

"We speak two languages in our house. Our child knows a lot of words in both languages, but she hasn't put more than two words together yet. We have to use both languages because my parents live with us and they always speak in Spanish. Is that delaying her speech?"

It may be delaying her speech a little; but when she does begin to talk, she will have a command of two languages. It is sometimes necessary to use only one language for children who are very slow in speech, but it seems that your child is making adequate progress. Not all children of two years speak in three-word sentences all of the time.

Social Development

"Our little boy seems to understand everything, but he doesn't put words together. He points and names over a hundred things and he understands anything we ask him to do, so we haven't been worried. He can do everything else very well. He can feed himself and even tries to put on some of his clothes. He tries to help around the house. If I sweep, he wants to sweep, too. We are pleased."

It is good that all of you as parents are noticing your own children's achievements and not expecting them to be exactly alike. Some are more advanced in speech, and some are developing faster in other areas.

The children's social horizons are widening, and that's very nice. They are beginning to make tentative contacts with other children in the park and beginning to visit with children in other homes. That, too, is quite an advance over the first year. Have you been noticing another evidence of growth: their growing need to do things by *themselves* when *they* are ready?

Personality Development

"Oh, yes! His favorite words now are 'Me do' when he wants to go up and down stairs or walk to the park. He's never ready when I want him to come for lunch or when I want to leave the park."

"We, too, have been noticing many instances of her wanting her own way. We are glad she has a mind of her own. We understand that she needs some autonomy and we try to give it to her wherever it's appropriate. There are times when she objects strenuously to doing something. We just accept the protest and try to give her the scenario of what is coming next. We've learned here to recognize her need for some autonomy and that she wasn't being a bad child if she wanted to decide some things herself."

"Well, my husband and I were brought up in the 'obedience school' and we had been warned that this year would be the onset of the 'terrible twos.' We seem to be weathering it all right, because we understand that at this age they begin to try their wings, so to speak, and need some independence— and this is not disobedience."

Parental recognition of the child's need for some autonomy, as well as his or her need for consistent limits and approval when accepting a suitable alternate activity, is really one of the most crucial contributions to the child's personality development that parents can make. You have all begun to work on this during the past year. That process makes it possible for a child to learn to accept authority without being made to feel that he or she is "bad." While limited in one area, the child learns that there is an alternate acceptable activity. Then, in later adult life, he or she will be able to deal appropriately with authority and with limitations and frustrations. Such an adult won't "fight" his or her boss or sulk if it rains on the day of a picnic; it will be possible to think of an alternate activity, such as going to the movies or a museum.

"We are concerned about having our child develop self-confidence and self-esteem. If he builds something with his blocks or returns a ball we throw, or just even comes to his meals when called, we recognize it with some positive comment."

That is a very important process; it helps the child develop a positive self-image. We began to talk about that when the baby was able to reach out and hold a toy. We commented on the importance of recognizing the achievement as appropriate for that age. This process has to be continuous, and it is very gratifying to see that parents are concerned with this aspect of personality. A child needs positive recognition in order to develop a good self-image. This helps him explore the world around him, to be involved in school, and to be self-motivated later in life.

Toilet Training

"We have been talking about the children's progress, but in my family the only progress that seems to count is bowel and bladder control. When can we expect our child to be trained?"

One or two of these children may achieve the ability to control these functions in the next few months; the majority will be closer to three years. Some of these children are beginning to inform the parent only *after* the evacuation of bladder or bowel has occurred and then ask for a change of diaper. That is an important step and should be greeted with approval, *not scolding for soiling.* If children are allowed to follow their own natural timetables, toilet training will be accomplished in just a few days. They will gain a sense of autonomy and responsibility for their own functions as well as a sense of achievement when parents show approval.

"Our son has reached the stage of telling me. But when we get to the bathroom, most of the time he can't perform until he is off the toilet seat and back in his diaper. My mother thinks I should keep him there until he has performed, but he cries to get off."

If you just go along with your son's signals and recognize the few successes he may have, making no comment over the failures, he will be able to function more easily. His toilet training will be successful when he is ready. Trying to force him may only impede the progress.

"That takes a burden off my mind, because that is the stage we are in. On some days we have successes once or twice a day; on other days, only failures."

Success should be recognized and failure overlooked! Each child is at a different level of maturation of the central nervous system. Some will mature faster than others; but, not pushed, they will all become toilet trained without having been made to feel disapproved of or incompetent over this issue. Child development specialists believe such feelings of inadequacy may lead to long-standing character problems in later life, which all of us wish to avoid.

Weaning from Bottles

"Well, now, what about bottles? My son takes most of his liquids from a cup after meals when I hold the cup, and sometimes he holds the cup himself. But first thing in the morning and to go to bed at night, he still wants his bottle. I'm perfectly satisfied with this arrangement, but my friends who have grown children say that it is wrong. They took the bottles away as soon as their children could drink from a cup. Most of them say it was before two years."

Again, we believe that the child's need should dictate the timing for weaning. It is appropriate for the child to learn to drink from the cup, but the child should give up the bottles when he or she is ready. Most children at two years still need the morning and evening bottles; some may require more. For some, the bottle is not so much a nutritional need as an emotional need: not to feel separated from Mother. This need should be respected for what it is; more time spent with Mother in other activities often cuts down the child's need for bottles.

"Well, when should a child be expected to give up all bottles?"

Most children are ready around three years of age; some may need them a little longer. Each child has his or her own timetable and special needs. Parents should relate to each child as an individual, and not to the advice of someone who does not know the child or understand the situation.

Changes and Developments to Expect in the Third Year

"Now that we have reviewed some of the accomplishments in the second year, what should we be looking forward to next year? Can you give us a little preview?"

Increasing Competence

That's a fair request. As we have just been saying, there will be progress in toilet training. The children will also relinquish most bottles, if not all. They will become more competent at self-feeding, and they will be able to put on some of their clothes.

In the area of motor activity, the children will be able to alternate feet

■   ■

when walking upstairs, and some will be able to pedal a tricycle by three. They will be able to make more complicated structures with their blocks. They may learn to discriminate and name colors.

The children's language development will be very exciting to parents because they will be able to express their ideas better in longer, more complicated sentences. They will begin to learn some nursery rhymes and songs. There will be an increase in their understanding of abstract concepts and ideas.

Increasing Sociability

Socially, they will begin to play more interactively with other children. They will begin to take turns, a process that will be more fully achieved from three to four years of age.

The children's likes and dislikes may become more pronounced, and they will be more vigorous in their protests, developments that may be annoying to parents at times. They will need the same consistency and firmness when limited, and the same recognition for achievement and approval for appropriate behavior. In this way a desire to achieve rather than rebel will become more appealing.

Increasing Autonomy

As the third year progresses, the children will be able to separate better from parents, in particular, and from home, in general. They will be able to play longer alone and at a greater distance from mother—sometimes away from home without mother.

It will be an interesting and challenging year. Now that you have all become so much more proficient and self-assured as parents and know and understand your children better, it should be a very good year. During this year, you will be preparing your children for greater independence and more relationships with other adults and peers. We advise you to savor and enjoy it. From age three on, your children will spend more and more time in school and away from home. You will have completed the "good start" that all of us want to give our children so that they may be more competent and caring adults.

Suggested Books for Children Twelve to Twenty-four Months

The verbal ability and concentration of children expand greatly between twelve and twenty-four months. The books on the following list vary from cloth and cardboard books with few or no words to paper books with simple story lines. If a child shows impatience or restlessness while looking at a particular book, the parent should try a different one. Children may have quite different interests, even at this early age, and the age at which each will enjoy a particular book will vary as well.

Parents should also try to find cardboard, cloth, and plastic foam-filled books that children can look at by themselves. Books with tabs, "push-ups," and "pop-outs" are too delicate for children of this age group. Parents and children can make their own books of pictures cut from magazines and pasted on cardboard. Children also enjoy looking at albums of photographs of themselves and hearing stories about themselves.

Adams, George, and Henning, Paul. *First Things.* New York: Platt and Munk.
At the Table; Going for a Ride; In the House; Trucks. 1981. Los Angeles: Price/Stern/Sloan (*cardboard*).
Baby's First Book. New York: Platt and Munk (*cardboard or cloth*).
Battaglia, Aurelius. 1976. *Come Walk with Me; I Look Out My Window; This Is My House; Let's Go Shopping; A Trip to the Zoo.* New York: Playskool Manufacturing Company (recommended by Pushaw, 1976).
The Bear; The Crane; The Train. 1979. Copenhagen: Carlsen (*cardboard, no words*).
Bonforte, Lisa. *Baby Animals.* New York: Golden Press (*cardboard*).
Brown, Margaret Wise. 1947. *Good Night Moon.* New York: Harper & Row.
———. 1950. *A Child's Good Night Book.* New York: Scott.
———. 1952. *The Duck.* Photographs by Ylla. New York: Harper & Row.
Bruna, Dick. *Dick Bruna's Animal Book.* London: Methuen Books (*cardboard*).
———. *My Meals.* A Dick Bruna Zig Zag Book. London: Methuen Books (*cardboard*).
Burningham, John. 1974. *The Rabbit.* New York: Thomas Y. Crowell.
———. 1975. *The Baby.* New York: Thomas Y. Crowell.
———. 1975. *The Blanket.* New York: Thomas Y. Crowell.

————. 1976. *The Cupboard.* New York: Thomas Y. Crowell.

Cellini, Joseph. 1958. *ABC.* New York: Grosset and Dunlap (*cardboard*).

Crews, Donald. 1978. *Freight Train.* New York: Morrow.

————. 1980. *Truck.* New York: Greenwillow Books.

Federico, Helen. 1960. *ABC.* New York: Golden (*cardboard*).

A First Book in My Garden; A First Book in My Kitchen. 1980. "Object Lesson" series. England: Brimax Books (*cardboard*).

Fujikama, Gyo. 1963. *Babies.* New York: Grosset and Dunlap (*cardboard*).

Gay, Zhenya. *Look!* New York: Viking.

The Golden Fire Engine Book. New York: Golden Press (*cardboard*).

Johnson, John E. *The Sky Is Blue: The Grass Is Green.* New York: Random House (*cloth*).

Kalan, Robert. 1979. *Blue Sea.* New York: Morrow.

Krauss, Ruth. 1945. *The Carrot Seed.* New York: Harper & Row.

————. 1948. *Bears.* New York: Harper & Row.

————. 1949. *The Happy Day.* New York: Harper & Row.

Kunhardt, Dorothy. *Pat the Bunny.* New York: Western.

————. *Tickle the Pig.* New York: Golden.

McNaught, Harry. 1976. *Baby Animals.* New York: Random House (*cardboard*).

Matthiesen, Thomas. 1968. *Things to See.* New York: Platt and Munk.

Miller, J. P. 1976. *Big and Little.* New York: Random House (*cardboard*).

————. *Farmer John's Animals.* New York: Random House (*cardboard*).

My First Toys. New York: Platt and Munk.

Najaka, Marlies Merk. 1980. *City Cat; Country Cat.* New York: McGraw-Hill (*cardboard*).

Nursery Rhymes. 1979. New York: Random House (*cardboard*).

Oxenbury, Helen. 1982. *Beach Day; Good Night, Good Morning; Monkey See, Monkey Do; Mother's Helper; Shopping Trip.* New York: Dial Press (*cardboard, no words*).

Pfloog, Jan. 1977. *Kittens.* New York: Random House (*cardboard*).

————. 1979. *Puppies.* New York: Random House (*cardboard*).

Pickett, Barbara, and Kovacs, D. 1981. *The Baby Strawberry Book of Pets.* New York: McGraw-Hill (*cardboard*).

————. 1981. *The Baby Strawberry Book of Baby Farm Animals.* New York: McGraw-Hill (*cardboard*).

Rey, H. A. *Anybody at Home?; Feed the Animals; See the Circus; Where's My Baby?* Boston: Houghton Mifflin.

Rice, Eve. 1977. *Sam Who Never Forgets.* New York: Morrow.

Richter, Mischa. 1978. *Quack?* New York: Harper & Row.

Risom, Ole. 1963. *I Am a Bunny.* New York: Golden Press (*cardboard*).

Scarry, Patsy. *My Teddy Bear Book.* New York: Golden Press.

Schlesinger, Alice. 1959. *Baby's Mother Goose.* New York: Grosset and Dunlap (*cardboard*).

Seiden, Art. 1962. *Kittens; Puppies.* New York: Grosset and Dunlap (*cardboard*).

"Show Baby" Series: *Bathtime; Bedtime; Mealtime; Playtime.* 1973. New York: Random House (*cardboard*).

Skarr, Grace. 1968. *What Do the Animals Say?* New York: Young Scott Books.

Steiner, Charlotte. *My Bunny Feels Soft.* New York: Alfred A. Knopf.

The Tall Book of Mother Goose. New York: Harper & Row.

Tensen, Ruth M. *Come to the Farm.* Chicago: Reilly and Lee.

Things That Go. New York: Platt and Munk (*cloth*).

Walley, Dean. *Pet Parade.* Kansas City: Hallmark Cards (*cardboard*).

———, and Cunningham, Edward. *Zoo Parade.* Kansas City: Hallmark Cards (*cardboard*).

Wells, Rosemary. *Max's First Word; Max's Ride; Max's Toys.* New York: Dial (*cardboard series*).

Wilkin, Eloise. 1981. *Rock-A-Bye, Baby.* New York: Random House. (*Simple games with rhymes to play with toddlers.*)

Williams, Garth. *Baby Animals.* New York: Western.

———. *Baby's First Book.* New York: Platt and Munk (*cardboard or cloth*).

———. *The Chicken Book.* New York: Delacorte.

Witte, Pat, and Witte, Eve. *The Touch Me Book.* New York: Western.

———. *Who Lives Here?* New York: Western.

Wynne, Patricia. 1977. *The Animal ABC.* New York: Random House (*cardboard*).

Zaffo, George. *The Giant Nursery Book of Things That Go.* Garden City, New York: Doubleday.

■   ■

Bibliography

Note: Titles preceded by an asterisk (*) are especially recommended for parents.

Abrahamson, David. 1969. *Emotional Care of Your Child.* New York: Trident Press.

Ainsworth, Mary D. Salter. 1965. Further research into the adverse effects of maternal deprivation. In *Child Care and Growth of Love,* 2d ed., ed. John Bowlby, 191–241. Harmondsworth, England: Penguin Books.

———. 1967. *Infancy in Uganda: Infant Care and the Growth of Attachment.* Baltimore: The Johns Hopkins University Press.

———. 1969. Object relations, dependency, and attachment: A theoretical review of the infant-mother relationship. *Child Development* 40:969–1025.

Ainsworth, Mary D. Salter, and Bell, Sylvia M. 1972. Attachment, exploration, and separation: Illustrated by behavior of one-year-olds in a strange situation. In *Readings in Child Development,* eds. Irving B. Weiner and David Elkind. New York: John Wiley & Sons.

*Ames, Louise Bates, and Chase, Joan Ames. 1973. *Don't Push Your Preschooler.* New York: Harper & Row.

Anglund, Sandra. 1968. Here, even infants go to school. *Today's Health.* March: 52–57.

Auerbach, Alice S. 1968. *Parents Learn Through Discussion.* New York: John Wiley & Sons.

Badger, Earladeen D. 1972. A mother's training program. *Children Today* (U.S. Department of Health, Education, and Welfare) 1/3:7–11, 35.

Bayley, Nancy. 1940. Mental growth in young children. *Yearbook of the National Society for the Study of Education* 39/2:11–47.

———. 1969. *Bayley Scales of Infant Development.* New York: Psychological Corporation.

Beadle, Muriel. 1970. *A Child's Mind.* New York: Doubleday.

Bel Geddes, Joan. 1974. *How to Parent Alone: A Guide for Single Parents.* Somers, Conn.: Seabury Press.

Bell, Richard Q. 1971. Stimulus control of parent or caretaker behavior by infant. *Developmental Psychology* 4:63–72.

Bell, Sylvia M., and Ainsworth, Mary D. Salter. 1972. Infant crying and maternal responsiveness. *Child Development* 44:1171–1190.

Bernstein, B. 1964. Aspects of language and learning in the genesis of the social process. In *Language in Culture and Society: A Reader in Linguistics and Anthropology,* ed. D. Hymes, 251–63. New York: Harper & Row.

Bettelheim, Bruno. 1962. *Dialogues with Mothers.* New York: Free Press.

Bijou, S. W. 1970. *Experiences and the Processes of Socialization.* New York: Academic Press.

Birch, Herbert G. 1970. *Disadvantaged Children: Health, Nutrition, and School Failure.* New York: Harcourt, Brace & World.

Blank, M. 1964. Some maternal influences on infants' rate of sensorimotor development. *Journal of the American Academy of Child Psychiatry* 3: 668–87.

Bloom, Benjamin S. 1964. *Stability and Change in Human Characteristics.* New York: John Wiley & Sons.

Bowlby, John. 1951. *Maternal Care and Mental Health: Report to World Health Organization.* New York: Columbia University Press.

———. 1958. Nature of a child's tie to his mother. *International Journal of Psychoanalysis* 39:350–73.

———. 1960. Grief and mourning in infancy and early childhood. In *The Psychoanalytic Study of the Child.* New York: International Universities Press.

———. 1969–80. *Attachment and Loss.* 3 vols. (*Attachment; Separation, Anxiety and Anger; Loss, Sadness and Depression.* New York: Basic Books.

*Brazelton, T. Berry. 1969. *Infants and Mothers.* New York: Delacorte.

*———. 1974. *Toddlers and Parents.* New York: Delacorte.

———. 1984. *To Listen to a Child.* Reading, Mass.: Addison-Wesley.

Bresnahan, Jean L., and Blum, William. 1971. Chaotic reinforcement: A socioeconomic leveler. *Developmental Psychology* 4:89–92.

Brim, Orville G., Jr. 1961. Methods of educating parents and their evaluation. In *Prevention of Mental Disorders in Children,* ed. G. Caplan, 122–41. New York: Basic Books.

———. 1965. *Education for Child Rearing.* Reprint. New York: Free Press.

Brody, Grace F. 1969. Maternal childrearing attitudes and child behavior. *Developmental Psychology* 1:66.

Brody, Sylvia. 1956. *Patterns of Mothering.* New York: International Universities Press.

Bronfenbrenner, Urie. 1970. *Two Worlds of Childhood.* New York: Russell Sage Foundation.

Bruner, Jerome S. 1968. *Processes of Cognitive Growth: Infancy.* Worcester, Mass.: Clark University Press.

*Calderone, Mary S., M.D., and Ramsay, James W., M.D. 1982. *Talking with Your Child About Sex. Questions and Answers for Children from Birth to Puberty.* New York: Random House.

Caldwell, Bettye M. 1972. What does research teach us about day care for children under three? *Children Today* (U.S. Department of Health, Education, and Welfare) 1/1:6–11.

Caldwell, Bettye M., and Ricciuti, N. N., eds. 1973. *Review of Child Development Research.* Vol. 3 of *Child Development and Social Policy.* Chicago: University of Chicago Press.

Call, Justin; Galenson, Eleanor; and Tyson, Robert L. 1984. *Basic Books.* Vol. 2. New York: Brunner/Mazel.

■   ■

*Caplan, Frank, ed. 1971. *The First Twelve Months of Life.* Princeton, N.J.: Edcom Systems, Inc.

Caplan, Gerald, ed. 1961. *Prevention of Mental Disorders in Children.* New York: Basic Books.

Chess, Stella, M.D., and Thomas, Alexander, M.D. 1984. *Origins of Evolution of Behavior Disorder.* New York: Brunner/Mazel.

———. 1980. *Dynamics of Psychological Development.* New York: Brunner/Mazel.

*Church, Joseph. 1973. *Understanding Your Child from Birth to Three: A Guide to Your Child's Psychological Development.* New York: Random House.

Clausen, John A., ed. 1968. *Socialization and Society.* Boston: Little, Brown.

*Comer, James, and Poussaint, Alvin. 1975. *Black Child Care.* New York: Stratford Press.

Cook, Thomas D., et al. 1975. *"Sesame Street" Revisited.* New York: Russell Sage Foundation.

Crandall, Virginia. 1972. Achievement behavior in young children. In *Readings in Child Development,* eds. Irving B. Weiner and David Elkind. New York: John Wiley & Sons.

Danziger, Kurt. 1971. *Socialization.* Reprint. Harmondsworth, England: Penguin Books.

Deutsch, Martin. 1960. *Minority Groups and Class Status as Related to Social and Personality Factors in Scholastic Achievement.* Ithaca, N.Y.: Society for Applied Anthropology.

———. 1964. Facilitating development in the preschool child: Social and psychological perspectives. *Merrill-Palmer Quarterly* 10:249–63.

———. 1965. The role of social class in language development and cognition. *American Journal of Orthopsychiatry* 35/1:78–88.

Dittman, Laura, ed. 1968. *Early Child Care.* New York: Atherton Press.

*Dodson, Fitzhugh. 1974. *How to Father.* New York: New American Library.

Ende, Robert N. 1983. *Rene A. Spitz: Ideologies from Infancy.* Selected papers. New York: International Universities Press.

Erikson, Erik H. 1963. *Childhood and Society.* 2d ed. Reprint. New York: W. W. Norton.

Escalona, Sibylle. 1968. *Roots of Individuality.* Chicago: Aldine Publishing.

Fantz, R. 1963. Pattern vision in newborn infants. *Science* 140:296–97.

Foss, B. N., ed. 1968. *Determinants of Infant Behavior IV.* New York: John Wiley & Sons.

*Fraiberg, Selma H. 1959. *The Magic Years.* New York: Charles Scribner & Sons.

———. 1977. *Every Child's Birthright: In Defense of Mothering.* New York: Basic Books.

*Galinsky, Ellen, and Hooks, William H. 1977. *The New Extended Family: Day Care That Works.* Boston: Houghton Mifflin.

Garmezy, Norma, and Ritter, Michael. 1983. *Stress of Coping and Development in Children.* New York: McGraw-Hill.

Garvey, Catherine. 1977. *Play.* Cambridge: Harvard University Press.

*Gesell, Arnold L. 1940. *The First Five Years of Life.* New York: Harper & Row.

■   ■

————. 1943. *Infant and Child Care in the Culture of Today.* New York: Harper & Row.

Gesell, Arnold L., and Amatruda, Catherine. 1947. *Developmental Diagnosis.* 2d ed. New York: Paul B. Hoeber.

*Glickman, Beatrice M., and Springer, Nesha B. 1978. *Who Cares for the Baby? Choices in Child Care.* New York: Schocken Books.

Goldstein, Joseph; Freud, Anna; and Solnit, Albert J. 1973. *Beyond the Best Interests of the Child.* Reprint. New York: Free Press.

Goslin, D. A., ed. 1969. *Handbook of Socialization Theory and Research.* New York: Rand-McNally.

*Green, Martin I. 1976. *A Sigh of Relief: The First-Aid Handbook for Childhood Emergencies.* New York: Bantam Books.

Greenspan, Stanley I., M.D. 1981. *Psychopathology and Adaptation in Infancy and Early Childhood.* New York: International Universities Press.

Greenspan, Stanley I., M.D., and Pollock, Georg H., eds. 1989, 1990. *The Course of Life.* Vols. 1 and 2 of *Infancy.* New York: International Universities Press.

Harlow, H. 1949. The formation of learning sets. *Psychological Review* 56: 51–65.

Hawke, Sharryl, and Knox, David. 1977. *One Child by Choice.* Englewood Cliffs, N.J.: Prentice-Hall.

Healy, Jane M. 1987. *Your Child's Growing Mind.* New York: Doubleday.

Hellmuth, Jerome, ed. 1970. *Cognitive Studies.* Vol. 1. New York: Brunner/Mazel.

Hess, R., and Shipman, V. 1965. Early experience and cognitive modes. *Child Development* 36:869.

*Hoffman, Dale. 1979. A guide to pre-nursery schools. *New York* magazine, October 15.

Hunt, J. McV. 1961. *Intelligence and Experience.* New York: Ronald Press.

————. 1971. Parent and child centers: Their basis in the behavioral and educational sciences. *American Journal of Orthopsychiatry* 41/1:13–38.

Johnson, Dale L., et al. 1974. The Houston parent-child development center: A parent education program for Mexican-American families. *American Journal of Orthopsychiatry* 44/1:121–28.

Kagan, Jerome. 1971. *Change and Continuity in Infancy.* New York: John Wiley & Sons.

Kagan, Jerome. 1984. *The Nature of the Child.* New York: Basic Books.

Kagan, Jerome; Kearsley, Richard B.; and Zelazo, Phillip R. 1978. *Infancy: Its Place in Human Development.* Cambridge: Harvard University Press.

Katz, I. 1967. The socialization of academic motivation in minority group children. In *Nebraska Symposium in Motivation,* ed. D. Levine, 133–91. Lincoln, Neb.: University of Nebraska Press.

Kessler, Jane W. 1970. Contributions of the mentally retarded toward a theory of cognitive development. In *Cognitive Studies,* ed. J. Hellmuth, vol. 1, 111–209. New York: Brunner/Mazel.

————. 1966. *Psychopathology of Childhood.* Englewood Cliffs, N.J.: Prentice-Hall.

Knobloch, Hilda, and Pasamanic, Benjamin, eds. 1974. *Gesell and Amatru-*

da's Developmental Diagnosis. 3d ed. Hagerstown, Md.: Harper & Row Medical.

Levy, David M. 1956. *Maternal Overprotection.* Reprint. New York: W. W. Norton.

Lewis, M. M. 1963. *Language, Thought, and Personality in Infancy and Childhood.* New York: Basic Books.

———. 1976. *Origins of Intelligence: Infancy and Early Childhood.* New York: Plenum Press.

*Lidz, Theodore. 1968. *The Person: His Development Through the Life Cycle.* New York: Basic Books.

*Lief, Nina R., and Fahs, Mary Ellen. 1991. *The First Year of Life.* New York: Walker and Company.

*Lief, Nina R., and Thomas, Rebecca Myers. 1991. *The Third Year of Life.* New York: Walker and Company.

Lief, Nina R., and Zarin-Ackerman, Judith. 1976. The effectiveness of a curriculum of parent education on a group of risk and non-risk mothers and infants. Paper presented at meeting of the American Association of Psychiatric Services for Children, 11 November 1976, San Francisco, California.

Lipsitt, L. 1966. Learning processes of human newborns. *Merrill-Palmer Quarterly* 12:45–71.

Litman, Frances. 1969. Environmental influences on the development of abilities. Excerpted from a Harvard Graduate School of Education Pre-School Project Paper presented at the Biennial Meeting of the Society for Research in Child Development, Santa Monica, California.

McClelland, D., et al. 1953. *The Achievement Motive.* New York: Appleton-Century-Crofts, Inc.

McGurk, Harry. 1974. Visual perception in young infants. In *New Perspectives in Child Development,* ed. Brian Foss. Baltimore, Md.: Penguin Books.

Madden, John; Levenstein, Phyllis; and Levenstein, Sidney. 1976. Longitudinal I.Q. outcomes of the mother-child home program—Verbal Interaction Project. *Child Development* 47/4:1015–25.

Mahler, Margaret S., and La Perriere, K. 1965. Mother-child interaction during separation. *Psychoanalytical Quarterly* 34: 483–98.

Mahler, Margaret S.; Pine, Fred; and Bergman, Ami. 1975. *The Psychological Birth of the Human Infant—Symbiosis and Individuation.* New York: Basic Books.

Malone, Charles A. 1967. Psychosocial characteristics of children from a development viewpoint. In *The Drifters,* ed. E. Pavenstedt, 105–24. Boston: Little, Brown.

*Marzollo, Jean. 1977. *Supertot: Creative Learning Activities for Children One to Three and Sympathetic Advice for Their Parents.* New York: Harper & Row.

Morris, Ann G. 1974. Conducting a parent education program in a pediatric clinic playroom. *Children Today* 3/6:11–14.

Murphy, Lois B. 1962. *The Widening World of Childhood.* New York: Basic Books.

————. 1963. Problems in recognizing emotional disturbances in children. *Child Welfare,* December 1963:473–87.

Neubauer, Peter B. 1968. The third year: the two-year-old. In *Early Child Care,* ed. L. Dittman, 57–67. New York: Atherton Press.

Newson, Elizabeth, and Newson, John. 1968. *Four-Year-Olds in an Urban Community.* Chicago: Aldine Publishing.

*Parke, Ross D. 1981. *Fathers.* Cambridge: Harvard University Press.

Pavenstedt, Eleanor. 1965. A comparison of childrearing environments of upper, lower and very-low lower class families. *American Journal of Orthopsychiatry* 35:89.

————. 1967. *The Drifters.* Boston: Little, Brown.

Piaget, Jean. 1950. *The Psychology of Intelligence.* New York: Harcourt, Brace.

————. 1970. The stages of the intellectual development of the child. In *Readings in Child Development and Personality,* 2d ed., eds. Paul H. Mussen, John J. Conger, and Jerome Kagan, 291–98. New York: Harper & Row.

Pine, Fred. 1971. On the separation process: Universal trends and individual differences. In *Separation-Individuation: Essays in Honor of Margaret S. Mahler,* eds. John B. McDivitt and Calvin F. Settlage, 113–30. New York: International Universities Press.

*Price, Jane. 1980. *How to Have a Child and Keep Your Job: A Candid Guide for Working Parents.* New York: Penguin Books.

Pringle, M. L. Kellmer, et al. 1967. *11,000 Seven-Year-Olds.* New York: Humanities Press.

Provence, S., and Litman, R. C. 1962. *Infants in Institutions.* New York: International Universities Press.

*Pulaski, Mary Ann Spencer. 1978. *Your Baby's Mind and How It Grows: Piaget's Theory for Parents.* New York: Harper & Row.

*Pushaw, David R. 1976. *Teach Your Child to Talk.* Fairfield, N.J.: CEBCO Standard Publishing.

*Rice, F. Philip. 1979. *The Working Mother's Guide to Child Development.* Englewood Cliffs, N.J.: Prentice-Hall.

Rowland, L. W. 1948. A first evaluation of Pierre the Pelican. *Health Pamphlets,* Louisiana Mental Health Studies, no. 1. New Orleans: Louisiana Society for Mental Health.

*Salk, Lee. 1971. *What Every Child Would Like His Parents to Know.* New York: David McKay Co.

Sarbin, Theodore R., and Allen, Vernon L. 1968. Role theory. In *Handbook of Social Psychology,* 2d ed., eds. Gardner Lindzey and Elliot Aronson, vol. 1, 488–567. Reading, Mass.: Addison-Wesley.

Schaefer, Earl S. 1970. Need for early and continuing education. In *Education of the Infant and Young Child,* ed. V. H. Denenberg. New York: Academic Press.

Sears, Robert R.; Maccoby, E. E.; and Levin, H. 1957. *Patterns of Childrearing.* New York and Evanston, Ill.: Row, Peterson.

Shapiro, David. 1981. *Autonomy and Rigid Character.* New York: Basic Books.

■   ■

*Singer, Dorothy; Singer, Jerome; and Zuckerman, Diana M. 1981. *Teaching Television: How to Use TV to Your Child's Advantage.* New York: The Dial Press.

Skinner, B. F. 1953. *Science and Human Behavior.* New York: Macmillan.

Smith, M. Brewster. 1968. Competence and socialization. In *Socialization and Society,* ed. J. A. Clausen, 270–320. Boston: Little, Brown.

Spitz, René A. 1945. Hospitalism and inquiry into the genesis of psychiatric conditions of early childhood. *Psychoanalytic Study of the Child* 1:53–74.

———. 1965. *The First Year of Life.* New York: International Universities Press.

*Spock, Benjamin. 1981. *Baby and Child Care.* New York: Pocket Books.

Steinfels, Margaret O'Brien. 1973. *Who's Minding the Children? The History and Politics of Day Care in America.* New York: Simon & Schuster.

Stern, Daniel. 1988. *The Interpersonal World of the Infant.* New York: Basic Books.

*Stone, Joseph, and Church, Joseph. 1968. *Childhood and Adolescence.* New York: Random House.

Talbot, Nathan B.; Kagan, Jerome; and Eisenberg, Leon. 1971. *Behavioral Science in Pediatric Medicine.* Philadelphia: Saunders.

Terman, Lewis M., and Merrill, M. 1972. *Stanford-Binet Intelligence Scale.* Form L-M. 3d revision. Boston: Houghton Mifflin.

*Thomas, Alexander; Chess, Stella; and Birch, Herbert G. 1968. *Temperament and Behavior Disorders in Children.* New York: New York University Press.

———. 1977. *Temperament and Development.* New York: Brunner/Mazel.

Weinraub, Marsha, and Lewis, Michael. 1977. *The Determinants of Children's Responses to Separation.* Monograph of the Society for Research in Child Development, no. 172.

*Weiss, Robert S. 1979. *Going It Alone: The Family Life and Social Situation of the Single Parent.* New York: Basic Books.

White, Burton L. 1970. Child development research: An edifice without foundation. In *Readings in Child Development and Personality,* 2d ed., eds. P. H. Mussen et al., 97–117. New York: Harper & Row.

*———. 1975. *The First Three Years of Life.* Englewood Cliffs, N.J.: Prentice-Hall.

White, Burton L., and Watts, Jean Carew. 1973. *Experience and Environment.* Vol. 1. Englewood Cliffs, N.J,: Prentice-Hall.

Wilson, Ronald S. 1972. Twins: Early mental development. *Science* 175/4024:914–17.

Winnicott, D. W. 1951. *Transitional Objects and Transitional Phenomena: A Study of the First Not-Me Possession.* In *Collected Papers.* New York: Basic Books.

Work, Henry H. 1972. Parent-child centers: a working reappraisal. *American Journal of Orthopsychiatry* 42/4:582–95.

Yarrow, Leon J. 1968. Conceptualizing the early environment. In *Early Child Care,* ed. L. C. Dittman. New York: Atherton Press.

■   ■

Zambrana, Ruth E.; Hurst, Martha; and Hite, Rodney. 1979. The working mother in contemporary perspective: a review of the literature. *Pediatrics* 64/6:862–70.

Zigler, Edward, and Child, Irvin L. 1969. Socialization. In *Handbook of Social Psychology,* 2d ed., eds. Gardner Lindzey and Elliott Aronson, vol. 3, 450–589. Reading, Mass.: Addison-Wesley.